T0330005

Biodiversity in the Balance

Ai miei genitori Rita e Giovanni, a cui devo, oltre alla fortuna di essere venuto al mondo, la mia istruzione, i miei valori etici fondamentali, e, a parziale loro rassicurazione per i lunghi anni di assenza da casa, l' amore per la lingua e la cultura del mio paese.

Biodiversity in the Balance

Land Use, National Development and Global Welfare

Raffaello Cervigni

The Ministry of Economy and Finance;
The World Bank; and
Centre for Social and Economic Research on the Global Environment
(CSERGE)

Edward Elgar
Cheltenham, UK • Northampton, MA, USA

© Raffaello Cervigni 2001

All rights reserved. No part of this publication may be reproduced, stored in a retrieval system or transmitted in any form or by any means, electronic, mechanical or photocopying, recording, or otherwise without the prior permission of the publisher.

Published by
Edward Elgar Publishing Limited
Glensanda House
Montpellier Parade
Cheltenham
Glos GL50 1UA
UK

Edward Elgar Publishing, Inc.
136 West Street
Suite 202
Northampton
Massachusetts 01060
USA

A catalogue record for this book
is available from the British Library

Library of Congress Cataloguing in Publication Data
Cervigni, Raffaello.
 Biodiversity in the balance : land use, national development, and global welfare / Raffaello Cervigni.
 p. cm.
 Includes bibliographical references and index.
 1. Land use, Rural—Environmental aspects—Developing countries. 2. Land use, Rural—Economic aspects—Developing countries. 3. Urbanization—Developing countries. 4. Biological diversity conservation—Developing countries. 5. Ecosystem management—Developing countries. 6. Sustainable development—Developing countries. I. Title.

HD1131 .C47 2002
333.76'09172'4—dc21   2001040764

ISBN 1 84064 345 5

Printed and bound in Great Britain by MPG Books Ltd, Bodmin, Cornwall

Contents

List of Figures   *ix*

List of Tables   *xi*

Preface   *xiii*

Acknowledgements   *xvii*

PART I. INTRODUCTION

1. Biodiversity conservation and loss: the background   3

1.1   The biodiversity problem   5
1.2   Defining diversity and loss   7
1.3   Biodiversity and human well-being   15
1.4   Economic activity and biodiversity loss   23
1.5   Summary   28

PART II. THEORETICAL ISSUES

2. Land use change, biodiversity loss, and economic analysis   35

2.1   Land conversion and biodiversity loss   35
2.2   Land conversion: a conceptual framework   39
2.3   Interventions to alter the incentives to land conversion   44
2.4   Conclusion: land use change in theory and in practice   52

Annex 2.1   Increasing rents from conservation compatible activities   55

3. Financing conservation: theoretical aspects   61

3.1   Biodiversity and incremental cost: a simple model   63

3.2   Some results using particular functional forms   78

3.3   Conclusions   84

Annex 3.1:   Deriving α and β 86

Annex 3.2:   Solutions of the model when utility is multiplicative   88

PART III. BIODIVERSITY LOSS AND CONSERVATION IN PRACTICE: A
         CASE STUDY IN MEXICO

4. The area: Sierra de Santa Marta, Veracruz, Mexico   95

4.1   Location and physical description   95

4.2   Biodiversity relevance   102

4.3   The socio-economic environment   106

Annex 4.1:   Background on Mexico's land tenure system   125

5. The process of land use change: modelling farm behaviour   129

5.1   The past: overview of the process of land use change   129

5.2   The present   138

5.3   Prospects for the future: modelling farm-level decisions   142

Annex 5.1:   Conceptual background of the linear programming models   160

Annex 5.2:   Deriving "corrected" profit margins   167

Annex 5.3:   Parameter selection   168

Annex 5.4:   Existing farms with land constraints   172

6. Land use changes: model predictions and policy design   181

6.1   A model for aggregating farm decisions over space and time 181

6.2   Results   189

6.3   Policy implications   196

6.4   Conclusions   200

Annex 6.1   The complete stock and flow model   207

Annex 6.2   Estimating the demand for temporary work   226

Annex 6.3   The income elasticity of cattle number demand   227

Annex 6.4   Pasture rotation   228

References   *235*

Index   *269*

List of Figures

Figure 1.1 The biodiversity problem   5
Figure 1.2 Diversity and ecosystem function: alternative views   20
Figure 1.3 Land management and diversity impacts over time   21
Figure 2.1 Bid-rent schedule for two competing land uses   41
Figure 2.2 Expansion of the development frontier: first stages   42
Figure 2.3 Frontier expansion: subsequent stages   44
Figure 2.4 Enforcing land use restrictions   50
Figure 2.5 The structure of an IFA   51
Figure 2.6 Increasing rent from conservation compatible activities   56
Figure 2.7 The solution to the rent-increasing problem   58
Figure 3.1 ROW's constrained and unconstrained optima   67
Figure 3.2 Domestic and global optima   69
Figure 3.3 Gross and net incremental cost   71
Figure 3.4 Equilibrium for rest of the world   74
Figure 3.5 Optimal claw-back factor   79
Figure 3.6 Domestic optimum vs. incremental cost financing   81
Figure 3.7 The case of price distortions   82
Figure 4.1 Location of the study area   96
Figure 4.2 Taxonomy of land users   110
Figure 5.1 Equilibrium of the agricultural household   162
Figure 5.2 Agricultural household and survival objectives   163
Figure 5.3 Transition matrix for land uses   174
Figure 6.1 Building blocks of the simulation model   182
Figure 6.2 Household sector: basic stock and flow structure   183
Figure 6.3 Decision tree for land conversion and use   186
Figure 6.4 The land use sector   189

Figure 6.5   Reference case: migration, settlers and landlessness   190

Figure 6.6   Reference case: land use (Has)   191

Figure 6.7   Reference case: forest in communal areas (Has)   192

Figure 6.8   Reference case: forest in private land (Has)   193

Figure 6.9   Reference case: palm extraction (million gruesas)   193

Figure 6.10 Formation of new households   208

Figure 6.11 Logistic growth of palm stock when the habitat shrinks   224

Figure 6.12 Pasture cycle   228

Figure 6.13 Distribution of stocking rates   230

List of Tables

Table 1.1   On-line references to biological diversity   4

Table 1.2   Estimates of the current rates of species loss   13

Table 1.3   Genetic uniformity in selected crops   14

Table 1.4   A typology of values of biodiversity   17

Table 2.1   Evidence on land use change world-wide, 1987-89   36

Table 2.2   Evidence on land use changes world-wide, 1992-94   38

Table 2.3   Compensation for foregone uses of land   49

Table 3.1   Assumptions about benefits generated by biodiversity   64

Table 3.2   Notation used in model of incremental cost   66

Table 4.1   Zoning and administrative units in the study area   99

Table 4.2   First stage sampling: selection of land units   101

Table 4.3   Second stage sampling   102

Table 4.4   Species recorded in the Los Tuxtlas region   105

Table 4.5   Types of land ownership   108

Table 4.6   Land parceling, various sources   109

Table 4.7   Landless population, various estimation criteria   112

Table 4.8   Land uses, zoning and municipios (hectares)   113

Table 4.9   Cropping patterns, area-wide estimates in hectares   115

Table 4.10 Cattle ranching: size and distribution of herds   116

Table 4.11 Gathering of non-timber forest products   118

Table 4.12 Trapping of live animals   119

Table 4.13 Hunting, area wide estimates   120

Table 4.14 Migration patterns and off-site employment   122

Table 4.15 Off-site employment and non-farm income   123

Table 5.1   Key features of the linear programming model   145

Table 5.2   New households: baseline case   148

Table 5.3   New households: improved employment prospects   149

Table 5.4   New households: improved access to credit   150

Table 5.5   New households: improved coffee prospects   152

Table 5.6   Evicted farmers: baseline and high employment cases   154

Table 5.7   Paradigm farm, assumed initial allocation of land   156

Table 5.8   Settled farms, baseline case   157

Table 5.9   Settled farms, improved livestock prospects   158

Table 5.10   Settled farms with compensation for foregone land use   159

Table 5.11   Parameters for linear programming model   168

Table 6.1   Impacts on land use of parameter changes   197

Table 6.2   Agriculture technology, tenure policies and land use   200

Preface

Biodiversity (a short hand for the variety of life forms on earth) has become over the last couple of decades the subject of a world-wide debate, due to mounting concerns about the negative consequences of its accelerating decline. There is a growing recognition that the contribution of biological resources both to sustainable national development and to the well being of the international community has been underestimated in the past. Ecological and biological research is increasingly pointing to the possibility that "low" diversity of life forms may threaten the satisfaction of material needs, imperil the life support functions of natural systems, and in general deprive present, and more likely future generations of material and spiritual benefits related to a biologically diverse planet.

At the same time, biodiversity is a concept that encompasses multiple scientific dimensions (genetic, species and ecosystem levels), multiple scales (local, national, international), and multiple justifications (materialistic, ethical, religious) for concern and action. As a result, there seems to be little clarity on what should constitute the objectives of public policies for biodiversity conservation and management.

One set of issues appears of particular interest, and will be addressed in this book. These revolve around the broad question of whether there are options to conserve the benefits of biodiversity without compromising the benefits of development. Specific questions that stem from this are: how much land may be allocated to productive uses without compromising the ability of biodiversity to contribute to human welfare? Will the development process continue to exert pressure on biodiversity, or will it generate incentives for its sustainable use? Does the international community have a role in facilitating the transition towards sustainability?

It will be argued that the answers to these questions depend on definitions of biodiversity adopted and assumptions on the relevance of its conservation for human wellbeing, and consequently, on the rationale for action.

Under more "stringent" notions of biodiversity and biodiversity conservation objectives, it is likely that sources of pressure resulting in possible "loss" of biodiversity will continue. The international community may have limited abilities to counter the process, primarily because the resources required to compensate developing countries for the opportunity costs of full nature conservation are likely to exceed the corresponding marginal benefits to donor countries.

However, it is possible to conceive "less stringent" definitions of biodiversity objectives. Few of the world's ecosystems are genuinely "pristine" (that is, untouched by human influences); and few if any of the ecosystems affected by human activities do not exhibit some degree of resilience, i.e. the ability to withstand external sources of stress without losing the ability to deliver life-support services (Perrings, 1998). Perhaps even more importantly, land use and natural resource management choices are rarely dichotomous; that is, of the type "conserve vs. develop; or "deforest vs. set aside". In real life, there will be a gradient of land management options, ranging from low-intensity, higher biodiversity uses, to high intensity, lower biodiversity uses. The key question then becomes to determine what combinations of land uses can meet the social and economic needs of developing nations without jeopardising the ability of natural systems to deliver their life-support functions.

This book contains a collection of writings, drafted throughout the period 1993-1998 on these issues. The introductory chapter (Chapter 1) summarises the main terms of the scientific and policy debate, highlighting areas of uncertainty and disagreement about the definition of biodiversity management objectives.

Conversion of forested areas to pasture and agriculture, especially in the tropics, has often been stressed as the single most important factor of habitat alteration likely to result in biodiversity loss. Chapter 2 proposes a framework to analyse the sequence of land use changes typically observed in a number of tropical countries; and discusses different policy interventions which could alter the incentives for land conversion.

Land conversion may improve the well being of some sectors of developing countries' society, but it is likely to make the rest of the world worse off. How can the international community provide the resources necessary for developing countries to modify their "baseline" course of action? The Convention on Biological Diversity stipulates that developing countries qualify for receiving financial support from developed countries to meet the "incremental cost" of undertaking activities that result in the conservation of biodiversity. Chapter 3 proposes a model that addresses the allocative and incentive implications of the incremental cost mechanism.

How does the process of land use change happen in real life, and what kind of options can be devised to provide local resource users with incentives for conservation and sustainable use of biodiversity? Part III of the book attempts to answer these questions based on a case study in the region of Sierra de Santa Marta, Mexico. It first discusses the social and economic factors that have been responsible over the last few decades for various processes of land use change and depletion of biological resources in the study area (Chapters 4 and 5); an economic model is then proposed for simulating, through use of linear programming techniques, further impacts at the farm level over the next decade (Chapter 5).

Based on a model of aggregation over space and time of individual household decisions, Chapter 6 considers the problem of the appropriate mix of conservation and sustainable use management options in the study area, discussing cost implications and possible funding sources. It further formulates tentative policy conclusions and sketches lines of possible future research.

Acknowledgements

Several individuals and organisations have provided the help, support and advice that have made this research possible. My Ph.D. supervisor at University College London, Professor David Pearce, has been an invaluable source of scholarly advice, professional example and personal encouragement. In addition to David, I have benefited from intellectual interactions with several other colleagues, while working for about two years in the stimulating research environment of the Centre for Social and Economic Research on the Global Environment (CSERGE) at University College London: in particular, I have been fortunate enough to share an office, long hours of work, a couple of field trips and lots of good times with Dominic Moran; Janet Roddy has been a timely and kind source of administrative support. In the department of Economics of University College London, John Pezzey and Malcom Pemberton have provided helpful advice on earlier versions of chapters 2 and 3.

During my stay at CSERGE, I have received financial support from Italy's Consiglio Nazionale delle Ricerche (CNR), from the British Council, and from the ENI - Enrico Mattei Foundation. All of these are gratefully acknowledged. Professor Luigi De Rosa in CNR has been a constant point of reference and support.

Much of part III of the book is based on work that I have undertaken during my assignment as a consultant to the Secretariat of the Global Environment Facility (GEF) in Washington DC. In particular, the choice of the Sierra de Santa Marta (SSM) in Mexico as the subject of the applied part of this research is motivated by my role of task manager, co-editor and co-author of a case study on sustainable development and biodiversity conservation in SSM.

The study was core-funded by the PRINCE program (see King, 1993, for information on the program) of the GEF, and conducted between 1995 and 1996 in a partnership involving the GEF, the Proyecto Sierra de Santa Marta (PSSM), a local non-governmental organisation, and CIMMYT, (Centro

Internacional para el Mejoramiento del Maiz y Trigo), an international research centre on maize and wheat in the CGIAR network.

In the GEF, I wish to thank Ian Johnson, Kenneth King and Mario Ramos for mentoring and advising, and for agreeing on a part-time work arrangement that has enabled me to make substantial progress on the write-up of the manuscript. Other people in the GEF from whom I have received valuable technical and administrative support include Lesly Rigaud, Lesley Wilson, Patrice Diakite and Anne Bohon-Flanagan.

My work experience in Mexico has been both a challenging and an extremely gratifying one. My first debt of gratitude is to the more than five hundred members of rural communities in the Sierra de Santa Marta, who have been interviewed in field surveys carried out for the GEF-PSSM-CIMMYT study, and have thus been the source of invaluable primary information. I am also sincerely grateful to the colleagues in the Proyecto Sierra de Santa Marta (PSSM) in Xalapa, Veracruz, with whom I have had the fortune of working for about a year and half. In particular, I have a debt of professional and human gratitude to Fernando Ramirez, Mayra Ledesma, Luisa Pare and Rafael Gutierrez.

Perhaps this will not be any compensation for the long hours of work that have been occasionally imposed on them, but I would like to say that I learnt a great deal from them: long conversations with Fernando and his colleagues have been the source of several of the ideas explored in the book.

Daniel Buckles, one of the founders of PSSM and a co-author of the GEF-PSSM-CIMMYT study, now with IDRC in Canada, has also been very helpful in creating the conditions for the development of the study. Diana Ponce Nava, in Mexico's Ministry for Environment and Natural Resources, has been an extremely valuable source of information and high level contacts.

In Washington, a lot of personal gratitude goes to Francesca Manno and Paolo Cappellacci, for their support and patience as friends. My wife Phoebe Millon has endured with me the final months of the writing up. The only feeling that surpasses my gratitude for her support is the acknowledgement of the fortune I had in meeting her.

Despite the long list of people that have been supporting my work in various ways, I remain the only one responsible for errors and omissions.

Credits
Some of the material contained in Chapter 2 forms parts of a CSERGE working paper (Cervigni, 1993); a later version of it has been published in a Spanish language journal (Cervigni, 1994). Chapter 3 is a modified version of

the article: Cervigni, R. (1998), "Incremental Cost in the Convention on Biological Diversity", *Environmental and Resource Economics*, 11: 217-241; kind permission from Kluwer Academic Publishers for the use of the article is gratefully acknowledged.

The description of the study area in Chapter 4, the summary of the historical process of habitat loss in Chapter 5, and the description of options for sustainable use of natural resources in Chapter 6 draw, among other sources, on the above mentioned GEF-sponsored study (Cervigni & Ramirez, 1997). The information collected for, and generated by, that research provides the background for the analysis, modelling exercises and conclusions of Chapters 4, 5 and 6, which amount to original contributions of this book, not included in the GEF-PSSM study.

PART I.

INTRODUCTION

1. Biodiversity conservation and loss: the background

There are probably few topics of the public debate on the environment that have generated over the last couple of decades as much interest as biological diversity, often abbreviated as biodiversity. Casual examination of the existing literature confirms this statement: reference books (Heywood, 1995) and bibliographies (Polasky, Jaspin et al., 1996) on the topic are becoming increasingly voluminous. Further evidence can be gathered if one tries to conduct some simple keyword searches on different on-line research tools, such as those listed in Table 1.1. The table reports the number of occurrences of the phrase "biological diversity" and of the word "biodiversity" in a number of repositories of information, such as catalogues of libraries managed by academic, government, and international organisations, databases of refereed journals, the World Wide Web[1].

Such a massive production of information indicates that the topic is regarded as important in the perception of governments, the academic and scientific community, and the public at large. In recent times, concerns about the conservation of biodiversity have brought about major international actions, such as the negotiation and signing of the Convention on Biological Diversity in 1992 and the establishment of the Global Environment Facility, replenished in 1994 for US\$ 2 billion and in 1998 for US\$ 2.75 billion for projects in four "global environment" focal areas, including conservation of biodiversity. The assistance strategy of multilateral organisations (World Bank, 1995) and of bilateral donors (Abramovitz, 1991) is being reshaped to take into account biodiversity concerns.

Despite the initiatives already undertaken, calls for further commitments to the cause of biodiversity conservation are often being made: estimates have been produced on the amount of resources needed to augment the sustainable development strategy laid out in Agenda 21 (UNCED, 1993)[2] with specific actions targeted at biodiversity conservation.

Table 1.1   *On-line references to biological diversity*

Source	Type/ Description	Items returned, "Biological diversity"	Items returned, "Biodiversity"
Northern Light	WWW search engine	198,258	285,841
Infoseek	WWW search engine	333,944	60,659
Lycos	WWW search engine	192,470	255,167
Jolis	Catalogue of World Bank's library system	35	369
LOCIS	Catalogue of Library of Congress	753	534
Econlit	Database of journals, books, and working papers on economics	51	267
ArticleFirst	Index of articles from nearly 12,500 journals	589	2,581

Source: author's searches, July 2000

But the large numbers of Table 1.1 also suggest that the topic is a complex one, and that it lends itself to a number of different analyses and types of scientific, political and policy approaches. Because of the consensus that biodiversity conservation is an important issue, and because of the significant amount of resource being mobilised to address it (and of the even larger amounts that are being called for), stakeholders of different constituencies are actively engaged in intense research, dissemination and persuasion campaigns, to steer the public debate (and the flow of funding) in the preferred directions. In spite of the growing attention to biodiversity and of the broad range of stakeholders, it is often argued that our understanding of the nature, causes and solutions to the problem is far from adequate.[3] The aim of this chapter is to provide a general overview of the nature of the problem of biodiversity. This should enable the reader to put into context the theoretical and empirical analysis presented in subsequent chapters.

1.1   THE BIODIVERSITY PROBLEM

Several overviews of the biodiversity problem have been produced throughout the late 1980s and the 1990s.[4] Most of them include a discussion of what the biodiversity problem consists of, and of why policy makers and the public should be concerned about it. The preamble of the Convention on Biological Diversity provides a useful summary of the key elements that are often highlighted to characterise the biodiversity problem:

> The Contracting Parties, (...) conscious of the importance of biological diversity for evolution and for maintaining life sustaining systems of the biosphere,(...) concerned that biological diversity is being significantly reduced by certain human activities, (...) aware that conservation and sustainable use of biological diversity is of critical importance for meeting the food, health and other needs of the growing world population, for which purpose access to and sharing of both genetic resources and technologies are essential, (...) have agreed as follows:(...) (UNEP, 1992).

This characterisation is reproduced in graphical form in Figure 1.1. Biodiversity is at the beginning of the reasoning (block A). It is often defined in short as the variety of life forms on earth.

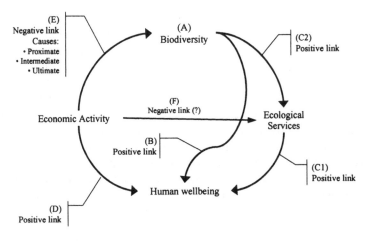

Figure 1.1   The biodiversity problem

Because the concept of "variety" can in turn be defined in a number of different ways, definitional issues are very relevant for a more precise specification of the problem, and will be addressed in more detail below (section 1.2). Biodiversity is hypothesised to influence in a positive way human well-being. Both a direct link and an indirect one are considered. In the first case, described by arrow (B), people derive material or spiritual enjoyment from having, or bequeathing, a biologically diverse planet. In the case of the indirect link, it is argued that material well-being depends on ecological services such as climate regulation, nutrient cycling, maintenance of hydrological cycles, and so forth (arrow C1). Nature's ability to provide these services, in turn, is assumed to have a positive relationship with biodiversity (arrow C2). Economic activity consists of consumption and production acts that increase human welfare (arrow D). However (and here is the crux of the debate), economic activities are also believed to have a negative influence on biodiversity via a range of proximate, intermediate and fundamental (or ultimate) causes: arrow E.

The rest of this chapter examines in further detail each of the "building blocks" of the biodiversity problem as characterised in Figure 1.1, discussing relevant evidence and literature. Before doing that, it is important to point out that the ultimate concern in this analysis is for *human* wellbeing. The worthiness of actions intended to conserve natural systems needs to be evaluated on the basis of their contribution to mankind's welfare. The conceptual and analytical valuation toolkits that can be used in this approach are based on social sciences like economics, anthropology, and sociology.

Despite its self-evident justification, this is not the only possible approach. Supporters of alternative paradigms, such as the Gaia hypothesis (Lovelock, 1987), argue that there need not be any justification of nature conservation in terms of human wellbeing. Conservation can be motivated by concerns for the well-being of the entire planet, regarded itself as a living organism; or by stewardship obligations that the human race would have towards other species and future generations. Under these premises, valuation exercises would not be conducted with the analytical tools of the social sciences; other disciplines such as ethics or theology would need to be employed.

1.2 DEFINING DIVERSITY AND LOSS

1.2.1 Defining diversity

As exemplified by the quotations listed in Text Box 1.1, one recurrent complaint in the biodiversity literature is that calls for biodiversity conservation are often not followed by an indication of what exactly should be conserved. In some cases, the absence of explicit definitions may be due to the fact that people use biodiversity as a "pseudocognate" term; that is, they assume that everybody else shares the same intuitive notion of what biodiversity means (Williams and Humphries, 1994).

Text Box 1.1: selected quotations on the problem of defining biodiversity

"Within six years, the word 'biodiversity' has exploded into the vocabulary of the popular press, governmental and intergovernmental reports, scientific papers and meetings. (...) It seems reasonable to ask of a word that is so widely used, just what is it supposed to mean." (Harper and Hawksworth, 1994)

"There is a broad consensus that biodiversity should be protected, but it is not at all clear what this means in policy and practical terms. This uncertainty is in part a consequence of divergent views as to the exact meaning of biological diversity." (Heywood, 1992)

"At the Earth summit in 1992, the more than 150 nations that signed the International Convention on Biological Diversity signalled their commitment to the conservation of biodiversity and their obligation to monitor its status. But do we have the means of measuring whether the objective of biodiversity conservation is being achieved? Indeed, do we even know what the objective of biodiversity conservation should be?" (Reid, 1994)

"When individuals or organisations stress the need to save nature or natural biodiversity, it is not always clear what are they talking about. Programs to safeguard pristine environments are chimerical." (Smith, 1996)

It has been argued that there are several intuitive shared notions of biodiversity (Harper and Hawksworth, 1994), as there are different disciplines that deal with biodiversity from different perspectives. Practitioners of evolutionary biology, taxonomy, systematics, ecology, genetics and population biology have different (and not always converging) approaches to biodiversity. The approach of community ecologists, for example (Magurran, 1988), leads to measures that combine information on species richness with information on relative abundance of each species; whereas conservationists emphasise vulnerability to extinction (Williams & Humphries, 1994).

It has also been argued that it is in fact desirable to have multiple views and definitions of biodiversity, as this broadens the constituency that supports the cause of conservation (Heywood, 1992). The counter-argument to this is, of course, that the political consensus created by a broad biodiversity constituency may be quickly dissipated by disagreement on policy prescriptions in presence of multiple definitions, entailing mutually exclusive choices on the operational use of scarce funds.

Partly because of the fact the biodiversity means different things to different scientists and different constituencies, definitions used in policy documents, scientific overviews and legal instruments are quite general, as exemplified by the quotes listed in Text Box 1.2.

Text Box 1.2: Definitions of biodiversity

"Biological diversity encompasses all species of plants, animals and micro-organisms and the ecosystems and ecological processes of which they are part. It is an umbrella term for the degree of nature's variety, including both the number and frequency of ecosystems, species or genes in a given assemblage." (McNeely, Miller, Reid, Mittermeier, and Werner, 1990)

"For the purposes of the Global Biodiversity Assessment, biodiversity is defined as the total diversity and variability of living things and of the system of which they are part." (Heywood and Baste, 1995)

"'Biological diversity' means the variability among living organisms from all sources including, inter alia, terrestrial, marine and other aquatic ecosystems and the ecological complexes of which they are part; this includes diversity within species, between species and of ecosystems. 'Biological resources' includes genetic resources, organisms or parts thereof, populations, or any other biotic component of ecosystems with actual or potential use or value for humanity." (UNEP, 1992)

A common feature of several definitions is the distinction of the genetic, species and ecosystem levels of biodiversity. Let us consider indicators that have been proposed for the measurement of diversity at these levels.

Indicators of genetic giversity

Indicators of genetic diversity have the purpose of measuring the degree of variability within different groupings of individuals (local collection of individuals, species, or higher taxonomic group). Genetic differences can be measured in terms of phenotypic traits, allelic frequencies, or DNA sequences.

Phenetic diversity is based on measures of phenotypes, individuals which share the same characteristics. These measures are usually functions of the variance of a particular trait, and often involve readily measurable morphological and physiological characteristics. The disadvantage of measures of phenetic diversity is that their genetic basis is often difficult to assess, and standardised comparisons are difficult when populations or taxa are measured for qualitatively different traits.

Allelic diversity. Variants of a same gene are called alleles. Allelic diversity may be measured at the individual level, or at the population level. Average expected heterozygousity (the probability that two alleles sampled at random will be different) is commonly used as an overall measure of diversity. A number of different indices and coefficients can be applied to the measurements to assess genetic distance (Antonovic, 1990).

Sequence variation. A portion of DNA is sequenced using the polymerase chain reaction technique (PCR). A very small amount of material, perhaps one cell, is required to obtain the DNA sequence data, so that only a drop of blood or single hair is required as a sample. Closely related species may share 95 percent or more of their nuclear DNA sequences, implying a great similarity in the overall genetic information.

Measurement of Species Diversity

There are a number of dimensions of diversity at the species level, including overall species richness, relative abundance and relatedness of different species. Often, species richness –the number of species within a region or given area– is used almost synonymously with species diversity.

In its ideal form, species richness would consist of a complete catalogue of all species occurring in the area under consideration, but this is not usually possible, unless it is a very small area. Species richness measures in practice therefore tend to be based on samples. Such samples consist of a complete catalogue of all organisms within a taxon found in a particular area, or it may consist of a measure of species density in a given sample plot, or a numerical species richness defined as the number of species per specified number of individuals or biomass.

A more informative measure of diversity would also incorporate the 'relatedness' of the species in a fauna (Williams & Humphries, 1994; Reid et al., 1993). The intuition is that the unit of value is not so much the species, as the evolutionary processes that have led to it. Two areas with the same number of species may not be equally valuable if one contains species which are "more diverse" from each other in terms of evolutionary processes.

Measures belonging to this group augment species richness with measures of the degree of genealogical difference. Derived from cladistic (family tree) methods, these measures include (a) the weighting of close-to-root species, (b) higher-taxon richness, (c) spanning-tree length and (d) taxonomic dispersion (Williams & Humphries, 1994). Close-to-root species and higher-taxon richness explicitly use polarity from the root of the tree to weight higher-ranking taxa or "relic" species as distinct survivors of long-independent lineages and original conduits of genetic information. In contrast, spanning tree length and taxonomic dispersion are more general tree measures of sub-tree "representativeness". Persisting conceptual difficulties in actual implementation of cladistic measures as well as scarcity of the necessary data imply that in the short run use of cruder indicators of richness of genera or families will be dominant in rapid assessment of species diversity.

Measurement of Community Diversity

Many environmentalists and ecologists put emphasis on conservation of biodiversity at the community level. Several different "units" of diversity are involved at the supra-species level, including the pattern of habitats in the community, relative abundance of species, age structure of populations, patterns of communities on the landscape, trophic structure, and patch dynamics. There are disadvantages as well as advantages in using measures of community diversity. One disadvantage is that unambiguous boundaries delineating the various units of diversity at the community level do not exist. On the other hand, the advantage is that by conserving biodiversity at the ecosystem level, not only are the constituent species preserved, but also the ecosystem functions and services protected. These include pollutant cycling, nutrient cycling and climate control, as well as non-consumptive recreation, scientific and aesthetic values (see for example, Norton and Ulanowocz, 1992).

Because of the many ways of defining biodiversity at community or ecosystem level, there is correspondingly a range of different approaches to measuring it. As observed in the literature (Reid et al., 1993), any number of community attributes are components of biodiversity and may deserve monitoring for specific objectives. There are several generic measures of community level diversity. These include biogeographical realms or provinces, based on the distribution of species, and ecoregions or ecozones, based on physical attributes such as soils and climate. These definitions may differ according to scale. For example, the world has been divided into biogeographical provinces, or more fine-grained classifications that may be more useful for policy-making. The latter include the definition of "hotspots", (Myers, 1983), based on the number of endemic species, and "megadiversity" states (Mittermeier & Werner, 1990).

1.2.2 Economics and diversity measurement

The problem of measuring diversity has recently been tackled by the economic literature. In particular, there have been a few attempts at formulating a measure of diversity of any given collection of species. The common starting point is the definition of a measure of dissimilarity, or distance,[5] among single *pairs* of species. The way in which the measure of diversity of the entire collection of species is defined depends on the way the pairwise distances are aggregated. Two approaches have been proposed (Pemberton, 1996).

The first one (Solow, Polasky et al., 1993) is based on the distinction of the original set of species in two subsets, one comprising the (potentially) extinct species, and the other comprising the surviving species. The preservation-diversity (PD) measure is (minus) the sum of the individual distance of the extinct species from the set of the surviving ones. If no species goes extinct, the index is equal to zero. The biodiversity management problem can then be easily formulated as one of maximizing the PD measure (i.e. making it as close as possible to zero) subject to a fixed conservation budget.

The second approach (Weitzman, 1992) does not take into account the set of extinct species, but only the set of existing ones. Given a set of species, Weitzman defines its measure of diversity as the length of the tightest or most parsimonious feasible reconstruction of the set, in the sense of being the minimal number of steps required to account for its evolution. The so-called "pure diversity" measure is the solution to a dynamic programming recursive problem in which a function of the point-to-set distance measure is being maximised.

Establishing rigorous definitions of a problem is clearly commendable, all the more so for one, such as biodiversity, where many alternative conceptual approaches compete for policy makers' attention, and for public and private funding alike. At the same time, the diversity measures briefly reviewed above seem to have particularly heavy requirement of data at the genetic level (often expensive to obtain or unavailable altogether), which considerably limits their applicability to many real-life decision problems.[6] Furthermore, in these approaches diversity is valued per se, irrespective of how much of it is required to maintain healthy ecosystems: a dimension which can in fact be a key consideration in defining trade-offs of ecosystem conservation versus development promotion.

1.2.3   Defining and measuring loss

Species loss
Species are lost when they become extinct. Hence, human-induced decreases in species diversity are measured by increases in extinction with respect to natural extinction processes. Because the total number of species is likely to vary over time, meaningful comparisons between current and past extinction must be based on rates. At any point in time t, the process of loss will be more severe than in pre-human times (h) if $E_t > E^h$, where E denotes extinction rates.

With regard to the first term of the comparison, background rates of extinction are mainly based on fossil records of marine invertebrate (Pimm, Russell et al., 1995).[7] Estimates of current extinction rates are troublesome for two reasons. The true value of the rate's denominator, i.e. the overall number of species existing at any given point in time, is not known.[8]

The numerator of the rate is the per-period number of species lost. Few estimates of extinctions are based on actually documented extinctions, which would in fact produce very low rates of loss (Heywood & Baste, 1995; Gentry, 1996).[9] Many studies estimate loss through models based on the species-area relationship. This relationship, the merits and limits of which will be elaborated upon in more detail in Chapter 2, stipulates that decreasing habitat size commands a decreasing number of species. This approach gives rise to predictions over the next century that the projected loss of species might be expected to be as high as 20 to 50% of the world's total (see Table 1.2) which represents a rate between 1,000 to 10,000 times the historical rate of extinction (Lugo, 1988; Barbault & Sastrapradja, 1995).

One aspect of particular relevance is that the species-area relationship estimates the number of species which will be *committed to extinction* as a result of habitat loss.

The ultimate occurrence of extinction, as well as its timing, however, is not an automatic result of land conversion, but will be affected by a number of variables, including demographic parameters of the population living in shrinking areas, and species and ecosystem management.

Genetic erosion
Each individual animal or plant belongs to a species. Yet, it differs from other individuals belonging to same species, according to the way it draws from the broad genetic pool shared by the species. The larger the genetic pool, the larger the chance of any given individual to possess traits improving the chance of resistance (and hence survival) to external stress factors, such as predators, climate, diseases, habitat disruptions and so forth.

Table 1.2   Estimates of the current rates of species loss

Estimate of Loss	Basis	Source
33-50% of species by 2000	forest area loss	Lovejoy (1980)
50% of species by 2000	forest area loss	Ehrlich (1981)
25-30% of species in 21st century	forest area loss	Myers (1989)
33% of species in 21st century	forest area loss	Simberloff (1986)

Source: Groombridge (1992) and references

It is often argued that human activities induce a reduction in the genetic variability of several species, especially of plants for use in agriculture. The "green revolution" has determined a dramatic increase in the productivity of the world's major crops through the introduction of a relatively small number of high-yielding varieties (HYV). As the area devoted to growing the HYV increased, traditional, unimproved, or lower yield cultivars tended to disappear, entailing the loss of potentially valuable genetic information stored in those varieties (Swanson, Pearce et al., 1994; Swanson, 1995). Table 1.3 provides examples of the extent of genetic uniformity for selected crops and countries.

Table 1.3	*Genetic uniformity in selected crops*

Crop	Country	Number of varieties
Rice	Sri Lanka	From 2,000 varieties in 1959 to 5 major varieties today; 75% of varieties descended form one maternal parent
Rice	India	From 30,000 varieties to 75% o f production from less than 10 varieties
Rice	Bangladesh	62% of varieties descended from one maternal parent
Rice	Indonesia	74% of varieties descended from one maternal parent
Wheat	USA	50% of crop in 9 varieties
Potato	USA	75% of crop in 4 varieties
Cotton	USA	50% of crop in 3 varieties
Soybeans	USA	50% of crop in 6 varieties

Source: Groombridge (1992) and references

The process of homogenization of plant for agriculture is a reason for concern (Groombridge, 1992), in that increases in crop yields have been accompanied by increase in their variability, allegedly due to increased susceptibility to pests, diseases and changes in weather patterns.

Loss at the community level
As discussed earlier, there are many different ways of classifying biological communities; for example, classifications based on community structure and function differ from classifications based on species composition (Bisby, Coddington et al., 1995). In terms of scale, global systems like life

zones (Holdridge, 1967), ecoregions (Bailey & Hogg, 1986) or bio-geographic realms and provinces (Udvardy, 1975) coexist with systems used at the regional scales, where landscapes are normally identified. Human activities that have an impact on biological community on the basis of a particular classification may go undetected when a different classification is used. For example, a reduction in landscape diversity due to the increase of a particular land use may not necessarily imply reduction in the diversity of bio-geographic provinces. Clarification of the relevant unit of classification and of the spatial scale of analysis is thus of particular importance to address the complex methodological issues related to measuring loss at the community level.

1.3 BIODIVERSITY AND HUMAN WELL-BEING

In much of the debate, biodiversity matters in so far as its decrease or loss affects human wellbeing. Much has been written in recent years on the value of biodiversity (see Perrings, Barbier et al., 1995; Pearce and Moran, 1994, for some surveys) and often different types (and magnitudes) of values have been estimated and fed into the debate. For the sake of clarity, it is useful to introduce some distinctions concerning the ways in which biodiversity may impact human wellbeing. First, impacts may be produced by *individual* components of biodiversity (genes, species ecosystems), or by their *aggregation*: strictly speaking, it is only the second notion that is relevant for biodiversity (diversity requires the presence of different units in a set).[10]

Secondly, human wellbeing may be affected by *actual* use of biodiversity in consumption or production activities (use values); or it may be affected by variations in biodiversity, *irrespective* and independently of actual use (non-use values). Some people are concerned about conserving a biological diverse planet for the sake of other current or potential users, of future generations, or of the wellbeing of animal and plant species. Use values in turn, may be associated to *current* uses of known biological resources, or to the possibility of *future* discovery of yet unknown biological resources (organic inputs for new drugs, or new varieties of agricultural plants).

A third distinction is the one illustrated graphically earlier, in Figure 1.1. This has to do with the nature of the link between biodiversity and human wellbeing. The link may be (a) *direct*, to the extent that people care, for purposes of their own's or other people's use, about a biologically diverse planet; (b) *indirect*, to the extent that people care about (or are affected by) not diversity per se; but rather the availability of ecological services, which in turn may depend upon genetic, species or ecosystem diversity. Finally, the various values of biodiversity may or may not be reflected in market prices. To the extent that they are not, market-based decisions will lead to non-optimal allocation of resources, and to under-provision of the various goods and services associated one way or another with biodiversity. Table 1.4 proposes a summary of the typology of the values of biological resources and of diversity discussed so far.

Direct linkages
Individual biological resources (both domesticated and from the wild) provide a host of goods and service of direct use to humans, including food, construction material, inputs for traditional and modern health care, etc. Several of these benefits are reflected in market prices, with values in developing countries ranging from less than $1 per ha per year, to $420 per ha per year (latex harvesting, Peru) (Perrings, Barbier et al., 1995). In addition to values reflected by market prices, biological resources provide further benefits not necessarily transacted in markets, as is the case with use of wild products for own consumption and use in subsistence-oriented communities. Individual species and ecosystem provide benefits in terms of recreation and tourism.

   Not all of the benefits of biodiversity accrue in the present, in relation to current uses. In fact, it is often argued that significant benefits might be obtained from future use of (individual) biological resources in the pharmaceutical and plant breeding industries, respectively as sources of "leads" for the development of drugs, and as sources of genetic material for the development of improved agricultural varieties.

   Estimating actual benefits from this type of future use depends on several variables. In the case of pharmaceutical values, these include probability and cost of discovery, market value of the resulting drugs, and royalty rates.

   Because of the uncertainty surrounding some of these variables, and because of the different methodologies that can be employed to estimate benefits (for example, based on average or marginal values of species), figures produced in the literature vary considerably.

Table 1.4   A typology of values of biodiversity

	Single biodiversity unit (single gene, species, ecosystem)	Collection of biodiversity units (mix of genes, species, ecosystems)
1. Use values:		
1.1 Current Use:		
Transacted in markets	* Example: products (agriculture, forestry or fishery) and services (nature tourism) traded in markets; * Value expressed by market prices	
Not transacted in markets	* Examples: biological resources used for own consumption (nutrition, construction, medicinal use) * Values can be inferred from related markets via production function, replacement cost techniques, etc.	*Example: value of a diverse set of genes, species, ecosystems to ensure survival of biological resources currently used; value of diversity to provide all other ecological services*
1.2 Possible future use:		
Markets available	* Example: bio-prospecting contracts	
Markets not available	* Example: *future* genetic information of possible use in agriculture, or pharmaceutical industries * Value estimated from projections of demands and likelihood of discovery	*Current insurance value associated to a diverse set of genes and species*
2. Non-use values:		
Expressed in monetary transactions	* Example: some donations to conservation organizations	
Not expressed in monetary transactions	* Existence value attached to individual biological units (species, ecosystems) and not expressed via monetary transactions (donations, etc.)	* Existence value attached to set of biodiversity units and not expressed via monetary transactions (donations, etc.)

Note: italicised entries denote indirect benefits of biodiversity

For example, Mendelsohn and Balick (1995) report a value of $48 per hectare; whereas Simpson, Sedjo and Reid (1996) estimate quickly declining marginal values of conservation as species increase (the value of the marginal species – and by extension the marginal hectare – approaches zero when the total number of species exceeds 600,000).

A further way in which individual biological resources or collections of them may generate benefits directly, is when people care for their protection irrespective of actual use (existence values). A specialised literature has burgeoned in the last couple of decades, to elicit estimates of existence values based on contingent valuation methodologies. According to the summary provided by Van Kooten and Bulte (2000), annual willingness to pay (WTP) ranges between $5 and $100 per individual. For a large number of individuals, the upper bound of the range may result in significant aggregate values. However, simply adding up values across different species may violate budget constraints; in addition, WTP is likely to be sensitive to the conservation status of the biological resources being valued. In particular, marginal WTP is likely to decline as species approach viable population sizes, as the degree of threat will be perceived as less immediate.

Indirect linkages: biodiversity and ecosystem functions
Another way, perhaps even more important, in which loss of biological resources may affect human welfare is through the linkage between biological resources and ecological function such as climate regulation, watershed protection, soil conservation, nutrient cycles, and so forth. Here again, there are two issues to be considered. The first is the value that any *specific* biological resource has in connection to the delivery of a well-identified ecological service. For example, a particular species of insect or bird may have a key role in delivering pollination service for a particular plant with commercial or subsistence value. The second possibility is that ecological services are provided by assemblages of species; so that subtracting species to the set will incrementally reduce the ability of the ecosystem to generate welfare-enhancing services. There may be a threshold level beyond which additional deletion of species leads the ecosystem to collapse. This is called the "rivet" hypothesis, in analogy to a plane in which several rivets can be taken away with little efect on the plane's ability to fly, until eventually one rivet too many will cause the plane's wings to fail.

The precise relationship between number of species (or other measures of biological diversity) and ecosystem function is the subject of considerable debate among ecologists (Mooney, Lubchenco et al., 1995) While there seems to be broad agreement on the fact that in a large variety of circumstances there is a non-negative relationship between the two sets of magnitudes, there is much less consensus on whether the functional link is monotonous, or whether it may "plateau off" beyond a certain level of species richness, making additional species beyond the threshold "redundant" in terms of ecosystem services. Figure 1.2 proposes a simplified account of the basic argument. The conventional view is represented by the ever-increasing upper curve: decreases in diversity always imply lower provision of ecosystem functions. However, an alternative paradigm has also been put forward (see Grime, 1997 for a discussion of recent evidence), which maintains that there may in fact be a critical level of diversity (d^*), associated with the presence of species with no substitutes for the delivery of particular ecological services. However, higher levels of diversity (that is, in excess of d^*) may in fact be found to be associated with non-increasing levels of ecological services.

The policy implication is that impacts of a given reduction in loss will critically depend on what is the initial level of diversity, *relative* to the critical level d^*. If initial diversity d_0 is located to the right of d^*, as in Figure 1.2, diversity losses in the tract d_0 - d^* are associated to non-decreasing provision of ecological services, and hence, most likely, to non-decreasing level of human welfare.

Despite the increasing attention of economists to the issue (see Perrings, Barbier et al., 1995, Simpson, 2000, Van Kooten and Bulte, 2000, for some reviews), attaching dollar figures to this type of biodiversity values is not easy. First, several valuation studies focus on ecological services in general, and not on those services that may be affected by changes in biodiversity. Secondly, many studies value total values of eco-services, rather than marginal values (i.e. the value of services provided by the marginal unit of land or the marginal species). This issue may have important implications when ecosystems with different levels of species richness are being analysed. In particular, in tropical ecosystems (typically richer in species than temperate ecosystems), the value of the marginal species in terms of securing the provision of ecological services may be relatively low, since the probability that it lies to the right of the critical threshold d^* is possibly higher than in ecosystems with lower diversity.

An often quoted recent attempt to estimate the value of ecological services is study by Costanza et al. (1997). This estimates that the earth's ecosystems (classified in 17 major categories) produce annual benefits worth \$33 trillion. Apart from the fact that the value estimated exceeds the world GDP (\$25 trillion for the reference year 1994), thereby introducing into the exercise a budget constraint violation, it is unclear how much of the total value estimated by the Costanza et al. study would be affected by changes in the underlying biodiversity traits of the ecosystems being analysed.

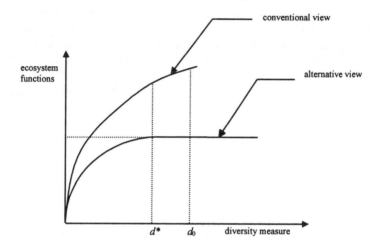

Figure 1.2   Diversity and ecosystem function: alternative views

A further aspect that complicates the task of estimating the indirect benefits of biodiversity conservation is the need to explicitly include *time* into the measure of value being considered. Any given management decision on natural resources (land use, species extraction) will be producing a different pattern over time of impacts on the diversity traits of the ecosystem, and in turn on ecological services. This pattern may include for example no effects initially, a subsequent decline in diversity, and later recovery, stabilisation, or further decline. To exemplify, in Figure 1.3 a management decision is taken at time t_0 (for example, a partial land clearing). No effect on baseline diversity levels (d^*) is observed until time t_1, when diversity starts to decline.

Depending on the type and intensity of the initial intervention, on the presence of further interventions, on the baseline characteristics of the ecosystem (including its resilience and hence ability to recover from shocks), and of a number of other factors, at time t_2 biological diversity may tend to recover its initial levels (pattern *a*), may stabilise at the lover diversity level *d'* (pattern *b*), or it may further decline (as in pattern *c*).

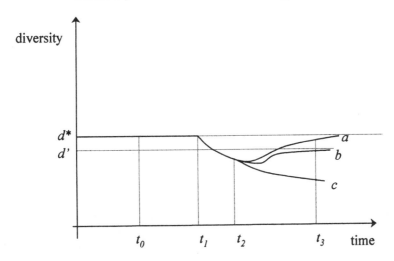

Figure 1.3   Land management and diversity impacts over time

As a result, value measures will lead to different management decisions depending on the time horizon over which they are applied. If the time horizon extends only until t_1, then probably decisions will be biased in favour of conversion, as no notable diversity effect is likely to be observed on that time horizon. Conversely, if the time horizon extends until t_2, then decisions may be more conservative because only diversity decline will be observed. Finally, over the broader time horizon $t_0 - t_3$, full (pattern *a*) or partial recovery (pattern *b*) of baseline diversity level may occur, so that management decisions may allow for more conversion than in the t_2 time horizon, but possibly less than in the first time horizon ($t_0 - t_1$), because of the possibility of the ever declining diversity pattern *c*.

Irreversibility and uncertainty
The above summary of the ecological debate leads to the conclusion that the current biological and ecological understanding of the linkages between diversity and ecosystem function is still considerably limited, and quite possibly unable to provide clear guidance to policy. The issue then becomes one of analysing how scientific uncertainty affects decision-making rules customarily applied in conditions of better information.

Even though it is only in recent years that the economic literature has focused on the actual term (and concept of) biodiversity, there have been lines of the literature that have addressed very similar issues related the desirability of revisiting the principles of benefit-cost analysis (BCA) for decisions that may entail the irretrievable loss of natural areas as a result of development.

Building on previous work on conservation (Krutilla, 1967) and on capital theory (Arrow, 1968), Fisher, Krutilla et al. (1972) show that the simple presence of irreversibility makes the case for less development; and that this result is strengthened if benefits from preservation are increasing over time, relative to benefits from development. Explicit modifications of standard BCA decision criteria are proposed by Porter (1982), when projects consist of developing a natural area and converting it to alternative uses, like industrial or agricultural activity.

A formal treatment of the nature of the conservation problem in presence of irreversibility is provided by Arrow and Fisher (1974) and Henry (1974). The most important feature of this branch of the literature is to take explicitly into account the one aspect of the conservation problem that, in addition to irreversibility, makes it particularly intractable for decision makers. That is, the information asymmetry between the preservation and development choices: while development benefits are, subject to reasonable approximation, known with certainty, preservation benefits are in most cases uncertain.

Yet, as is shown in subsequent contributions[11] that refine the basic ideas of Arrow, Fisher and Henry, it turns out that, under a set of assumptions about the features[12] of the decision problem, it is the very presence of uncertainty and irreversibility at the same time that makes optimal development lower than in standard situations (i.e. in situations with no uncertainty and irreversibility).

The key concept that supports this result is quasi-option value. This is defined as the expected value of information, *conditional* on the decision of not developing in the first place. For the class of decision problems studied by Arrow, Fisher and Hanemann, quasi-option value is non-negative, which implies that there is always a non-negative gain (i.e., there is never a loss) attached to the choice of postponing development until more information is available on the benefits from preservation.

In addition to quasi-option value, there have been other approaches that advocate a conservative revision of criteria to be adopted in development decisions. The Safe Minimum Standards (SMS) literature (Southgate, 1991) uses methods of decision theory (in particular the MiniMax criterion) to justify avoidance of decisions that lead to irreversible consequences (such as species extinction) "unless the social costs of doing so are unacceptably large". In the area of environmental law and regulation, the "precautionary principle" has been often championed as the appropriate way for the environmental regulatory community to deal with the problem of uncertainty. The principle states that rather than await certainty, regulators should act in anticipation of any potential environmental harm in order to prevent it (Costanza, 1994).

1.4   ECONOMIC ACTIVITY AND BIODIVERSITY LOSS

Biodiversity matters to human wellbeing, as discussed in previous sections. But does human activity determine the loss of biodiversity? And if so, how? A significant amount of effort has been devoted to analysing the causes of biodiversity loss (see for example, McNeely et al., 1995; Pearce and Moran, 1994; World Resources Institute, 1992; Forester and Machlis, 1996; Ostrom, 1995; Stedman-Edwards, 1997; World Resources Institute, 1992). Many of the contributors to this literature develop lists of social and economic "causes" that are considered responsible for biodiversity loss; they then propose a ranking of those causes according to their position in a causation chain leading from "root causes" to actual biodiversity loss. Finally, they argue that unless action is taken to address the ultimate causes of loss (such as population growth, consumption patterns, global trade, inequitable entitlements to land and other natural resources, market failure, etc.) biodiversity will continue to disappear (see for example McNeely, Gadgil et al., 1995; Barbier, Burgess, and Folke, 1994; Pearce and Moran, 1994).

To be sure, the task of analysing the social and economic causes of biodiversity loss is made complex by a number of factors. First, there is the issue of clarifying "what causes of what loss". As discussed earlier, biodiversity is a multi-dimensional notion, encompassing management objectives at the genetic, species and ecosystem level. Although it is likely that significant areas of overlap exist, it is not a foregone conclusion that one set of explanations fits all of the dimensions of the biodiversity concept. For example, the causes of loss of genes may not necessarily coincide with the causes of ecosystem loss. Secondly, there is the issue of actually documenting loss before explaining its causes. There are relatively few species that are actually known to have become extinct as a result of human interventions (see note 9 on page 32). Much of the debate on the relationship between economic activity and biodiversity impacts relates to the fact that some management actions such as land conversion may *commit* species to extinction. But as argued earlier, the ultimate *outcome* of extinction will depend on a number of circumstances that precede and follow the human induced perturbation of the ecosystem.

For the sake of brevity, two areas of the economic literature will be briefly discussed here, which have addressed in recent times aspects of direct or indirect relevance for the analysis of the causes of biodiversity loss. A first branch of the literature focuses on the economic analysis of activities that lead to the extinction of *species*. Another area of the literature analyses the causes of a key phenomenon thought to result, via habitat perturbation, in biodiversity loss; namely, tropical deforestation.

1.4.1   Extinction theories

The seminal work in this area by Gordon and Clark (Gordon, 1954; Clark, 1973a; Clark, 1973b) focuses on fish extinction due to over-harvesting. In Clark's analysis, over-harvesting may occur under two different assumptions about the prevailing property right regime.

Under open access to fish stocks, the harvesting equilibrium will be determined by the "zero rent" condition, (and not by the "zero *marginal* rent" condition that an individual, profit-maximiser stockowner would select). If the harvesting rate corresponding to the zero rent point exceeds the Maximum Sustainable Yield (MSY) harvesting level, the stock will be depleted to extinction.

Extinction can also occur under private ownership if the growth rate of the species stock is lower than the single owner's discount rate. If the "rate of return" to the resource (i.e. the resource's growth rate) is less than the interest rate (discount rate, opportunity cost of capital and interest rate are all equal here), it will make sense to "mine" the resource to extinction, and invest the proceeds in higher yielding assets in the capital market or elsewhere.

One of the policy implications of Clark's model is that for low growth species, the higher the market price, the higher the likelihood of extinction. Therefore, policies aimed at conservation need to lower the resource's sale price. A theory of extinction that reaches the opposite policy conclusion has been proposed by Swanson (Swanson, 1994; Swanson, 1990).

A key feature of Swanson's theory is to highlight that resource management decisions are taken not only on the basis of the net return to the resource's use, but also on the basis of the opportunity cost, i.e. the return to *alternative* uses of the resource. While this observation may have little bearing on marine environments that have few alternative uses, it makes a significant difference when it comes to land-based species: land has a number of alternative (and often mutually exclusive) uses.

If the opportunity cost of maintaining an area in a wilderness state (i.e. the foregone revenues from agriculture or urban development) are high, it will make sense for the resource user or manager to give up the land use with lower returns. The policy implication is that species will survive only if activities compatible with their conservation command high enough returns to compete with alternative land uses.

1.4.2   The causes of tropical deforestation

Loss of forests in the tropics has been at the centre of a world-wide public and policy debate over the last quarter of the 20th century in connection to its possible detrimental consequences in ecological, social and economic terms. Despite conceptual and practical problems surrounding the definition and measurement of concept such as "forest", forest "conversion" and "degradation", available global data from FAO suggests that in the tropics annual rates of deforestation have averaged 0.8% in the period 1980-1991, which gives a total of some 140 million ha of forest lost in that period (an area the size of a country like Peru).

Calls for private and public action to slow down the loss of tropical forests are motivated by concerns that deforestation may result in disruption of tropical ecosystems and associated reduced provision of ecological services at a local scale (watershed protection, micro-climate stabilisation), as well as at a global one (carbon sequestration). In addition, it is often remarked that immediate beneficiaries of the ecological and economic benefits (e.g. source of food, building material, etc.) of tropical forests are segments of tropical countries' population of special vulnerability, such as poor, subsistence-oriented communities, often of indigenous descent.

More to the point of the present research, deforestation has also been associated with biodiversity loss, primarily on account of the high number of species per unit of land area often documented in the tropics. Mainly on the basis of theoretical constructs such as the island bio-geography theory and the associated "species-area" relationship (both to be discussed in more detail in Chapter 2), it has been argued that loss of tropical forests is bound to result sooner or later in loss of species, "committed" to extinction by the loss or severe disruption of their habitat.

The social and economic causes of tropical deforestation are the subject of a voluminous literature. Earlier contributions are summarised by Brown and Pearce (1994); because of its thorough coverage of the more recent literature, the main findings of the review by Kaimowitz and Angelsen (1998) will be summarized here. The authors revisit the distinction frequently made in the literature between direct (proximate), intermediate and ultimate causes of deforestation:

(i) Proximate Causes

These are human actions that result in the elimination of tropical woody vegetation. Causes belonging to this group include timber logging for commercial purposes, collection of fuel-wood, extraction of lumber as construction material, forest clearing for agriculture or cattle ranching. In terms of decision-making analysis, these correspond to the *choice variables* for the various types of economic agents (e.g., households, firms) involved in decisions on natural resource use. For example, given her resource endowment, preferences, technology available, input and output prices, attitude towards risk, etc., a farmer will select how much of the resources under her control (time, labour, cash, etc.) will be invested in converting natural forest to pasture or agricultural land.

(ii) Intermediate Causes

These include the *parameters* that influence economic agents in their decision making processes: output and input prices (including labour cost), regimes of access to resources (including land tenure), availability of information, accessibility of land and other natural resources.

An important cause in this group is the inadequate functioning of the price mechanism, for example in the case of prices not reflecting the external cost of deforestation in terms of its impact on the provision of ecological services (aquifer recharge, protection of watershed from flash floods, micro-climate regulation, and of course for the present purposes, biodiversity conservation).

Another important set of "intermediate" causes is the lack of information, institutions and resources that could allow sustainable management of tropical forests. Knowledge of ecosystems' value in terms of their life-support functions may be inadequate, both among the general public, and among policy makers (information failures). Even if there is private and public awareness of the importance of conservation, the required institutions, and the necessary endowment of material and human capital may not be available. Among the missing institutions, special importance is traditionally given to absent or ill-defined property rights on land, or on natural resources like water, forests, and air.

(iii) Ultimate Causes

These are the macro-economic variables and policy instruments that determine the parameters of the agents' decision making processes (and hence influence their choices albeit in an indirect fashion). Ultimate or underlying causes include demographic patterns (including migration flows), fiscal, exchange rate, monetary and sectorial policies, world market prices, and technology.

These are the causes ultimately responsible for generating social and economic incentives that do not favour forest conservation. Several authors agree in singling out a few number of key causes: human attitudes towards natural resources, population growth, natural resource consumption patterns, global trade, inequitable distribution of income and wealth, global institutional and market failure (World Resources Institute, 1992; McNeely, Gadgil et al., 1995).

Kaimowitz and Angelsen review over 140 deforestation models, which they classify according to the scale of analysis (micro level, including household, farm, or firm level; regional level; and national level); and according to the methodology employed to examine the relationship between causes investigated and deforestation outcomes. The various methodologies include analytical modelling (which develops deforestation hypotheses based on underlying behavioural assumption, but does not test hypotheses against empirical evidence), simulation techniques (including linear and non-linear programming, and general equilibrium modelling), and regression analysis.

They find several areas of consensus among the models reviewed: in particular, deforestation tends to be greater when forested lands are more accessible, when the prices of agricultural products and timber are higher, when rural wages are lower, and when trade arrangements are more open. At the same time, they suggest that in the reviewed literature there is no consensus on the deforestation impact of input prices (including land markets), tenure arrangements, productivity growth, and poverty (as measured by household income).

One caveat is in order on the possibility of extrapolating the conclusions of this literature to the causes of biodiversity loss. Arguing that any given cause of tropical deforestation is *also* a cause of biodiversity loss is legitimate to the extent that there is a documented mechanism to map, under different circumstances, any given change in forest cover into a corresponding change of a specified biodiversity objective function (at the genetic, species or ecosystem level). In particular, the resulting change in biodiversity expected to follow from a change in forest cover should be inferred from a known mechanism of species loss, such as extinction (Barbault and Sastrapradja, 1995).

1.5 SUMMARY

This chapter has provided a summary of the main aspects of the biodiversity debate. It has reviewed the conceptual and practical issues surrounding the definition and measurement of biodiversity. It has discussed the reasons for concerns about excessive loss of biodiversity, which relate to the direct and indirect positive contributions of biodiversity to human welfare.

One of the main conclusions of this chapter's review is that scientific knowledge currently available is not sufficient to guide decision makers in choices related to uses of natural resources that may have impacts on biodiversity. Two points seem of particular importance. First: biodiversity loss is seldom *observed*; most often it is *inferred* (especially form processes of land use change). Second: even if loss of biodiversity *does* in fact take place, we do not know precisely how much human welfare is being, or will be, lost as a result.

While there is widespread concern (and often good evidence) that overexploitation of species and conversion of natural habitat produces extinction of species, genetic erosion and ecosystem loss, there is no straightforward criterion to establish where to stop the process of conversion of nature to human use. Both extremes of outright preservation and of full development seem to be out of the question: the former because it would be prohibitively expensive in the terms of opportunity cost of foregone development, the latter because of the unacceptably high risks of compromising the delivery of critical ecosystem services. There must be some middle ground that balances off current benefits accruing to those who gain from nature conversion, with future benefits accruing to social groups that depend (in present or future generations) on biodiversity for their material or spiritual wellbeing.

The task of coming up with the scientific insight and the empirical data necessary to determine where that middle ground may be, is certainly daunting, and it is unlikely that anything close to it may be feasible in the foreseeable future. This is the reason why, given current limits to our understanding of biodiversity and its effects on human welfare, "Safe Minimum Standards" or the "Precautionary Principle" have been put forward as pragmatic guides for action. However, in the many developing country situations where postponing conversion of wilderness areas would entail destitution or starvation, Safe Minimum Standards are not viable, because the consequences of their application would indeed be "unacceptably high social costs".

Under those circumstances, what, if any, could be the role of applied research? Even if we cannot say how much is the biodiversity loss that will ultimately result in loss of human welfare, at least we can investigate two ancillary questions, namely: (a) what are the social and economic processes that drive processes believed to be the proximate causes of biodiversity loss (mainly land use change and species exploitation); (b) how much biodiversity is likely to become lost as a result of those processes.

Given the importance attached by the ecological and biological literature to habitat modifications, this book focuses on social and economic processes that determine land use decisions. In particular, Chapter 2 analyses the sequence of land use changes typically observed in a number of tropical countries, and discusses interventions that could alter the incentives for land conversion. Based on the Mexico case study material presented in Chapter 4, chapters 5 and 6 propose quantitative models for analysing land use decisions at the farm level, and for their aggregation over space and time.

NOTES

1. The actual numbers need to be interpreted with caution, since they are likely to conceal multiple counting of the same items. Nevertheless, they provide an order of magnitude of the volume of information that is currently generated and gathered on the topic of biodiversity.
2. The Secretariat of the UN Conference on Environment and Development has estimated the average annual costs (1993-2000) of implementing Agenda 21 in developing countries to be over \$600 billion, including about \$125 billion on grant or concessional terms from the international community. The Conference secretariat has also estimated that the average total annual cost (1993-2000) of implementing activities related to biodiversity conservation to be about \$3.5 billion, including about \$1.75 billion from the international community on grant or concessional terms. All of these figures are indicative and order-of-magnitude

estimates only, and have not been reviewed by governments. Actual costs will depend upon, inter alia, the specific strategies and programmes governments decide upon for implementation. It may be argued that some portion of the second figure (i.e. the cost of actions specifically targeted at biodiversity conservation) may be reduced by appropriate allocation of resources included in the first figure, which determines a "baseline" course of actions countries would undertake to pursue national sustainable development objectives. Issues related to the determination of "baseline", "alternative" and "incremental cost" of biodiversity conservation are addressed in theoretical terms in Chapter 3.

3. The Preamble to the Convention on Biological Diversity express the Contracting Parties' awareness "of the general lack of information and knowledge regarding biological diversity and of the urgent need to develop scientific, technical and institutional capacities to provide the basic understanding upon which to plan and implement appropriate measures".

4. See for example Ehrlich (1988); Wilson (1988); Reid and Miller (1989); McNeely et al. (1990); Groombridge (1992); World Resources Institute (1992); Perrings, Mäler et al. (1994); Heywood (1995); Van Kooten and Bulte (2000).

5. The measurement of pair-wise distance is often based on genetic methods, such as DNA-DNA hybridization.

6. For an application of Weitzman's pure diversity measure to a situation where the required genetic data is available, see Weitzman (1993).

7. An alternative approach for estimating rates of loss in pre-industrial times is to use the species-area relationship (see below in the text) and use information on past land conversion and likely habitat losses.

8. It is thought that there are somewhere between 5 to 80 million species on earth. A conservative estimate is 13-14 million of which just 1.75 million have been described, some in only rudimentary detail (Barbault and Sastrapradja, 1995)

9. "The rate at which species are likely to become extinct in the near future is very uncertain. If we look at the number of recorded species extinctions since 1600 it is barely four figures, which contrasts with several predictions of imminent or actual massive extinctions that have been made in the period 1980-95, based mainly on a species-area model derived from the field of island biogeography" (Heywood, 1992). Gentry (1996) observes that "(...) to date, gratifyingly few extinctions of plant species are known to have occurred. We might still have time to save nearly all plant species of the neotropics". According to Edwards (1995), a total of 626 extinctions of species (50% of them invertebrates) have been documented during the period 1600-1994 (quoted by Van Kooten and Bulte, 2000).

10. However, diversity may matter also for single-resource values, to the extent that species with no individual use and hence value are required for the survival of the species actually used.

11. See Fisher and Hanemann (1986) and Hanemann (1989).

12. In particular, (a) only two periods are considered; (b) in both of them, there are only two discrete choices: either no development or full development; (c) new information is obtained by preserving, *and not* by developing.

PART II.

THEORETICAL ISSUES

2. Land use change, biodiversity loss, and economic analysis

Given the importance attached by the ecological and biological literature to habitat modifications as a threat to biodiversity conservation, it is important to analyse the social and economic processes that determine land use decisions. This chapter analyses the sequence of land use changes typically observed in a number of tropical countries, and discusses interventions that could alter the incentives for land conversion.

2.1 LAND CONVERSION AND BIODIVERSITY LOSS

There is abundant evidence suggesting that land use change phenomena are widespread worldwide. Many developing countries in Asia, Africa and Latin America host the remains of primary forests and other pristine areas especially rich in diverse biological resources. In those continents, conversion of land to productive activities like agriculture, pasture and other uses has been particularly intense during the seventies and eighties, as summarised in Table 2.1.

Much of the literature focuses on the role of conversion of land from a pristine state to productive activities as a major proximate cause of loss (see for example Groombridge, 1992; Lugo, 1988; McNeely, Gadgil et al., 1995). The theoretical rationale for this is provided by the island biogeography theory (MacArthur and Wilson, 1967).

According to this theory, there is a more or less stable functional link (the species-area relation) between the extension of an area biologically homogenous and the number of species resident therein. The form of the species-area relation commonly adopted is $S = \alpha A^{\beta}$, where S is the number of species, A is the size of the area, and α and β are, respectively, a proportionality and an elasticity parameter. The latter is empirically estimated to range in the interval 0.15-0.35. In particular, with a value of β of approximately 1/4, a 90% reduction of the size of an "island", say forest, should produce a halving of the number of species.

Table 2.1   *Evidence on land use change world-wide, 1987-89*

	Cropland	Permanent pasture	Forest and woodland	Other land
World	1,478 (2.2%)	3,323 (0.1%)	4,095 (-1.8%)	4,233 (1.0%)
Africa	186 (4.4%)	891 (0.5%)	686 (-3.6%)	1,200 (1.9%)
North Central America	274 (1.1%)	369 (3.1%)	715 (1%)	780 (-2.5%)
South America	142 (10.9%)	478 (4.1%)	896 (-4.6%)	238 (4.7%)
Asia	454 (0.8%)	694 (-0.3%)	539 (-5.3%)	1,044 (2.8%)
Europe	140 (-1.3%)	83 (-4.0%)	157 (1.1%)	93 (3.8%)
USSR	232 (-0.2%)	371 (-0.6%)	945 (1.7%)	679 (-1.9%)
Oceania	49 (11.65%)	437 (-3.1%)	157 (-0.6%)	199 (5.05)

Note: All figures in million hectares; figures in brackets are percentage changes since 1977-1979

Source: World Resources Institute (1992)

There are at least two problems with estimates of species loss based on the species-area relation; these problems are associated with the A variable, and with the α parameter, respectively. Looking at A, first, how does it change over time? What is an appropriate measure of the "island's" size that ought to be considered in the calculation? Consider the case of tropical forests, which are among the richest areas of the world in terms of biological resources.

Predictions of future extinction depend crucially upon assumptions about deforestation rates; as usual in these cases, simple fitting of a regression curve on past deforestation data may or may not be appropriate, depending on the way demographic, economic and policy variables are supposed to affect deforestation.

Furthermore, it is commonly asserted that the size of tropical "islands" should decrease when deforestation is taking place. However, it is often argued that there are not only two possible states of the land, i.e. forested and deforested land, but more than that. In particular, not all the logged forest has to be considered unforested land, since a part of it turns into secondary forest fallow; moreover, a proportion, even if small, of cleared land is converted every year into secondary fallow forest through natural regeneration or human intervention (Lugo, 1988).[1]

A further reason why species-area curves may overestimate extinctions is that these curves are based on single taxa, and it is likely that assemblages of species will exhibit different relationships which can not be captured by simply adding up curves (Lugo, Parrotta et al., 1993).

Consider now the α parameter in the species-area relation. This represents a scale factor on which the unit effect of size variation is applied, so that the overall effect on the number of species can be derived. If we interpret the S variable as the proportion of species resident in the island relative to the total number of species in a wider geographic region, say the tropics, as a function of the size of the island, α becomes the ratio between the number of species initially existing in a given "island", and the total.

It is the case that such a ratio exhibits wide variation across different types of habitats; there is evidence, for example, that species richness doubles from dry to moist forests, and triples from dry to wet forests. To quote again Lugo (1988), in estimating extinction rates, it should not be assumed 'that all tropical forests are subject to the same rate of deforestation, respond uniformly to the same reduction in area, or turn into sterile pavement once converted'.

Despite the fact that the documented evidence of species extinction through deforestation or other forms of land use change, is limited, there is consensus that habitat loss causes several species to be "ommitted to extinction". However, the time to reach a new equilibrium characterised by a lower species number is unknown (McNeely, Gadgil et al., 1995). This may be a particularly important element in policy design, on account of the fact that rates of land use change exhibit variability over time. Periods of intense conversion of forests to agriculture or pasture may be followed by periods of

Biodiversity in the balance

slower change, and even of reconversion of land to its previous state. Global land use data suggest that in the late eighties to early nineties, the rate of conversion of forests has been slower than in the previous decade, and that in some regions, especially in the American continent, previously farmed land might have returned under forest cover: see Table 2.2 for an illustration.

Table 2.2   Evidence on land use changes world-wide, 1992-94

	Cropland	Permanent Pasture	Forest and Woodland	Other Land
World	1,466 (2.0%)	3,410 (3.2%)	4,177 (-2.2%)	3,992 (-1.0%)
Africa	189 (6.5%)	889 (0%)	713 (-0.3%)	1,171 (-0.8%)
North America	233 (-1.1%)	267 (-1.2%)	749 (2.9%)	588 (-2.6%)
Central America	40 (5.4%)	98 (6.2%)	74 (1.2%)	86 (-9.2%)
South America	113 (9%)	495 (3.0%)	935 (0.6%)	209 (-12.3%)
Asia	520 (na)	1,051 (na)	557 (na)	957 (na)
Europe	317 (na)	178 (na)	948 (na)	816 (na)
Oceania	51 (1.4%)	430 (-2.8%)	200 (-0.2%)	165 (6.3%)

Note: All figures in million hectares; figures in brackets are percentage changes since 1982-1984. Figures for the World do not include Antarctica

Source: World Resources Institute (1998) World Resources 1998-99: A Guide to the Global Environment. New York: Oxford University Press

In summary, the species-area relationship (SAR) indicates a correlation between size of an area and number of species to be found in that area.

However, accurate quantitative predictions of extinction should be based on models incorporating the known mechanisms of extinction (Barbault & Sastrapradja, 1995).

Subject to these qualifications, the island bio-geography theory, together with the empirically ascertained relevance of land use changes, still provides powerful arguments for being concerned about land use change. It is therefore necessary to analyse more closely the process of land conversion. This could be helpful in proposing interventions at the national and international level to mitigate this important cause of biodiversity loss. In what follows, the problem will be addressed, of what measures should be taken to prevent land conversion. It will be assumed that the geographical areas where interventions are warranted have been identified on the basis of some proper ecological or biological criterion.

2.2   LAND CONVERSION: A CONCEPTUAL FRAMEWORK

As reviewed in Chapter 1, recent theories of extinction are based on an analysis of the allocation of land among competing uses (Swanson, 1990; Swanson, 1994). These theories are consistent with the basic postulate of economic theory, that resources are allocated among competing uses in such a way that economic returns from them could be maximised. Allocation of resources among land uses should be no exception. Accordingly, standard land use theory (as illustrated for example in Hartwick and Olewiler, 1986; Randall and Castle, 1985) suggests that land use decisions are guided by the criterion of maximising W, the net present value of activities carried out on land over the relevant time horizon:

$$W = \int_{t_0}^{T} e^{-\rho t} \big(R_h(t) \big) dt \tag{2.1}$$

where t_0 and T are the initial and terminal point of the relevant time horizon, ρ is the discount rate, $R_h(t)$ is the total of rents in the parcel of size h in time period t.

Rents, i.e. the revenues from land in excess of the input (labour and capital) cost, vary not only over time, but also across different land uses: agriculture (and within agriculture across different crops), ranching, logging, and so forth. The reason of this variation is that each use is characterised by different input requirements, and hence different labour and capital costs per unit of output, different price of the final output, and finally different transportation costs, depending on the distance from the market of the area where the activities are carried out. For use i, rent is then defined by:

$$R_i = y_i (p_i - w l_i - t_i x) \qquad (2.2)$$

where R is rent per unit of land (rent per unit of output, in brackets, times output per unit of land, y);
p is price of the output;
t is transportation costs per unit of distance;
x is distance of the production site from the market;
l is the labour requirement per unit of output;
w is the wage rate.

This simple formulation assumes that there is a fixed input proportions technology, that capital inputs are limited to transportation capital, and that neither unit transportation costs, t, nor fertility (output per unit of land, y) vary with distance. In what follows, the analysis of the incentives to land conversion will be mainly referred to developing countries' frontier regions between agriculture and pristine areas. In those situations, the adoption of traditional production techniques is quite widespread, and access to alternative techniques pretty much constrained by institutional, financial and cultural factors. This justifies the assumption of a fixed factor proportion technology.

It is interesting to emphasise the last determinant of cost (i.e. distance) for three reasons. Firstly, because we are interested in the balance between developed and undeveloped (forested) land. When productive activities take place in locations further and further away from the market, the frontier between cleared and forested land moves ahead, and the size of the forested area shrinks. So, increasing distance from the market of activities requiring land clearing is a proxy for decrease in conservation.

Secondly, unit transportation cost is a parameter that can be influenced by policy through road building; therefore, policy can in some cases have a crucial role in determining land use changes.[2]

Thirdly, we can use a diagrammatic tool known as "bid-rent function", which has the advantage of a very intuitive interpretation. Consider Figure 2.1: the variable x on the horizontal axis represents distance from a hypothetical market central location; on the vertical axis there are rents from land. The two downward sloping lines are the graphical counterpart of equation (2.2) for two possible competing land uses, 1 and 2. For distances in the interval $[0, x_1)$, land will be used for activity 1, as rents from that use are higher. For distances in the interval $[x_1, x_2]$, land use 2 will prevail. For distances $x>x_2$, none of the two activities is profitable, and land will be left idle. The bid-rent function tells us what pattern of land use will result from maximisation of rents; in Figure 2.1, the bid-rent function is given by the line ABx_2.

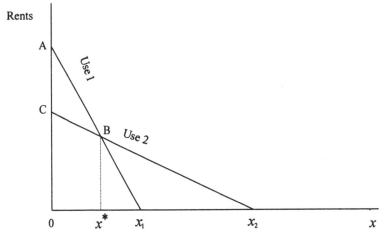

Figure 2.1   Bid-rent schedule for two competing land uses

The bid rent function could be used to conduct a very simple diagrammatic analysis of a pattern of land use change typically occurring in areas with relative abundance of pristine (mainly forested land), and undergoing a process of colonisation. This pattern is known as the "peasant pioneer cycle", and consists of a number of stages including logging, mineral extraction and/or annual cropping, ranching, and, as a possible but not inevitable last stage, abandoning land in favour of other, still virgin areas, where the cycle restarts. In this sequence, given relative abundance of land with normally undefined property rights, capital and labour are employed to a great extent to "mine the nutrients" contained in the forest's soil, rather than being invested in maintaining the soil productivity. This phenomenon is often summarised by the phrase "it is cheaper to bring the farm to the nutrients, than to bring the nutrients to the farm". In recent times, the pioneer cycle has been convincingly used by Schneider (1992) to explain deforestation in Brazil's Amazon.

Consider the four panels of Figure 2.2 and Figure 2.3. They are meant to be only an example, useful to clarify ideas, but without claims of complete realism. Starting from panel 1 in Figure 2.2, an area is covered entirely by forest over the tract $0-\bar{x}$. Until distance x_e extractivism (i.e. sustainable harvesting of non-timber forest products), which does not imply clearing, is profitable; for $x>x_e$ no activity is viable, and the forest is left in its virgin state.

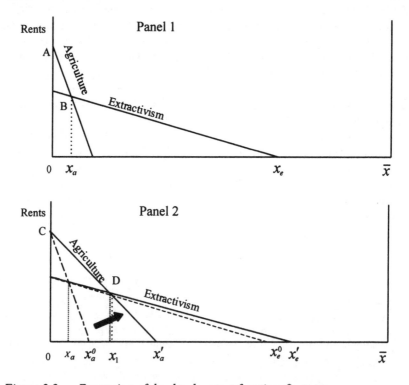

Figure 2.2   Expansion of the development frontier: first stages

Agriculture has a lower labour input requirement (higher vertical intercept), but much higher transportation costs (few roads are initially available) than extractivism. The reason for this assumption is that in the case of agriculture, transportation costs have a more substantial component of input transportation cost (pesticides, irrigation, technical assistance and so on). As a result, agriculture is more profitable only in proximity of the market, i.e. in the interval $[0, x_a]$, in which there are incentives to deforest. The bid-rent frontier is ABx_e.

In panel 2, a road building program has taken place. This has relevant implications for the slope of the rent functions. Namely, it tends to decrease transportation costs, that is, to make the rent curves flatter. However, it is likely that agriculture will benefit more from the road building program, so that its horizontal intercept will shift rightwards *more* (from x_a^0 to x'_a) than the extractivism rent curve will do (from x_e^0 to x'_e). The new bid-rent function is now CDx'_e, so that it will pay to convert land to agriculture (and to deforest) in the interval $[0, x_1]$ (note that to keep matters simple, deforestation costs are deliberately ignored).

In panel 3 (Figure 2.3), the fall in agriculture's productivity – due to nutrient mining - is represented by means of an increase in labour input requirement per unit of output, that is, a lower vertical intercept of the rent function. This has the effect of making profitable another activity with higher transportation costs (say ranching, or cultivation of a different type of crop), in the interval $[0, x'_1]$. Agriculture is now confined to the interval $[x'_1, x_1]$. Note that as deforestation has been carried out over the range $[0, x_1]$, the rent function for extractivism is no longer drawn for that tract. The bid-rent line is now $FGJHx'_e$, with a jump at J.

Consider now panel 4. Nutrient mining continues in the cleared area, so that both farming and ranching productivity decline; when they approximate zero, land is relinquished (interval $[0, x_1]$). In the meanwhile, population density has increased: road building and the prospect of rising income may have encouraged colonisation, or proliferation of urban agglomerates; cleared land may have become accessible to placer miners (like the Amazon's *garimpeiros*). These factors, in turn, increase demand for agriculture commodities, and, thus, with upward sloping supply, their price. In terms of the diagram, this has the effect of shifting the rent function upwards, so that new deforestation in the interval $[x_1, x_2]$ is called for, and the size of the extractivist area shrinks to $x'_e - x_2$. Now the bid-rent line is LMx'_e. The process may iterate until extractivism ceases to be profitable and goes completely out of business, while the development frontier approaches $\bar{x}$.

2.3   INTERVENTIONS TO ALTER THE INCENTIVES TO LAND CONVERSION

The simplified framework of the rent-bid function captures some of the essential elements of the problem of land conversion: the competition among alternative activities for land use, and the impact of the various types of costs on land use patterns. In any particular area of interest for biodiversity conservation, a large number of productive activities will be possible, but they can be divided in two groups, conservation compatible activities (CC), like sustainable harvesting of timber and/or non timber forest products, agroforestry, or ecotourism, and non-conservation-compatible (NCC), e.g. shifting agriculture, unsustainable logging.[3] CC do not require land conversion, whereas NCC do. For simplicity, we will assume that all NCC and all CC activities can be aggregated in two groups. Rents accruing from NCC activities are represented by the r_1 function; rents generated by CC activities are represented by the r_2 function (see again Figure 2.1).

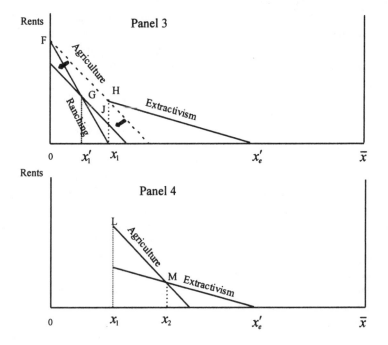

Figure 2.3   Frontier expansion: subsequent stages

It will also be assumed that the area of interest has just been made accessible, say by road building, so that in principle both land use options are open to private resource users. In the absence of any intervention, land users would find it profitable to convert land to NCC activities up to distance x^*. How would it be possible to avoid conversion in the interval $[0, x^*]^4$, i.e., to induce land users to carry out activity 2 in the entire area? In order to answer this question, it is necessary to understand what are the forces determining the divergence in the two rent gradients.

There are a number of reasons why NCC dominate CC over a relevant tract, i.e. $r_1 > r_2$ in $x \in [0, x^*)$. Summarising some of the aspects discussed above in the section on the causes of biodiversity loss, these are briefly reviewed below.

i) Policy distortions

The first and most obvious reason for dominance of NCC activities is that the associated returns may be artificially inflated by policy interventions. If activity 1 is agriculture, subsidised credit or fertiliser purchase clearly has the effect of reducing input costs, shifting the r_1 function upwards, and encouraging more land conversion than would otherwise be the case. Removing policy distortions would shift r_1 downwards, and reduce the gap with the r_2 function.

ii) Property rights

Another usual explanation of the observed pattern of land conversion is the absence of property rights. Consider the case of land formally claimed by the state, but subject to an open access regime. Farmers willing to expand cultivation face at most the cost of clearing and converting land to agriculture. If they were to expand cultivation on parcels of land with clearly defined property rights, they would have to pay a rental fee to the legitimate owner; or if the latter were to cultivate the land himself, he would have to impute some costs in terms of foregone rental value to the agricultural activity carried out. Obviously in the presence of formally defined property rights, a rental cost should be imputed to CC activities as well. But so long as $f_1 > f_2$, where f_i is the rental cost from activity i, less land conversion would take place than in the open access regime.[5]

iii) Yield decline

This type of factor has particular relevance in dynamic settings. In many tropical areas, traditional cultivation techniques lead to a rapid decline in the soil's nutrient content, and hence to a drop in yields per hectare. When yields decline, and no other source of cash income is available, farmers may need to convert new land to cultivation. They will do so if the cost of conversion is lower than the cost of investing in soil conservation techniques. The latter cost, in turn, may be raised by market imperfections like credit constraints.

iv) "Fundamental" difference in returns

In all of the above cases, NCC generate higher returns due to some form of market or institutional imperfections, like policy distortions, ill-defined property rights, or credit constraints preventing the adoption of soil conservation techniques. It may be the case that even without all these distortion factors, a fundamental imbalance in the relative returns of NCC vs. CC activities persists. The rest of this chapter will address the issue of how to generate incentives for CC activities when "spontaneous" incentives would favour NCC activities. This issue is likely to be of interest to the International Community (IC): to the extent that biodiversity generates transnational externalities, IC might consider transferring resources to countries hosting biodiversity to improve the chances of conservation.

Two possibilities might be considered: a) IC might provide resources necessary for shifting the r_2 function upwards up to the point where no NCC activity is attractive to individual land users; b) IC might simply compensate land users for the opportunity cost of conservation, i.e. for the difference in rents in the region $x \in [0, x^*)$.

Before considering these two possibilities individually, it is important to note one common feature. In every scheme of biodiversity conservation, the international community is assumed to provide resources to be used for protecting biodiversity. The international community, however, cannot use the funds itself to achieve the desired objective, but requires the co-operation of some counterparts in the country hosting the biological resources to be protected. These counterparts could be the national state, public authorities at the local level, or land users, acting in isolation, or possibly organised in a local NGO. These parties would have to administer the resources provided by the international community to increase the profitability of CC activities, or to distribute them among land users who would bear the opportunity costs of not converting land.

The international community has imperfect knowledge of some of the characteristics of its country counterparts. For example, it will not know exactly what are the costs and benefits of activities which are currently carried out in the area to be conserved, nor will it know the costs and benefits of suggested conservation compatible activities. (In terms of the preceding analysis, the international community will not know with certainty the location of the r_i curves).

Furthermore, the international community will not be able to monitor closely the behaviour of the counterparts. In particular, it may not be possible to monitor the state's investment in infrastructure enhancing the profitability of CC activities. All the international community may be able to observe *ex post*, is the outcome in terms of changes in land use of its agreement with the state or with land users. This information, too, may not be completely reliable. For example, it is not always straightforward to acquire uncontroversial data on deforestation. Land reconnaissance may be costly, and the use of remote sensing techniques is often constrained by weather induced biases.

Even if the conservation outcome is easily measurable, it may not be possible to establish a one-to-one relationship between that conservation outcome and the "onservation effort" of the party which has entered an agreement with the international community. For instance, land owners may refrain from carrying out NCC activities, and yet a high degree of land conversion may be observed due to the encroachment of squatters (and to inadequate state effort to enforce legitimate owners' property rights).[6]

The following section proposes a simple model to analyse compensation of land users for the foregone benefits from land conversion. The annex to this chapter discusses ways to increase the profitability of CC activities.

2.3.1   Compensating foregone development benefits

In some cases the option of altering the pattern of relative returns of CC vs. NCC activities will not be viable.[7] This may be so for various reasons. First, the cost of increasing rents from CC uses of land may turn out to be too high. This is likely to happen when activities like agroforestry or non-timber forest products face very poor market prospects, very unfavourable soil or weather conditions, or when the required institutional infrastructure (e.g. extension, capacity building) is absent and very costly to establish from scratch. Another possibility could be that activities not requiring land conversion are in fact economically viable, but they are deemed incompatible with conservation. Many countries establish sanctuaries or biosphere reserves where no economic activity is allowed, apart from strictly controlled access for scientific or educational purposes.

In what follows, we will still consider the problem in terms of choice between two competing land uses. Again with reference to a rent bid function approach, the problem is how to deter conversion in the tract where this would be profitable, $[0, x^*]$ in Figure 2.1, given that the possibility of increasing returns from conservation-compatible activities is now precluded. The answer is obviously that land users in the relevant tract will have to be compensated for the foregone conversion benefits. The case of no activity allowed at all in the conservation area is a special case of the one considered here. In particular, compensation should be paid gross of the benefits from activity 2 if this is regarded as not compatible with conservation; net, if activity 2 is allowed.

In the latter case, compensation T is given by:

$$T = \int_0^{x^*} (r_1(x) - r_2(x)) dx = \frac{(a_1 - a_2)^2}{2(t_1 - t_2)} \qquad (2.3)$$

When only activity 2 is allowed, by redistributing amount T among land users residing in the tract $[0, x^*]$ it should be possible to make everybody as well off as in the no-intervention case.

One problem[8] with this solution is enforcement, which is not costless, as implicitly assumed above, and thus not necessarily complete. Land users entitled to compensation may have an incentive to carry out activity 1 in the tract $[0, x^*]$ *and* collect their share of T, the total overall compensation. The organisations involved in the scheme will therefore have to provide the resources necessary to enforce it.

The simplest way to capture some aspects of the problem is to imagine land users facing an expected utility maximisation problem, where a choice has to be made between two options (cheat, no cheat), and where there are only two states of the world (detect, no detect). If land users "cheat", that is, collect payment but do not respect zoning, they may be detected with probability p; it is assumed that detection always implies conviction, and that no wrongful detection is possible. If land users are detected, they face a penalty, the monetary equivalent of which is the fine f. Land users are compensated in the amount c for the opportunity cost of conservation at their location x: $c(x) = r_1(x) - r_2(x)$. The fine is for simplicity assumed to be a multiple of c: $f(x) = \mu c(x)$. That is, detected cheaters will have to return compensation received, plus, if $\mu > 1$, a fine proportional to it. Actions, events, probability, pay-offs and utility are summarised in Table 2.3. Utility will be assumed equal to pay-offs only under risk neutrality.

Table 2.3   Compensation for foregone uses of land

Action	Event	Probability	Pay-off	Utility
Cheat, ch	detected	p	$r_i(x) - c(x)(\mu - 1)$	$U(r_i(x) - c(x)(\mu-1))$
	not detected	$1 - p$	$r_i(x) + c(x)$	$U(r_i(x) + c(x))$
Do not cheat, nch	not detected	1	$r_2(x) + c(x) = r_i(x)$	$U(r_i(x))$

The expected values are: $E(ch) = r_1(x) + c(x)(1 - \mu p)$; $E(nch) = r_1(x)$. So, assuming risk neutrality, at any distance land users will not cheat if $E(nch) \geq E(ch)$, which implies:

$$\mu p \geq 1 \qquad (2.4)$$

This has the obvious interpretation that the expected value of the penalty must be larger than compensation, at any location x.

What is the cost of enforcing land use restrictions? The probability of detection p is assumed to be an increasing, concave function of l, labour employed to patrol; the function is bounded from above as p can not exceed unity: $p = p(l)$; $p' > 0$; $p'' < 0$; $p(\infty) = 1$. For a given μ, labour required to enforce zoning, l, solves:

$$p(\hat{l}) = \frac{1}{\mu} \qquad (2.5)$$

However enforcement will be more difficult, and hence more costly, as distance from the central business location increases. Denoting with τ the cost per unit of distance of transporting a unit of labour, the enforcement cost per "enforcing unit of labour" (l), $e(x)$ at location x is: $e(x) = 1 + \tau x$ where the wage rate has been normalised to one. Total enforcement cost is:

$$E(\hat{l}) = \int_0^{\overset{\bullet}{x}} e(x)dx = \left[x^* \left(1 + \frac{\tau^2}{2} x^* \right) \right] \tag{2.6}$$

The total cost of the scheme, S, is thus given by the sum of compensation and monitoring cost: $S = T + E(l)$. The cost of the scheme will clearly be sensitive to risk attitudes (see Figure 2.4 for a graphical illustration).

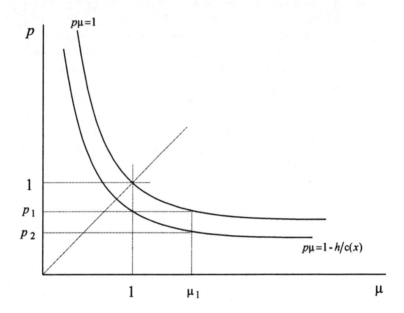

Figure 2.4   Enforcing land use restrictions

For instance, in the case of risk aversion, the enforcement condition becomes:

$$\eta(x) \geq \eta(x) + c(x)(1 - \mu p) - h \tag{2.7}$$

with h denoting the certainty equivalent of the "cheating gamble". This gives $\mu \geq 1 - h/c(x)$, which implies that at any level of penalty rate μ, the required probability of detection, labour input, and enforcement cost is less than in the risk-neutrality case (see Figure 2.4). The reverse will be true in the risk-loving case.

2.3.2 Tradable development rights and franchise agreements

The previous section has sketched a very simple framework, which could be used to analyse schemes of restrictions on land use. To carry the analysis forward, it is necessary to consider how such a scheme could actually work. One possible form compensation could take is purchase of development rights. This option has recently been the object of some attention in the literature (Katzman and Cale, 1990; Panayotou, 1994). The idea is essentially that landowners could be asked to give up their rights on some uses of land (e.g. burning the forest, or developing land beyond a given level of intensity) in exchange for a money payment. The state could also be involved in the management of the scheme, as in the case of the suggested International Franchise Agreements (IFAs) (Swanson, 1992).

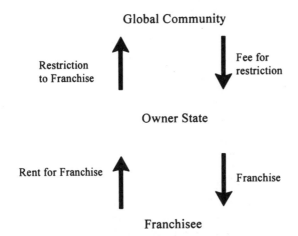

Figure 2.5   The structure of an IFA

An IFA is a concession, by the state, of exclusive rights on land to a franchisee, with limitation on allowable uses in the interest of a third party. As explained by Swanson (1992):

> in the case of the Brazilian Amazon, the franchise would be a limited term of use of a specified property within that region subject to specific restrictions. The grantor would be the owner-state (O-S), e.g. Brazil. The franchisee would be the entity allocated the franchise. The third party is the global community, represented by bilateral agreement between an international organisation such

as the World Bank, and Brazil. The IFA operates by the O-S dividing the total development rights for the particular parcel of land between the GC and the Franchisee in a way that maximises the O-S's return from that land. The O-S then collects a rental payment from the franchisee for its use of the franchise, and a rental payment from GC for the restrictions placed upon that franchise. Both "holders" of development rights (franchisee and GC) have an incentive to police their own allocations; the owner-state has the incentive to respond to intrusions on its holders' rights in order to maximise the value of its auctioned rights in the future (and to receive the future rental streams from both rights allocations). This mechanism allows the expression of GC's preferences within O-S in an incentive compatible fashion, which is the solution to the underlying problem.

The structure of an IFA is represented in Figure 2.5. According to the International Franchise Agreement (IFA) approach, the owner state confers exclusive rights on land to a franchisee in exchange for a payment, and it imposes restrictions on admitted uses in exchange for a compensation fee paid by a third party (the international community).

The mix of charges for admitted uses and compensations for prohibited uses would affect the individual perception of returns from alternative activities. The decision on whether to engage in an admitted activity or in an illegal one will depend on the policing effort of the body responsible for the enforcement for the restriction. It will also depend on the share of compensation fee the owner state will decide to transfer to local resource users.

Tradable development rights and IFAs seem a promising option for future conservation policies. One indispensable condition for the implementation of these schemes is the existence of clearly defined (and enforced) property rights on land. Such a condition does not yet fully hold in several developing countries, which, like Mexico (the subject of the case study of Chapters 4 to 6) are still in the process of modifying land tenure legislation and/or implementing land titles regularization programs.

2.4   CONCLUSION: LAND USE CHANGE IN THEORY AND IN PRACTICE

Based on the strong empirical evidence of land use changes throughout the world, this chapter has summarized the theoretical link between land use changes and biodiversity loss, proposed a diagrammatic interpretation of a typical sequence of land conversion prevailing in developing countries, and discussed options for tilting the balance of incentives in favour of activities compatible with conservation of biodiversity.

The analysis of this chapter, primarily theoretical, will be complemented by the empirical part of the book (Chapters 4 to 6). Using primary field data from Mexico, both the analysis of land use change processes, and the discussion of strategies to conserve biodiversity will be reformulated and adapted to local circumstances, in an attempt to add realism to the ideas discussed in this chapter.

Regarding the analysis of the process of change, a first issue has to do with the spectrum of land uses considered. Casting the problem in terms of binary choice between conservation and development is an oversimplification. In reality, there is a continuum of intensity of human uses, ranging from high intensity uses, such as urban development, to low or no-intensity, such as primary forests. Each use will have different impacts on biodiversity, as it will create the conditions for the survival of some plant and animal communities, and for the decline, and eventually extinction, of others.[9]

Because of this variety of impacts, the choice of the optimal mix of land uses will be dictated by the particular biodiversity conservation objective selected by policy makers. Even if there seems to be no clear consensus among ecologists about the "right" objective function, and thus about the optimal land use mix, it is nevertheless important to analyze social and economic processes that determine the allocation of total land available to all the uses included in the spectrum of human activities, not just the uses at its two extremes. The results of such an exercise could be used as input for policy making.

On the basis of an analysis of farm-level resource allocation decisions, a model will be proposed for predicting changes in selected land use types of the study area, including primary forest, second growth vegetation, farm land and pasture.

A second element concerns land tenure. The peasant pioneer sequence discussed in this chapter assumes the absence of property rights on land. In reality, several countries in Latin America and elsewhere are considering or implementing land reforms aimed at improving tenure security. Establishment of property rights is likely to decrease one source of incentives for conversion.

However, it may also be important to address the situation that occurs in the transition from open access to the new tenure system, especially when households without secure tenure face the risk of eviction, and don't have many employment opportunities outside the rural sector. Chapters 4, 5 and 6 will discuss the possible implications in terms of pressure on natural resources, of the title regularization program currently being implemented in Mexico.

Concerning the alteration of incentives for conservation and development, the Mexico case study will look not only at ways for improving the attractiveness of activities compatible with conservation, but also at technological options for reducing the land intensity of activities, such as ranching or agriculture, that have detrimental impacts on diversity.

ANNEX 2.1 INCREASING RENTS FROM CONSERVATION COMPATIBLE ACTIVITIES

In the very simplified version of the rent-bid function approach outlined in section 2.2, the position of the rent-bid line is determined by two parameters: the slope and the vertical intercept. Equation (2.2) could be expressed as:

$$\frac{r_i}{y_i} = a_i - t_i x; \quad with: a_i = p_i - w z_i \tag{2.8}$$

Rents per unit of output, r_i/y_i, are a direct function of a_i, the price margin over labour cost per unit of output, and, at any given distance x, an inverse function of t_i, the transport cost per unit of output.

As illustrated by Figure 2.6, activity 1 is profitable in $x \varepsilon [0, x^*]$, whereas activity 2 is only profitable in $x \varepsilon [x^*, a_2/b_2]$. The attractiveness of activity 2 will clearly change if the parameters a_2 and t_2 change. What is the combination of shifts in the slope and intercept of rent gradient 2 that would eliminate the incentives towards land conversion? A first possibility is to make activity 2 *everywhere* more profitable than activity 1. This would happen if the vertical intercept shifts upwards until a_1, while the horizontal intercept stays constant at a_2/b_2.

In Figure 2.6, the resulting rent gradient is given by $r_2'(x)$. However, this line lies everywhere above both r_1 and r_2, and therefore generates a larger amount of benefits than the initial case. The intervention to conserve biodiversity thus makes local communities better off.[10] The question then arises as to how should the rent gradient 2 shift in order to generate the same amount of benefits prevailing in the no-intervention case. That is, what is the incremental cost of the intervention *net* of domestic benefits?

The total cost of intervention, C, will depend on the cost of raising the vertical intercept, that is the cost of increasing the price-labour cost margin; and on the cost of flattening the rent function, that is the cost of infrastructure investments to reduce transport cost: $C=C(a, t)$. Assuming that the price of the output, p, and the wage rate, w, are not affected by the intervention examined, the only way to increase the margin is to reduce $z = l/y$, the labour requirement per unit of output. To simplify further, we can use w as the numeraire, so that the margin becomes $a = p - z$.

Biodiversity in the balance

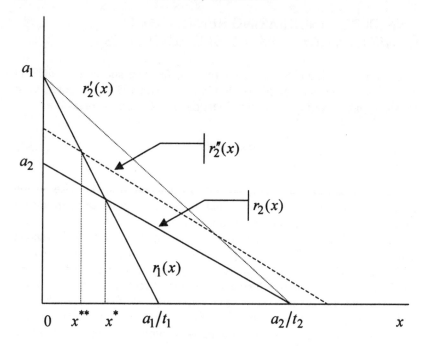

Figure 2.6   Increasing rent from conservation compatible activities

Rents prevailing in the no intervention case are the sum, M, of the rents from activity 1 between 0 and x^*, and of the rents from activity 2 between x^* and a_2/t_2:

$$M = \int_0^{x^*}(a_1 - t_1 x)dx + \int_{x^*}^{a_2/b_2}(a_2 - t_2 x)dx = \frac{1}{2}\left[\frac{(a_1 - a_2)^2}{(t_1 - t_2)} + \frac{a_2^2}{t_2}\right] \quad (2.9)$$

The problem for the provider of the funds is to minimise the overall cost of the intervention, subject to the constraint that total rents deriving from the "new" CC activity, $r = a - tx$, will be no less than "old" total rents, M. The constraint can be expressed as:

$$\int_0^{\frac{a}{t}}(a - tx)dx \geq M \quad \Rightarrow \quad \frac{a^2}{2t} \geq M \quad (2.10)$$

From the lagrangeian of the problem:

$$\Lambda = C(z,t) + \lambda \left(M - \frac{(p-z)}{2t} \right)$$
(2.11)

the first order conditions are:

$$C_z + \lambda \frac{(p-z)}{t} = 0;$$

$$C_t + \lambda \frac{(p-z)^2}{2t^2} = 0$$
(2.12)

$$M - \frac{(p-z)^2}{2t} = 0$$

Solving for the margin and for the unit transport cost one gets:

$$(p-z)^* = M \frac{C_z}{C_t}; \quad t^* = \frac{M}{2} \left(\frac{C_z}{C_t} \right)^2$$
(2.13)

The second order conditions impose some requirement on the cost function.[11] Assuming a particular quadratic form for the cost function allows a simple graphic interpretation of the result. Suppose that the cost of changing any of the two parameters is given by the square of the deviation from the initial values, z_2 and t_2, and the that the two cost components are summed:

$$C = (z - z_2)^2 + (t - t_2)^2$$
(2.14)

The cost function is then represented by concentric circles in the space (a, t), with total cost increasing on circles of larger diameter (see Figure 2.7). The original parameters z_2 and t_2 lie to the left of the shaded area where total rents are no less than M, as, by assumption, total rents under r_2 are less than M. The point of tangency between the iso-cost circles and the constraint line is the solution to the minimisation problem.

The solution (a^*, t^*) generates the same amount of aggregate benefits of the no-intervention case at minimum investment cost, given the cost function

C $(\cdot)$. However, the rent bid function r_2'' generated by the (a^*, b^*) parameters will not, in general, be individually incentive compatible. Depending on the marginal cost ratio C_z/C_t, the new line will cross the r_1 line somewhere to the left or the right of x^*, i.e. the development frontier in the no-intervention case. Let us call this new "frontier" x^{**}. Land users to the left of x^{**} will still have an incentive to convert, as $r_1 > r_2'$ in $x \in [0, x^{**}]$ (see again Figure 2.6).

However, this will not be the case if there is a single owner of land, be it a private individual, or a community which redistributes income among its members. In this case, the individual or the community will be indifferent between the situation with, and without, the intervention, as, by construction, the overall amount of rents is fixed at M.

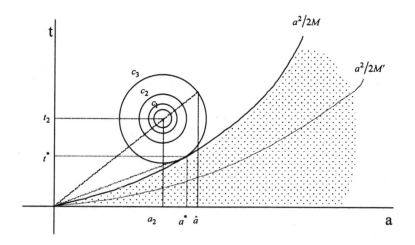

Figure 2.7   The solution to the rent-increasing problem

If there are many uncoordinated land users, then r_2 will have to be more profitable than r_1 over the entire tract $[0, x_2]$, as in the case of the r'_2 function constructed above. Whether or not the "individual" solution is more costly than the "community" solution depends on the value of a_1. To see this, consider that imposing the requirement of a fixed horizontal intercept is equivalent to fixing the ratio a/t at a_2/t_2. This is represented in Figure 2.7 by the line joining the origin and the point (a_2, t_2).

The cost of the "no-community solution" will be determined by the intersection between that line through the origin and the line $a=a_1$. There is only one vale of a_1 (assuming $a_1 > a_2$) such that the cost of the two solutions is the same. This is given by $\hat{a}$, which is the solution of the couple of equations $C(a, t)=C^*$ and $a/t=a_2/t_2$, where C^* is the cost of the solution (a^*, t^*). That is, $\hat{a}$ is at the same time on the line from the origin with slope a_2/t_2, and on the iso-cost line identified by a^*. Figure 2.7 displays the location of $\hat{a}$. If $a_1 > \hat{a}$, then the individual solution is more expensive than the community solution.

In the simple framework outlined in this section, the international community has the option of preventing land conversion by modifying the rent gradient of CC activities. It has been shown that under some circumstances, the cost of the intervention is lower if land is managed by a community that redistributes rents among its members, rather than being managed by uncoordinated individual users.[12]

NOTES

1. The role of second growth regeneration in mitigating the impacts of deforestation is questioned by some analysts: (Myers, 1994) notes that abandonment of cleared land, which is required for regeneration, is rare in much of West Africa, East Africa, and Southern and Southeast Asia, where population pressures are greatest. However, quoting Browder (1989), he concedes that in the Brazilian Amazon in 1988, between 20 and 40 percent of deforested lands were starting to feature secondary forest recovery.

2. Indeed, this has seemed to be the case in the Amazon (see, for example, Mahar, 1989; Schneider, 1992).

3. Clearly, what activities could be included in each group will crucially depend on the definition of biodiversity that is being adopted. Under particularly stringent definitions of the "diversity" objective function, few, if any, activities could be included in the CC group. In that case, the problem of avoiding land conversion is essentially one of imposing legal restrictions on land use, and establishing a protected status. The problem of the effectiveness of these restrictions will be addressed below.

4. Note that when a process like the pioneer sequence is in action, conversion will take place initially only in the tract $[0, x^*]$, but it will successively affect a much larger area.

5. See Southgate (1990) for a more formal treatment of the effect of property rights definition on frontier expansion.

6. All these considerations suggest that the problem of trading conservation between the international community and a domestic counterpart could be analysed in the context of principal-agent theory (see Rees, 1985 for an overview). This theory deals with problems of choices which a subject, called the principal, find advantageous to delegate to another subject, called the agent. The principal faces

uncertainty on the characteristics (adverse selection) or on the action (moral hazard) of the agent, and has the problem of devising a payment mechanism for the agent which optimally combines incentives to provide effort - given limited observability - with incentives to enter the contract, given risky outcomes of agent's actions. Occasional reference will be made to problems of uncertainty and limited observability, but a more complete analysis of the problem in terms of principal agent, which may well be the subject of a separate research, will not be attempted here.

7. Even if the option of changing the relative returns of NCC vs CC activities is available, it still may be interesting to compare its merit in terms of cost or effectiveness with the alternative of compensating land users for the foregone development benefits.

8. An additional issue, not addressed here, one concerns information: how many land users reside in the tract $[0, x^*]$? What is the exact pattern of the r_1-r_2 function therein?

9. An interesting observation made by recent scientific literature, is that low and moderate intenisty regimes of land uses, such as extraction from secondary forests, or agroforestry systems, have an important role in biodiversity conservation, perhaps not substitute, but at least complementary, to the role of pristine ecosystems (Brown and Lugo, 1990; Gomez Pompa, Whitmore, and Hadley, 1991; Smith, 1996; Nepstad, Uhl et al., 1991; Estrada. A. , Coates - Estrada et al., 1993). Some authors have even highlighted the role of selected agricultural systems as reservoirs of diversity of particular associations of plants and animals (Srivastava, Smith, and Forno, 1996; Paoletti, Pimentel et al., 1992; Paoletti and Pimentel, 1992; Pimentel, Stachow et al., 1992).

10. In terms of the incremental cost analysis of Chapter 3, in such an intervention there are incremental benefits that are not netted out from the resource transferred; i.e. the γ parameter is less than 1.

11. Assuming separability of the cost function, i.e. $C_{zt} = C_{tz} = 0$, the bordered Hessian is given by:

$$\frac{-4C_t^2\left(C_t^3 + C_{tt}C_z^2 M + C_t^2 C_{zz} M\right)}{C_z^4 M}$$

which has to be negative for the stationary values to be a minimum.

12. An implicit assumption in this conclusion is that the community has the ability to monitor the behaviour of its members, and preventing land users residing in the tract $[0, x^{**}]$ from carrying out activity 1 *and* claiming a share of overall rents M.

3. Financing conservation: theoretical aspects

Conservation of biological resources generates local, national and international benefits.[1] Country-level activities, which result in depletion of biodiversity, generate transboundary externalities affecting the rest of the world. This chapter addresses the issue of how those externalities can be internalised through the "incremental cost" mechanism; it does not deal with the problem of how the international community could reach agreement (or fail to do so) on sharing of the cost of conservation. This topic has been analysed elsewhere in the literature (see for example Barrett, 1994).

The existence of transboundary externalities associated with biodiversity conservation justifies the need for co-ordinated action at the international level. The Convention on Biological Diversity (CBD) is the most important attempt to date to promote such collective action. The Convention stipulates that all the signatories have an obligation to undertake a number of actions to conserve biological resources. It also requests developed countries to provide developing countries with the resources necessary for them to comply with the convention. An institutional structure is established to manage the resulting financial transfers from the former group of countries to the latter. The institution that operates on an interim basis the financial mechanism of the Convention is the Global Environment Facility (GEF).

The specific criterion regulating the financial mechanism of the convention is the "incremental cost" principle, which is also adopted by two other major environmental conventions, the Montreal Protocol on Ozone Depleting Substances, and the Framework Convention on Climate Change. Article 20 of the CBD dictates that developed countries will provide resources to enable developing countries to meet the "full agreed incremental cost" to them of undertaking the conservation measures required by the convention.

During its "pilot phase" (1991-1994), the Global Environment Facility has been funding projects for about US$ 730 million, with biodiversity conservation projects amounting to 45% of the total.[2] Funds have been

61

disbursed on the basis of "full", rather than "incremental" costing. In recent times, policy negotiations and applied research[3] have been undertaken to foster the complete application of the financial provisions of article 20. These have been prompted by the move from "pilot" to "operational" phase of the GEF, which has been restructured and replenished for US$ 2 billion in early 1994, and by progresses towards the full implementation of the Convention. The debate has revolved around the exact meaning and scope of the notion of incremental cost, and its applicability to the biodiversity context.

The Convention provides little guidance for the discussions, as none of the terms used in introducing incremental cost is further defined. Despite this indeterminacy, there is some consensus[4] that in broad terms incremental cost encompasses all the costs of actions that countries undertake because of the Convention, and that they would otherwise not undertake. Incremental cost is thus defined by contrast with a (hypothetical) baseline representing the situation without the Convention.

To make this simple definition more operational, some further element has to be added. First, conservation actions might generate benefits as well as costs to the countries undertaking them. Should these additional benefits be netted out of incremental cost? The phrase "agreed full" could refer to the percentage of domestic benefits to be deducted from the transfer of resources meeting incremental cost.

Second, there is the issue of the baseline. When the existing price system is distorted in such a way to encourage depletion of biological diversity, should the baseline be evaluated net or gross of distortions?

In both cases, there is a trade-off between likelihood of effective conservation and cost efficiency.

If domestic incremental benefits are not deducted from the amount of resources transferred from developed to developing countries, countries hosting biological resources will end up better off with the transfer than without it, and will have more incentive to comply with the convention. On the other hand, the cost per unit of additional conservation will be higher, and, for a given size of the budget available, less biological resources will be conserved.

Similarly, a distorted baseline is more likely to be acceptable to the host country. This will be so if, by using undistorted shadow prices in calculating incremental cost, compensated resource users end up worse off than in the baseline. At the same time, a distorted baseline is likely to result in higher unit cost of conservation, and again, less biodiversity conserved overall.

To address these issues in a more systematic fashion, a simple partial equilibrium, demand-side model is proposed here, with only two agents: a representative country hosting biological diversity, and a homogenous international community, interested in higher levels of conservation than those prevailing in the status quo.

Section 3.1 introduces the basic model and defines three situations: the domestic optimum, which prevails before the Convention; a hypothetical Global Optimum, and finally the situation prevailing after the ratification of the convention.

To fully characterise the latter situation, section 3.1.4 introduces two further ways in which the financial mechanism of the Convention could possibly work. The distinction depends upon the way the host country may act in the implementation process. The host may either commit itself to a given level of conservation and try to get the highest level of compensation corresponding to that level (quantity-taking behaviour). Or it may take the amount of resource transferred as given, and then choose the utility-maximising level of conservation (transfer-taking behaviour). The main idea is that the equilibrium level of conservation is endogenous to the trading process between the host country and Rest of the World, and will not necessarily coincide with the global optimum.

Section 3.1.5 introduces domestic price distortions into the analysis. Section 3.2 proposes simple functional forms for the utility of the host country and of the international community. This makes it possible to draw some specific conclusions on the comparative merits of the domestic optimum and the incremental cost scheme, in both the absence and presence of domestic price distortions. Section 3.3 provides some tentative conclusions.

3.1 BIODIVERSITY AND INCREMENTAL COST: A SIMPLE MODEL

There are two countries: one host country, H, which conserves an environmental commodity (biological resources), generating global benefits, and the Rest of the world, ROW. Utility in both the host country and the rest of the world depends upon consumption of a single non-environmental good (x for H and X for ROW) and upon conservation of biological resources, q. We can think of q as some suitable measure of natural systems' health (e.g. percentage of land maintained in relatively undisturbed conditions), which can be used a proxy for conservation of biodiversity. The literature normally highlights that benefits of biodiversity can be classified according to the spatial level where they accrue (national and international), and according to their nature (social or private).

Table 3.1   Assumptions about benefits generated by biodiversity

Type of benefits	Level at which benefits accrue	
	National	International
Private	Yes	No
Social	No (see text)	Yes

As indicated by Table 3.1, the choice has been made to include only some of those benefits in the present analysis. In particular, this model concentrates on allocative distortions related to the international externalities of conservation: the level of q is selected by the host country but affects *ROW*'s utility (for example, via existence values), and so is an externality for the latter. From the point of view of the host country, it is assumed that q mainly generates privately appropriable benefits. For example, if q is the percentage of land under forest cover, any given level of q will be associated with some level of sustainable timber harvesting, or extraction of non-timber forest products. To the extent that these types of benefits are easily monetized and readily transformed into income and wealth, this approach is consistent with the preamble of the Convention on Biological Diversity. This stresses that "economic and social development and poverty eradication are the first and overriding priorities of developing countries", so that, by implication, uses of biodiversity more directly related to those priorities have pre-eminence in determining the position of developing countries in conservation-related negotiations.

There are of course also important domestic social values stemming from biodiversity conservation, for example watershed protection or micro-climate stabilisation.[5] Often domestic externalities from conservation are especially important at the local or sub-national level, but are not perceived at the national level in a way strong enough to shape the country's negotiating position. This may be so for political economy factors. Consider for example, logging concessions to be granted in a fragile watershed. Local communities, who will be affected most by the possibly resulting disruption of the watershed, may be not as effective in defending their interest with the government as the lobby of the logging concessionaires.

For the time being, domestic social benefits will be assumed irrelevant in determining the host's negotiation position. Section 3.1.5 will modify this assumption, in that it will take into account more general distortions in the pricing system of the host country.

In summary, this model studies the way in which the host and *ROW* negotiate about the provision of international benefits from conservation. To characterise the problem, we identify three situations. In the first one, which exemplifies the situation prior to the Convention on Biological Diversity, both parties operate in isolation. The host country decides on the optimal combination of x and q on the basis of its own preferences and income only. The Rest of the World takes the level of q selected by the host as given, and is constrained to spend all of its income on good X.

The second situation represents the hypothetical global optimum, in which a benevolent world dictator determines the optimal provision of the man-made goods, x and X, and of the environmental commodity q, taking into account both parties' preferences.

Finally the third situation is the one arising out of the Convention on Biological Diversity, which establishes a financial mechanism to encourage conservation in countries hosting biological resources.

The model can be intended as analysing resource allocations over a number of possible conservation projects large enough to justify the use of continuous variables. These projects are to be co-funded by a single representative host country and the Rest of the World. The analysis is static, and purports to identify equilibrium allocation outcomes and welfare implications for host and *ROW* in the various situations considered. The results obtained here can be used as inputs for future work attempting to deal with the topic at hand through dynamic analysis tools, so as to take into account issues of commitment and credibility which are not addressed here. The notation used in what follows is summarised for convenience in Table 1.1.

3.1.1 Before the convention

In accordance with the assumptions spelled out above on the domestic benefits of q, we will assume that the privately appropriable benefits of conservation are reflected in a market price p_q (this can be thought of as a composite price index of conservation-compatible goods, e.g. sustainably harvested timber, non timber forest products, etc.). The possibility that p_q does not reflect the social value of q will be addressed in section 3.1.5.

Table 3.2   Notation used in model of incremental cost

H:	Host Country
ROW:	Rest of the World
q:	Quantity of environmental commodity with global benefits
P_q:	Price of environmental commodity
x:	Quantity of non-environmental good consumed by Host
P_x:	Price of good x
X:	Quantity of market good consumed by Rest of the World
P:	Vector of prices in host country (p_x, p_q)
b:	Income of host country
B:	Income of Rest of the world
$u(.)$:	Host country utility function
$U(.)$:	Rest of the World utility function
u_i, u_{ij}:	First, second derivatives of function u with respect to variable i, and variable i and j
U_i, U_{ij}:	First, second derivatives of function U with respect to variable i, and variable i and j
$E(.)$:	Expenditure function of host country
γ:	"Clawback" factor indicating the share of domestic benefits deduction from incremental cost
δ:	Price-distortion factor
σ:	Factor indicating a subsidy rate paid by ROW
$\phi(q)$:	"Parametric" utility function for the Host. It answers the question: for given prices, what level of utility can be reached when q is chosen optimally?
$Variable_d$:	Indicates level of the given variable determined as a result of domestic optimisation in host country
$Variable_g$:	Indicates level of the given variable determined as a result of global optimisation
$Variable_\gamma$:	Indicates level of the given variable determined as a result of incremental cost compensation; when $\gamma=\gamma_0$, under transfer taking behaviour; when $\gamma=\gamma^*$, under quantity taking behaviour

The problem of the Host country is then:

$$\underset{q,x}{\text{Max}} \ u(q,x) \quad \text{s.t.} \quad p_x x + p_q q = b \tag{3.1}$$

The Host country's equilibrium is assumed to exist and is represented by the pair (x_d, q_d), with associated utility level u_d. The problem of the Rest of the world is:

$$\underset{X}{\text{Max}} \ U(q_d, X) \quad \text{s.t.} \quad p_x X = B \tag{3.2}$$

The rest of the world is quantity constrained by the host's choice of q_d, and is thus forced to spend of all its income on good X. The resulting equilibrium is therefore given by the pair $(X_d = B/p_x, q_d)$. Figure 3.1 illustrates the host's equilibrium and the Rest of the World constrained equilibrium.

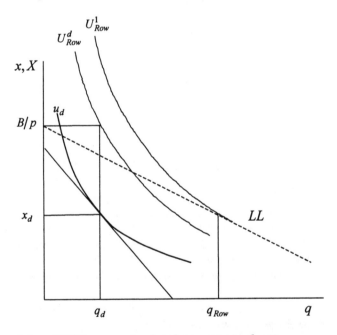

Figure 3.1   ROW's constrained and unconstrained optima

ROW faces a horizontal budget constraint; if there was the possibility of introducing a downward sloping budget constraint (i.e. if *ROW* were enabled to spend some of its income on q), *ROW* might achieve higher utility. For example, in Figure 3.1, the hypothetical linear budget constraint *LL* induces *ROW* to optimise at $q_{row} > q_d$, and enables it to reach a higher indifference curve, $U^1_{row} > U^1_d$. The interpretation suggested here to the Convention on Biological Diversity (see below for details) is thus that it introduces a way of relaxing *ROW's* quantity constraint, and of making its budget constraint downward sloping.[6]

3.1.2   The global optimum

In this situation, it is assumed that both host's and *ROW*'s welfare are taken into account in determining the equilibrium combination of x, X and q. For simplicity, let us assume a Benthamite utilitarian global welfare function, whereby utilities are given equal weights and summed. The problem is given by:

$$\text{Max}_{q,x,X}\ u(x,q)+U(X,q)\quad \text{s.t.}\ \ p_x\left(x+X\right)+p_q q=b+B \qquad (3.3)$$

First order conditions for a global optimum are:

$$\frac{u_q}{u_x}+\frac{U_q}{U_X}=\frac{p_q}{p_x};\quad U_X=u_x;\quad B+b=p_x(X+x)+p_q q \qquad (3.4)$$

The first condition has the interpretation that the sum of the marginal rates of substitution must be equal to the price ratio. This is the familiar (Samuelson, 1954) rule for the optimal provision of public goods. The Global optimum, which satisfies the above condition is the vector: (x_g, X_g, q_g). The corresponding utility levels are given by u_g and U_g. The global optimum is displayed in Figure 3.2: host's and *ROW*'s indifference curves sum vertically to generate the global indifference curves $U+u$. The global optimum is identified by the point of tangency of the function $U+u$ with the aggregated budget constraint.

3.1.3   After the convention

The Convention on Biological Diversity stipulates a number of measures[7] contracting parties should undertake to conserve biological resources. Furthermore, it establishes that developed countries are to provide "new and additional" financial resources to meet the "full agreed incremental cost" incurred by developing countries in complying with the convention (i.e. undertaking the indicated conservation measures, thereby providing a level of conservation q higher than q_d).

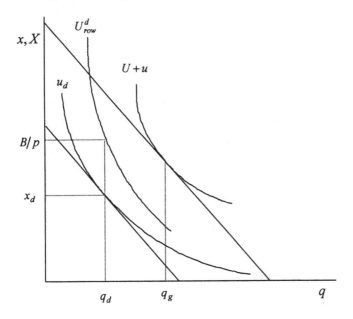

Figure 3.2   Domestic and global optima

This provision of the convention effectively introduces the possibility of a "trade" in conservation between developed and developing countries: the latter will agree to conserve more than they would otherwise do, and, in exchange, the former meet the corresponding incremental cost. Unfortunately, the terms of the transaction are far from being precise, since, in introducing the concept of incremental cost, the Convention fails to define:

   (a) incremental *to what* (i.e. what is the baseline);
   (b) what does "agreed full" mean;
   (c) cost of getting where: that is, how much further than q_d should the host's conservation effort be pushed?

As summarized in Pearce and Cervigni (1994), and discussed in Glowka et al. (1994), a variety of differing interpretations has been proposed in recent times on these issues, which are still the subject of political and legal controversies. For the present purposes, we will assume:

(a) The baseline situation is the domestic optimum (x_d, q_d). Until section 3.1.5, it will be assumed that there are no price distortions affecting the determination of the domestic optimum.

(b) In general, actions to conserve biological resources will generate benefits as well as costs. We will thus assume that "agreed full" means there will be an agreement between Host and Rest of the World as to what percentage of incremental domestic benefits has to be deducted from the incremental cost. In the context of the present model, "cost" is the expenditure necessary for purchasing a particular combination of goods q and x; "benefit" is the level of utility associated with the selected basket of goods. If the host were to select a level of conservation higher than q_d, it would incur a cost (i.e., spending more than b), but it would also gain a benefit (reaching a utility level higher than u_d).

The notion of "agreed full incremental cost" can then be translated in the following way: for any level of conservation q in excess of the domestic optimum, *ROW* will have to provide a transfer $T(q)$ equal to the gross incremental cost minus an "agreed" fraction γ, varying between 0 and 1, of any incremental benefit:

$$T(q) = e(p,\phi(q)) - e(p,u_d) - \gamma(e(p,\phi(q)) - \tilde{e}(p,u_d,q)) \qquad (3.5)$$

The symbols have the following meaning: $e(.)$ is the expenditure function for the host country; normally, the arguments of the expenditure function are prices and utility. Instead of being a parameter, utility ϕ is here expressed as a function of q. The function $\phi(q)$ indicates, for given prices, the level of utility that would be reached when the Host optimally chooses conservation level q (and when it is endowed with the necessary income, which is precisely $e(p, \phi(q))$. The function $\tilde{e}(\cdot)$ is the *constrained* expenditure function, i.e. is the solution to the problem:

$$\underset{x}{\text{Min}}\ p_x x + p_q q \quad \text{s.t.}\ u \geq u_d, \quad q : \text{parameter} \qquad (3.6)$$

Its arguments are prices p, the "reference" level of the domestic utility u_d, and conservation q. The function $\tilde{e}(\cdot)$ indicates the minimum expenditure necessary to keep the host's utility constant at u_d when conservation level q is chosen.[8] No transfer is forthcoming if conservation does not increase:

$T(q_d)=0$. The graphical interpretation of the $T(q)$ function is provided in Figure 3.3.

The host's initial income (evaluated in terms of good x) is A. For the host to be willing to reach the generic conservation level $q>q_d$ it must be given at least income B-A, which will leave it on the original indifference curve (corresponding to the domestic optimum, u_d). Keeping q constant, any income in excess of B will make the host better off; income C is defined as the income level at which the host would freely choose conservation level q. So, the difference C-A is interpreted here as the gross incremental cost of moving from q_d to q.

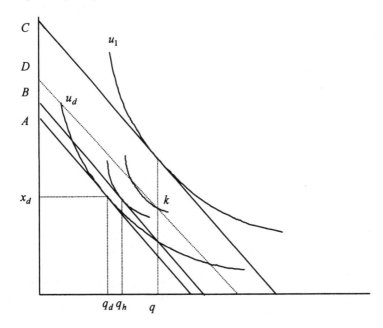

Note: $B - A = Net$ Incremental Cost; $C - A = Gross$ Incremental Cost

Figure 3.3   Gross and net incremental cost

The term γ is a "claw-back" factor indicating what percentage of domestic incremental benefits are deducted from the transfer. When $\gamma=0$, no incremental benefit is deducted, and the transfer is equal to the gross incremental cost; in Figure 3.3, the transfer is equal to C-A.

When $\gamma=1$, all of the incremental benefits are deducted, and the transfer is equal to the net incremental cost, which, in Figure 3.3 is equal to B-A. Notice that for any $q>q_d$ by definition of the function $\phi(q)$ the host optimises only for $\gamma=0$; however, sub-optimal choices of $\gamma>0$ can still make the host better off, relative to the domestic optimum. For example, in Figure 3.3 a transfer of D-A, which corresponds to some value of γ intermediate between 0 and 1, leads the host to the sub-optimal, but welfare-improving, point k (it lies on an indifference curve higher than u_d).

3.1.4   "Quantity-" and "transfer-taking" behaviour

Question (c) in section 3.1.3, concerning the level of conservation induced by the convention, deserves further discussion. One interpretation of the convention is that its purpose is to achieve the global optimum.[9] The relevant incremental cost is then the cost of moving from q_d to q_g, whatever this cost may be. Under this interpretation, host and Rest of the World would bargain only about the way domestic incremental benefits should be considered, that is, they bargain about the level of γ.

However, the Rest of the World will want to go for the global optimum only if this is compatible with its budget constraint; similarly, the host might not want it either, if this makes it worse off than the domestic optimum.

Therefore, the present model proposes a description of the negotiation process between Host and Rest of the World, rather than assuming that the automatic outcome of the Convention on Biodiversity is the achievement of the global optimum q_g. For simplicity, we will assume that negotiation can work in two ways: the host may either commit itself to a particular level of conservation q in excess of q_d and then negotiate the compensation accordingly (*ROW* chooses q and Host claims $T(q)$); or it may take compensation as given and select conservation accordingly (*ROW* offers T and Hosts chooses $q(T)$). In the first case, the Host can be defined as a "quantity taker"; in the second, a "transfer taker". In order to concentrate on equilibrium outcomes, we will assume that the cost to *ROW* of monitoring the actual enforcement of the host's commitments are negligible, and that, as a result, the host has little incentive to deviate from its conservation pledges. Issues of credibility and possible reneging of promises are of course important in the present context, and the assumption of perfect information might be relaxed in a more complex model. However, the main objective of the present analysis is to illustrate the allocative implications of the incremental cost mechanism, not the difficulties associated with its implementation.

We will first examine the case where the Host is quantity taker, and see what level of γ and of conservation q will prevail in equilibrium. If the Host is a quantity taker, it will commit itself to whatever level of conservation *ROW* will decide to finance, but it will then try to get as much incremental domestic benefits as possible (i.e. a value of γ as low as possible). Even if it would seem that for the host the best policy would always be to have all of the incremental benefits (i.e. γ=0), this will not in fact be necessarily the case, as we will see below, as the conservation level (and hence the availability of incremental benefits) is dependent on the value of γ agreed upon. The problem for *ROW* becomes:

$$\underset{X,q}{\text{Max}}\, U(X,q) \quad \text{s.t.} \ p_x X + T(q) = B \tag{3.7}$$

Note that according to (3.5), $T(q)$ is a function of the unconstrained and constrained expenditure function, $e(q)$ and $\widetilde{e}(q)$. These in turn, involve the optimising behaviour of the host, so that, in fact, *ROW* faces its own budget constraint, *plus* the constraint implicitly defined by $T(q)$. Optimality requires:

$$\frac{U_q}{U_X} = \frac{1}{p_x}\left\{(1-\gamma)(p_q + p_x \alpha) + \gamma\,(p_q - p_x \beta)\right\};$$

$$\tag{3.8}$$

$$\alpha = \frac{u_q u_{qx} - u_x u_{qq}}{u_x u_{qx} - u_q u_{xx}}; \quad \beta = \left.\frac{u_q}{u_x}\right|_{u=u_d}$$

(The derivation of the quantities α and β is reported in Annex 3.1). Assuming an interior solution, this is represented by the pair (X_θ, q_γ), which depend on the value of γ. Diagrammatically, as γ changes, so does the budget constraint faced by *ROW* in its optimisation problem; Figure 3.4 illustrates a case in which, when γ decreases, the budget constraint moves downwards, and the equilibrium level of conservation decreases.

If, in particular, γ=1, i.e. the resource transfer is equal to the incremental cost *net* of incremental domestic benefits, the condition contained in (3.8) becomes:

$$\frac{U_q}{U_X} + \left.\frac{u_q}{u_x}\right|_{u=u_d} = \frac{p_q}{p_x} \tag{3.9}$$

Comparing this to condition (3.4), it turns out that when incremental cost is paid net, the equilibrium level of conservation coincides with the global optimum. However, the equilibrium values of x and X will in general differ from the global optimum case. This is so because, as the utility of the host is kept constant, the equilibrium level of good x must be lower than in the global optimum case, otherwise the host would be better off than in the domestic optimum case.

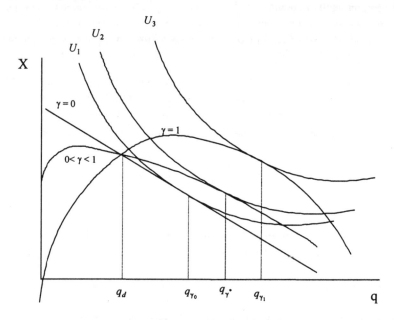

Note: The diagram depicts ROW's indifference curves and budget line in the q-X space. As the clawback factor γ changes, so does the budget constraint faced by ROW in its optimisation problem. In the particular case depicted in the diagram, where ROW's utility is multiplicative ($U = qX$), when γ decreases, the budget constraint moves downwards, and the equilibrium level of conservation decreases. The value q_{γ_0} defines the transfer-taking solution; the quantity-taking solution q_{γ^*} will be somewhere in between q_{γ_0} and q_{γ_1}.

Figure 3.4   Equilibrium for rest of the world

This observation enables us to comment on the debate net vs. gross incremental cost.[10] The standard argument in favour of net incremental cost is its cost-effectiveness: more conservation can be achieved for any dollar spent when international resources are used to pay only the net cost of incremental conservation measures. In this model this argument is valid if we assume that the host country is a quantity taker, and it has no control over the "clawback" factor γ, or that it is willing to accept the value γ=1.

Indeed, if the host has decided to follow a "quantity-taker" behaviour, it will be more likely to try and negotiate the clawback factor γ in such a way that it can maximise its own utility.

From the point of view of the host, there are two forces at work, which interestingly push in opposite directions:

– on one hand, a smaller γ will take away less domestic benefits from the transfer, and thus make *H* better off;

– on the other hand, a smaller γ will induce *ROW* to choose a lower level of q_{row}, thereby reducing the size of the cake available to *H*, and making it worse off.

In other words, as γ decreases, *H*'s slice of the "compensation cake" increases, but the size of the cake decreases. The host will then want to balance off, at the margin, size and slice effect. The quantity q_γ is defined by (3.8); the equilibrium value of the non environmental good consumed in the host country, x_γ, can be derived by plugging q_γ in to the host's budget constraint:

$$p_x x + p_q q_\gamma = b + T(q_\gamma) = (1-\gamma)e(q_\gamma) + \gamma \tilde{e}(q_\gamma) \qquad (3.10)$$

and solving for x (the second equality in the above expression results from re-arranging (3.5), and noting that $e(p, u_d) = b$). Substituting both q_γ and x_γ into the host's utility function, we obtain an indirect utility function, v, which depends on prices, income and the clawback factor γ:

$$v(p_q, p_x, b, B, \gamma) = u(x_\gamma, q_\gamma) \qquad (3.11)$$

Assuming that the second order conditions are satisfied, the optimal value of the claw-back factor can be obtained by equating the derivative of v with respect to γ to zero, and solving for γ. That is, finding the value of γ that solves:

$$\frac{u_q}{u_x} = -\frac{dx/d\gamma}{dq/d\gamma} \qquad (3.12)$$

Conditions contained in (3.8) and (3.12) jointly define the solution to the model in the quantity-taking case. The Host selects the optimal claw-back factor, γ^*, taking *ROW*'s optimisation as given; *ROW*, in turn, decides the optimal level of conservation q_{γ^*} once the Host has chosen γ^*.

Suppose now that the Host is a "transfer-taker". That is, for any particular value of the transfer, it will select the utility-maximising values of q (and of x). The graphical interpretation (refer back to Figure 3.3) is that for any given budget line parallel to the original one (and to the right of it), the host will select the point of tangency with the highest possible indifference curve. For instance, when the host receives income B-A in Figure 3.3 (which would be the net incremental cost of the move from q_d to q) it will choose conservation level q_h. Formally, the problem is analogous to (3.1), except that the income available to the Host is now given by $b + t(q)$. The host's new problem thus reads:

$$\underset{x,q}{\text{Max}}\, u(x,q) \quad \text{s.t.} \quad p_x x + p_q q = b + t(q) \tag{3.13}$$

When the host is transfer taker, it maximises its own utility subject to the budget b *plus* the transfer $t(q)$. The transfer t(q) is defined as the amount of income in excess of the resources available domestically that would induce the host to choose, in an unconstrained fashion, conservation level q. It follows that:

$$t(q) = e(q) - b \quad \Rightarrow \quad t(q) = T(q)\big|_{\gamma=0} \tag{3.14}$$

That is, the transfer taking behaviour can be analysed with the quantity-taking model provided that γ is set equal to zero, i.e. provided that incremental cost is being paid gross. So we can define the transfer-taking solution as $q_{\gamma 0}$. A natural question is whether the host will be better off choosing the quantity-taking, rather than the transfer-taking strategy. One would suspect that the transfer-taking option, which entails optimising behaviour, will be preferable to the transfer-taking solution, since the latter induces the host to a quantity-constrained, and hence sub-optimal, behaviour. However, the transfer-taking solution depends upon the additional amount of resources that *ROW* decides to make available, on which the host has no control. If this amount is small, so will be the utility gain that the host will achieve vis a vis the initial welfare level in the domestic equilibrium. By introducing explicit specifications for the utility functions, it is possible to see cases where the quantity-taking strategy dominates the transfer-taking behaviour in terms of welfare improvements of the domestic equilibrium. An example of this possibility is provided in section 3.2.1.

3.1.5   Allowing for price distortions in the host country

The model has so far assumed that the prices p_x and p_q correctly reflect the social scarcity values of goods x and q in the host country However, for many developing countries hosting biological resources, this assumption may not be appropriate.

Typically, there will be two, often coexisting, type of distortions.[11] The first source of distortions regards the price of good x. In many cases, consumption of the non-environmental good x will be encouraged by governments of host countries because of its beneficial effects on growth, or because of concerns about poverty. In this case the true social scarcity cost, p_x, will be lowered of a subsidy factor δ_x.

Regarding q, it is often argued that conservation levels are sub-optimal not only internationally, but also from the developing country point of view. There are both equity and efficiency reasons to argue that developing country should conserve more of their biodiversity. In terms of equity, the "sustainable use industry" (e.g. agroforestry, non-timber forest products) is often associated with sectors of the economy which are marginalized both geographically (poorly accessible areas) and socially (indigenous people). Geographic remoteness and inadequate access to market channels are likely to result in high production costs and competitive disadvantage vis-à-vis other, non conservation compatible industries. A way to improve the living conditions of people living in marginal areas would be to improve the market prospects of their sustainable industries.

In terms of efficiency, it is often argued that sustainable use activities generate local ecological benefits (watershed protection, micro-climate stabilisation). To the extent that these benefits are not internalised by the sustainable use industry, less incentives for conservation will prevail.

In terms of the present analysis, we can capture both effects by augmenting the "correct" price, p_q, with a distortion factor $(1+\delta_q)$, with $\delta_q > 0$. The resulting price, $p'_q = p_q(1+\delta_q)$ will be higher (and therefore demand for q in equilibrium lower), both because of higher production and transaction costs in the sustainable use industry, and because producers are unable to reduce those costs by capturing the social benefits of their activity.

In principle, domestic public policy can lower δ_q either on equity grounds, by improving market access for marginal sustainable producers; or on efficiency grounds, by introducing internalisation mechanisms, e.g. charging off-site water users for ecological services provided upstream by sustainable producers. Taken together, the two distortions will modify the budget constraint as follows:

$$p_x(1-\delta_x)x + p_q(1+\delta_q)q = b; \qquad 0 < \delta_x < 1; \quad \delta_q > 0 \qquad (3.15)$$

With respect to the present model, the qualitative effect of introducing distortions into the host's budget constraint will be that the domestic optimum will be characterised by a lower level of q and higher level of x compared to the situation without distortions. Depending on its preferences, the host may be better or worse off than in the no-distortions case, whereas *ROW* will surely be worse off, as it will be quantity-constrained to a lower level of conservation. An interesting question is whether this effect on the baseline will also alter the host's and *ROW*'s incentives for negotiating an increased provision of conservation on the basis of an incremental cost scheme. Some insights can be gained by imposing specific forms onto the utility functions of host and *ROW*, and carrying out some numerical and diagrammatic simulations. This is the objective of next section.

3.2   SOME RESULTS USING PARTICULAR FUNCTIONAL FORMS

Let us impose some specific functional forms on the utility functions of the HostHos country and of the Rest of the World. In order to get tractable algebraic derivations in presence of non-linearities in the budget constraints, we have supposed that utility for both parties is multiplicative in both commodities:

$$u(x,q) = xq; \quad U(X,q) = Xq \qquad (3.16)$$

A first interesting result that can be illustrated diagrammatically concerns the relationship between the optimal claw-back and B (which has the interpretation of relative difference in incomes if b is assumed as the *numeraire* (see Annex 3.2 for algebraic derivations). As can be seen in Figure 3.5, the larger the relative difference in incomes, the lower the optimal claw-back factor, and the closer the equilibrium transfer to gross incremental cost.

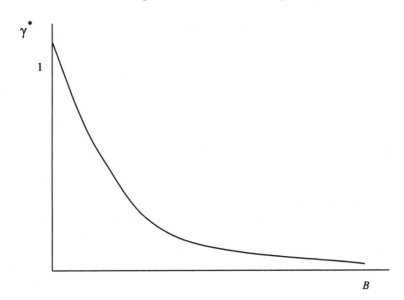

Figure 3.5   Optimal claw-back factor

Interpretation: when the income differential is small, the size effect dominates, and γ^* is close to 1; at high income differentials, the slice effect dominates, and γ^* approaches zero. When there is little international finance available for conservation, there will be little scope for diverting part of it from outright conservation to increasing the well-being of the host. By claiming a large share of incremental benefits, the host loses in terms of reduction of the cake's size more than it gains in terms of increase in its slice. Conversely, when *ROW* makes more finance available, the host will be able to get a larger slice (i.e. a lower γ) without affecting the overall size of the cake too much.

Will the host do better under quantity or transfer taking behaviour? According to the above analysis, the transfer taking solution can be obtained by imposing $\gamma = 0$ onto the quantity taking solution. As shown in Figure 3.5, $\gamma = 0$ is an optimal choice from the point of view of the host only when the difference in relative incomes approaches infinity. Therefore, we can infer that for finite values of B, the host is better off under quantity, and not transfer, taking behaviour.

3.2.1   Domestic optimum vs. incremental cost financing

While it is intuitively clear that *ROW* has an incentive to enter into a negotiation with the host to move away from its baseline quantity constrained equilibrium (as illustrated in section 3.1.1), why would the host embark in a bargaining process, when the baseline situation is already an optimum for it?

Indications have been obtained for the multiplicative utility case by carrying out some numerical analysis of the model with the software Mathematica 2.0. Such an analysis confirms that the answer is gains from trade: both parties are better off with the ICS than with the domestic optimum. By inserting the optimal value γ^* into the indirect utility function $v(.)$ we can express the latter in terms of relative prices and relative incomes only: $v_{\gamma^*}(B, p_x)$. And similarly for *ROW*'s indirect utility function: $V_{\gamma^*}(B, p_x)$. (Again, p_q and b have been set equal to unity.)

For both Host and *ROW*, we can plot the ratio of indirect utilities obtained in the two situations, v_{γ^*}/v_d and V_{γ^*}/V_d, as a function of relative incomes (or as a function of B only, when b is normalised to unity). As shown by Figure 3.6, both curves exceed unity for all values of $B>0$.

3.2.2   Price distortions

Case (a): Host and *ROW* agree on the baseline
This result that ICS dominates the domestic optimum still holds in the case of price distortions, if these are present both in the baseline domestic optimum and in the alternative ICS: the graph of Figure 3.6 would not be modified by the inclusion of the distortion coefficients. In other words, if host and *ROW* agree on the baseline (be it distorted or undistorted), they will also both be willing to adopt ICS.

Case (b): Host and *ROW* disagree
However, host and *ROW* may not necessarily agree on whether or not distortions should be included in the baseline.[12] *ROW*, for example, could argue that under art. 11 of the Biodiversity Convention, developing countries have an obligation to introduce incentives for biodiversity conservation, which would also include the elimination of existing disincentives for conservation, like price distortions. In this case, *ROW* may not be willing to negotiate an ICS unless distortions are previously removed in the host country. If this is the case, however, the host will still evaluate the attractiveness of the ICS with reference to the distorted domestic optimum, which is for its purposes the significant baseline.

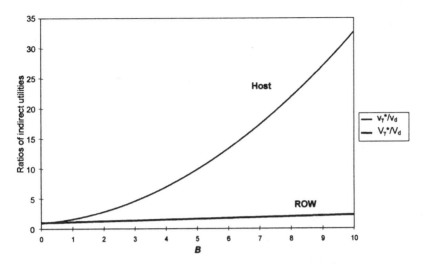

Figure 3.6   Domestic optimum vs. incremental cost financing

Therefore, a separate numerical analysis of the model has been carried out, to compare the attractiveness for each of the two parties of the two alternatives: distorted domestic optimum, undistorted ICS. To obtain results visualizable in a two-dimensional space, we picked two key parameters (relative incomes and distortion factors affecting conservation).

We then constructed the locus of values of the parameters where each party is indifferent between the two schemes under consideration, i.e. where the ratio of indirect utilities is equal to unity. For values of the parameters outside of that locus, one scheme will dominate the other. If the region of dominance of a given scheme is the same for both parties, then in that region there will be "consensus" on the relative attractiveness of that scheme.

The results are provided in Figure 3.7, which depicts the two parties' curves of indifference between undistorted ICS and distorted domestic optimum in the B - δ_q space. The intermediate line is *ROW*'s indifference curve; the upper and lower lines are the host's indifference curves for values of $\delta_x = 0.9$ and $\delta_x = 0.1$, respectively. Above the relevant indifference curve, each party is better off with the undistorted ICS; below it, with the distorted domestic optimum.

For any $\delta_q > 0$, *ROW* is always better off by paying the undistorted transfer. The host, however, will be better off in the domestic optimum when δ_x is high. For instance, the host will prefer the distorted domestic optimum for all values of the parameters below the upper curve, if $\delta_x{=}0.9$. The indifference curve of the host gives us an idea of the kind of incentives necessary for it to accept an ICS negotiated on the basis of an undistorted baseline.

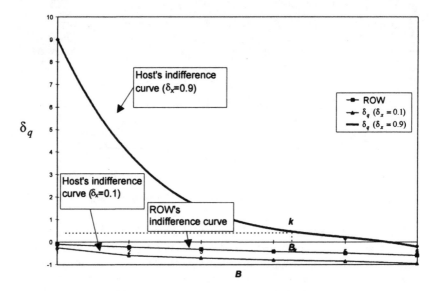

Figure 3.7   The case of price distortions

For example, when δ_x =0.9 and δ_q =0.5 (point k), conservation finance of at least B_k is required for the host to accept an undistorted ICS. Any amount less than B_k will make the host better off with the distorted baseline, and therefore unwilling to enter an ICS scheme. The diagram also confirms the intuition that incremental cost funding will be made cheaper by domestic policies aimed at supporting the "sustainable use" industry, or by policy reforms that reduce pricing distortions in the rest of the economy.

Policies of the first type would result in a lower δ_q , which would permit an upward movement along a given indifference curve; policies of the second type would result in lower δ_x, and hence a downward shift of the relevant indifference curve. In both cases, lower levels of financial commitment from the international community would be needed, other things being equal, to induce the host to choose higher conservation levels, to be funded by an incremental cost system.

Discussion

Conservation of biological diversity depends upon both domestic policy reform and upon the financial support of the international community. The appropriate way in which these two types of effort should be combined is a complex issue, which would probably deserve to be dealt with separately. The diagrammatic analysis presented above has illustrated the type and direction of the incentives at work. A more systematic treatment of the issue would necessitate spelling out the sequential decision trees faced by host and *ROW*, specifying the payoffs resulting from alternative strategies, and, for those branches of the host's decision tree where policy reforms are present, modelling costs and benefits to different domestic stakeholders of those reforms.

In the present context, however, it may be interesting to discuss a few policy issues. The connection between international funding for conservation and pre-existing domestic disincentives has long been a hotly debated topic, with significant political ramifications in the international negotiation arena.

On the one hand, a large body of the literature (Repetto and Gillis, 1988; Pearce and Warford, 1993) points to the key role played over the last few decades by developing countries' credit, fiscal and pricing policies in generating negative incentives for natural resource management in general, and biodiversity conservation in particular.

On the other hand, developing countries have quite often asserted in a number of negotiating fora (Earth Summit, Convention on Biological Diversity, GEF Council) that the principle of "additionality" –which implies that resources over and above conventional aid flows should be mobilized to tackle the new global environmental issues, and which underpins for example the establishment of the GEF–, should not result in "new conditionality".

To balance off these tensions, a number of compromise statements have been incorporated in international legal and policy documents. The Biodiversity Convention, for example, while calling contracting parties to undertake measures "that act as incentives for the conservation and sustainable use of components of biological diversity" (art. 11), reaffirms that "States have, in accordance with the Charter of the United Nations and the principles of international law, the sovereign right to exploit their own resources pursuant to their own environmental policies" (art. 3).

The GEF council, in approving the overall policy on incremental cost, has recommended that in implementing it "the notion of 'environmental reasonableness' be a guiding principle so as not to penalise progressive environmental action in recipient countries" (Global Environment Facility, 1995).

However, the relationship between developed and developing countries in the area of policy reform need not be necessarily antagonistic. There may well be sectors of developing country societies (indigenous people, NGOs, academics) that would actually support policy measures promoting sustainable uses of natural resources compatible with conservation; in some cases policy reforms are not undertaken because of infra-government co-ordination problems, or because of the lack of a systematic framework for assessing the impact of the various sectors of the economy on the conservation of natural resources.

The international community may effectively promote conservation by facilitating the process of policy reform, and more generally the process of integrating global environmental concerns into sectoral development planning (World Bank, 1995). Seed money could be used to promote stakeholder dialogue and improve stakeholders' understanding of the economy-environment interactions. This, of course, opens up a fascinating and mostly uncharted area for theoretical and applied research. Regarding the latter, the issue of promoting the establishment of a progressive environmental baseline will be addressed by the case study of this book (Chapters 4 to 6).

3.3   CONCLUSIONS

By ratifying the Convention on Biological Diversity, the international community has taken substantial commitments towards conservation of biological resources. The convention also recognises that a major share of the resulting financial burden must be borne by the rich nations.

However, the formulation of the financial provisions of the Convention has been left in vague terms. The compromise incorporated in the phrase "full agreed incremental cost" reflects the tension between developing countries' claims that there is little for them to gain from conservation, and developed countries aversion to fund baseline development activities, rather than conservation.

The present model, by providing a particular interpretation of the financial provisions of the Convention, has indicated a way in which those conflicting interests can be balanced. It has been shown that both *ROW* and host will have incentives for agreeing on a transfer of resources that entails only partial deduction of domestic incremental benefits. This transfer, despite failing to reach the utilitarian global optimum, still represents a Pareto improvement over the pre-convention status quo.

By imposing a particular multiplicative functional form on the utility of both host and *ROW*, additional results can be obtained. It has been shown that the optimal transfer implies a claw-back factor decreasing with relative income differentials, and that incremental cost financing dominates the domestic optimum even when price distortions are present in the host country. If removal of price distortions is a precondition for incremental cost funding, the analysis has illustrated the magnitude of incentives necessary for the host to give up the distorted baseline.

Theoretically, the indeterminacy of the Convention can be resolved straightforwardly with some simple analytical tool, as suggested by this chapter. However, it is quite likely that efficiency arguments like those put forward here are not the only ones that matter in the search for agreements on the way to fully implement the Convention. Other considerations (equity, strategic behaviour, pay-offs at stake in other negotiating tables), will also play an important role in the appropriate institutional and policy fora.

ANNEX 3.1:   DERIVING α AND β

The expenditure function e (p_x, p_q, u) can be also be defined as a function of q: that is, what is the minimum expenditure necessary to optimally choose conservation level q at given prices? We know that at the optimum, it must be true that:

$$\frac{u_q}{u_x} = \frac{p_q}{p_x} \tag{3.17}$$

This condition implicitly defines x as a function of q: $x=x(q)$. We can thus substitute in the expression of the budget constraint:

$$p_x x(q) + p_q q = e(p_x, p_q, q) \tag{3.18}$$

The derivative with respect to q of the expenditure function defined in this way is:

$$\frac{\partial e}{\partial q} = p_x \frac{dx}{dq} + p_q \tag{3.19}$$

The derivative dx/dq can be obtained by totally differentiating (3.17):

$$\frac{u_x u_{qq} - u_q u_{xq}}{(u_x)^2} dq + \frac{u_x u_{qx} - u_q u_{xx}}{(u_x)^2} dx = 0 \tag{3.20}$$

which gives the expression of α reported in the text:

$$\frac{dx}{dq} = \frac{u_q u_{qx} - u_x u_{qq}}{u_x u_{qx} - u_q u_{xx}} = \alpha \tag{3.21}$$

Regarding the constrained expenditure function, $\tilde{e}(p_x, p_q, u_d)$ this can also be expressed as a function of q: at given prices, what is the minimum expenditure that keeps the host at the initial level of utility u_d while conservation is at level q? When utility is constant, i.e.:

$$u(x,q) = u_d \qquad (3.22)$$

x is implicitly defined as a function of q: $x = \tilde{x}(q)$. Substituting into the budget constraint, we get:

$$p_x \tilde{x}(q) + p_q q = \tilde{e}(q) \qquad (3.23)$$

The derivative of the constrained expenditure function with respect to q is then:

$$\frac{d\tilde{e}}{dq} = p_q + p_x \frac{d\tilde{x}}{dq} = p_q - p_x \frac{u_q}{u_x}\bigg|_{u=u_d} = p_q - p_x \beta \qquad (3.24)$$

where the derivative dx/dq has been calculated by totally differentiating condition (3.23).

ANNEX 3.2: SOLUTIONS OF THE MODEL WHEN UTILITY IS MULTIPLICATIVE

When utility is multiplicative, as assumed in (3.16), it can be easily shown that the domestic optimum is given by:

$$x_d = \frac{b}{2\,p_x}; \quad q_d = \frac{b}{2\,p_q} \quad v_d(b,p) = \frac{b^2}{4\,p_q\,p_x} \qquad (3.25)$$

Where $v_d(\cdot)$ indicates indirect utility. The quantity-constrained optimum of *ROW* is:

$$X_d = \frac{B}{p_x}; \quad V_d(B,b,p) = \frac{Bb}{2\,p_q\,p_x} \qquad (3.26)$$

When the host is quantity taker, the problem for *ROW* becomes:

$$\underset{X,q}{\text{Max }} X_q \quad \text{s.t.} \quad p_x X + (2-\gamma)\,p_q\,q + \gamma\frac{b^2}{4\,p_q\,q} = B + b \qquad (3.27)$$

To see how, from expression (3.7), which applies to the general case, one arrives at expression (3.27), which applies to this particular case, note the value that the terms defined by (3.5) take on when utility is multiplicative:

$$e(p,\phi(q)) = 2pq; \quad \tilde{e}(p,u_d,q) = \frac{b^2}{4\,p_q\,q} + p_q\,q \qquad (3.28)$$

Also, note that $e(p, u_d)$ is equal to b by definition. The solutions to this problem can be shown to be:

$$q_\gamma = \frac{(B+b)}{2(2-\gamma)\,p_q}; \quad X_\gamma = \frac{(B+b)^2 - \gamma(2-\gamma)\,b^2}{2(B+b)\,p_x};$$

$$x_\gamma = \frac{(1-\gamma)[(B+b)^2 + \gamma\,b^2(3-\gamma)] + \gamma\,b^2}{2(2-\gamma)(B+b)\,p_x} \qquad (3.29)$$

Notice that for $\gamma = 1$, we in fact get $q_\gamma = q_g$, and $x_\gamma + X_\gamma = (x+X)_g$, i.e. the equilibrium values in the quantity-taking case coincide with the global optimum. Plugging these values back into the host's utility function, we obtain an indirect utility function with prices, incomes, and the claw-back factor γ as arguments:

$$v(B,b,p,\gamma) = \frac{b^2\gamma^3 - (B^2 + 4b^2)\gamma^2 + (3b^2 - 2Bb)\gamma + (B+b)^2}{4(\gamma-2)^2 p_q p_x} \qquad (3.30)$$

Differentiating this expression with respect to γ, and, to simplify the algebra, expressing prices in terms of p_q and incomes in terms of b (i.e. letting $p_q = b = 1$), we get:

$$\frac{\partial v}{\partial \gamma} = \frac{\gamma^3 + (B^2 - 6)\gamma^2 + (2B+13)\gamma - 8}{4(\gamma-2)^3 p_x} \qquad (3.31)$$

By equating the numerator of that expression to zero, we get an equation of third degree, which admits three roots: two complex, and one real. Discarding the complex roots, we obtain:

$$\gamma^* = 2 - \frac{(B+1)^2 + 9M^2}{\sqrt{3}M};$$

$$M = \left(\sqrt{3}\left[(B+1)^4(B^2 + 2B + 28)\right]^{1/2} - 9(B+1)^2\right)^{1/3} \qquad (3.32)$$

where γ^* is expressed in terms of B, which, as b is the income numeraire, has the interpretation of the relative difference in income between *ROW* and host.

NOTES

1. For some overviews on the economic values of biological resources, see Cervigni (1993), Pearce (1993), Pearce and Moran (1994).
2. Funds in the other GEF focal areas have been divided as follows: Climate Change 36%, International Waters 16%, Ozone depleting substances phaseout 1%, Multiple Areas 2%. (Global Environment Facility, 1994 and other years).

3. An example of the latter is the Program for measuring Incremental Cost for the Environment (PRINCE), core-funded and managed by the GEF. Started in 1993, PRINCE is a program of technical studies aimed at testing methodologies, undertaking case studies and disseminating results in the area of incremental cost (King, 1993c). In the biodiversity area, case studies have been carried out in Mexico (Cervigni and Ramirez, 1996), Indonesia, Malaysia and Vanuatu (Giesen and King, 1997).

4. See, for example, Pearce and Barrett (1993), King (1993), Pearce, Cervigni and Moran (1994).

5. It is plausible to assume that in most developing countries use values (both direct and indirect) will be the most relevant in determining preferences for biodiversity conservation. Non-use values, such as existence value, are likely to be relevant in countries with higher per capita income.

6. In the interpretation of the present model, the Convention on Biological Diversity introduces a particular, quantity-based, mechanism for the international financing of biodiversity conservation. In principle, one could also consider some other, price-based, instrument to induce the host to push conservation beyond q_d. One possibility is a fixed subsidy rate σ (with $0<\sigma<1$) for *any* unit of conservation in excess of the domestic optimum q_d. A previous, longer version of this paper (Cervigni, 1995) provides a more detailed analysis of the issue, with a number of quantitative results obtained by considering specific functional forms.

7. These are specified, with various degree of detail, in articles 6 through 19, and fall below the headings of: General Measures, Identification and Monitoring, In-Situ Conservation, Ex-Situ Conservation, Sustainable use of Components of Biological Diversity, Incentive Measures, Research and Training, Public Education and Awareness, Impact Assessment and Minimising Adverse Impacts, Access to Genetic Resources, Access to and Transfer to Technology, Exchange of Information, Technical and Scientific Co-operation, Handling of Biotechnology.

8. It may be argued that the loss of utility associated with any sub-optimal choice of q (i.e. to any non-zero level of γ), is itself a cost to the host country, hence eligible for incremental cost compensation. This argument is valid *only* if the principle is accepted that incremental cost should always be paid *gross* of incremental domestic benefits. But as mentioned before, there is no explicit indication in the Convention of Biological Diversity that this should be the case. Indeed, one of the purposes of the model is to suggest a possible way out of the indeterminacies of the Convention.

9. The Convention on Biological Diversity does not use the expression "global benefits". However, the preamble to the Convention affirms that "the conservation of biological diversity is a *common concern* of mankind", and stresses the "intrinsic" value of biodiversity, and its importance "for the evolution and for maintaining the life sustaining system of the biosphere". That is, it stresses the "public good" components of the value of biological diversity. Critics

of this viewpoint out that the preamble does not impose binding commitments upon signatories in the same way the actual text of the convention does.

10. See, for instance, El-Serafy (1994), King (1994), Pearce, Cervigni and Moran (1994), Glowka et al. (1994)

11. The existence of external economies and diseconomies is often conceptualized in the literature by a divergence between private and social marginal benefits. The analysis in the text focuses on cost; this is for reasons of consistency with the approach of this paper, where the mechanism for internalizing transboundary externalities of conservation depends on the expenditure function of the host. As explained in the text, this, in turn, is affected by changes in the cost of purchasing goods x and q, caused by price distortions.

12. See the discussion at the end of this section for an overview of the policy and political issues involved in reaching agreement on the baseline.

PART III.

BIODIVERSITY LOSS AND CONSERVATION IN PRACTICE: A CASE STUDY IN MEXICO

4. The area: Sierra de Santa Marta, Veracruz, Mexico

Part I of the book has discussed some of the key conceptual, definitional and methodological issues of the debate on biodiversity conservation. Part II has provided theoretical analysis of two of the issues introduced in Part I: causes of loss and funding of mitigation activities. In particular, Chapter 2 has identified and discussed social and economic factors responsible for land use change processes likely to result in biodiversity loss. Chapter 3 has proposed a model for analysing the functioning of the main tool for conservation funding (incremental cost) used in the context of the Convention on Biological Diversity.

Part III of this research addresses issues of land conversion, biodiversity loss and options for conservation in a real-life case study. It consists of three chapters. Chapter 4 introduces the case study area: Sierra de Santa Marta, located in the southern part of the State of Veracruz, Mexico. Chapter 5 discusses the social and economic factors that have been responsible over the last few decades for various processes of land use change and depletion of biological resources in the study area, as well as proposing a model for simulating further impacts over the next couple of decades. Finally, Chapter 6 develops a model for aggregating farm decisions over space and time, and discusses options for a biodiversity conservation and management strategy which would tackle the causes of change analysed in Chapters 4 and 5.

This chapter provides essential information on the case study area, Sierra de Santa Marta (SSM).[1]

4.1 LOCATION AND PHYSICAL DESCRIPTION

The Sierra de Santa Marta lies on the Gulf of Mexico, about 150 kilometres to the south-east of the Port of Veracruz, in the western foothills of Lake Catemaco, and about 40 kilometres to the north-west of the cities of Coatzacoalcos and Minatitlán. Administratively, it belongs to the municipalities of Catemaco, Mecayapan, Soteapan, and Pajapan. It is also identified as Sierra de Soteapan in various sources.

SSM belongs to a broader physiographic structure known as the Mountainous Volcanic System of Los Tuxtlas. The name "Los Tuxtlas" refers to an area that includes the three volcanoes of San Martin Tuxtlas, Santa Marta and San Martin Pajapan. The last two (which correspond to the better preserved portion of Los Tuxtlas) are included in the present study area, whereas the first one is not. [2]

The co-ordinates of Sierra de Santa Marta are 18° 05' and 18° 33' north latitude and 94° 37' and 95° 03' west longitude. Its natural boundaries are the Gulf of Mexico on the north and east, the depression of the Sontecomapan lagoon to the north-west, Lake Catemaco to the west, the Veracruz coastal plain to the south, and the Ostión lagoon to the south-west (see Figure 4.1).

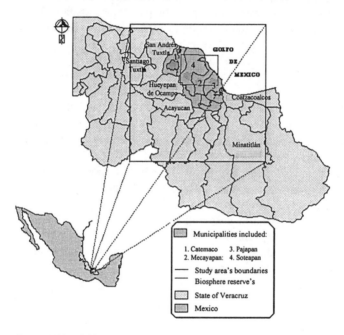

Source: PSSM (1995)

Figure 4.1   Location of the study area

The area covers 135,812 hectares, of which 82,300 hectares were declared a protected forest and wildlife refuge zone under the decree of April 28, 1980. In 1988 it was reclassified as a special biosphere reserve, and in 1998 a new protection decree was issued.[3] The boundaries of the present study area were defined by combining criteria related to land tenure, and the need for a territorial and hydrographic continuum. The zone contains 90 land units, including communities, ejidos, and private properties (see section 4.3.2 and Annex 4.1 for clarifications on land tenure categories); among towns, villages and other forms of human settlements, the total number of centres of residence is 110.

In the eastern and north hillsides, the annual average rainfall reaches 6,000 mm (in the highest elevations), and decreases gradually along lower altitudinal gradients: in the south-west a minimum annual average rainfall of 1,300 mm in is recorded, so that three humidity provinces are therefore found in the SSM: Wet, Very Wet and Rainy.

Zoning

This sub-section introduces a subdivision of the study area into ecological and socio-economic zones. This is instrumental to the rest of this chapter, since in several cases the presentation of the socio-economic data under consideration will feature breakdowns by zones.

The proposed zoning is based on ecological, geographical and land tenure considerations, and is the result of previous extensive cartographic and ground-truthing work undertaken by a local non-governmental organisation in the early 1990s.[4] In accordance with broad UNESCO methodological guidelines on biosphere reserves, three basic zones are identified: (i) a nucleus or core zone, (ii) a buffer zone, and (iii) a zone of influence. The characteristics of the zones proposed for the Sierra de Santa Marta are summarised below.

Nucleus zone. It includes areas that best conserve their natural conditions and cover sufficient land to allow for the maintenance of biotic communities and the ecological processes to sustain them.

Buffer zone. This includes forested areas that protect the nucleus zone, and mitigates the effects of human activities in the core zone. The buffer zone offers additional space for conservation of species and local migratory movements of fauna. Human settlements, farming and livestock areas are also present.

Influence zone. This area includes most of the largest population centres of the study area. The resident population interacts in various ways with communities and natural resources of the buffer zone, and in some cases with the nucleus zone as well. The influence zone includes natural or modified areas devoted to activities such as agriculture, livestock, gathering, hunting, forest exploitation, and fishing.

The fate of some of SSM's most valuable biodiversity will depend in a significant way on land use decisions taken in the nucleus and buffer zones. Nevertheless, there are good reasons to include also the influence zone in the analysis. First, the influence zone still contains areas covered by vegetation types (primary forest fragments, second growth forest, coffee groves) that can complement the protection function of the buffer zone. Second, buffer and nucleus zones are connected to the influence zone through a web of social and economic linkages, including land tenure and migration patterns, exchanges of goods and labour, so that an analysis of land use decisions constrained to the buffer and nucleus zones is unlikely to be complete. The categorization of land in zoning units overlaps with the administrative division of the study area across municipalities, as illustrated by Table 4.1.

Each of the entries in Table 4.1 defines "zoning and administrative units" (ZAUs). This double system of classification, which will be used repeatedly throughout the rest of Part III of the book, is an important one. The zoning classifications can be used for purposes of analysis of trends and of planning alternative scenarios. On the other hand, the administrative classification is especially important for policy purposes: whatever the development strategy may be, this will need to be implemented, politically and institutionally, at the individual municipio level.

4.1.1   Sources of information

The material presented in this chapter as well as the analysis carried out in the rest of the book rely on a number of sources of information. These range from census data to official documents to specialised bibliography. In cases where Federal or State programs are mentioned, which at data collection time were still under preparation, information obtained through interviews with public officials or other sources is also used. Data on land areas, land use and vegetation cover was obtained from an ad-hoc Geographical Information System (PSSM, 1995).[5]

Field surveys
One major source of primary data is the fieldwork carried out in the study area.[6] Two types of surveys were undertaken during August and September of 1995. The first survey consisted of interviews with 531 heads of household

in 47 communities. The questionnaire comprised questions on household composition, agriculture, forest and livestock activities, as well as fishing, hunting, live animal trapping, and sources of off-farm income. The other type of survey was administered to 74 key informants in 41 communities. In this survey, community-level information was sought on land tenure, land inheritance and parcelling modalities, availability of, and access to, rural services and infrastructure.

Table 4.1   Zoning and administrative units in the study area

Zone	Municipio	Land units	Area (has)	Area (% of total)
Nucleus	Federal land	1	152	0.11%
Nucleus	Catemaco	1	3,064	2.26%
Nucleus	Mecayapan	2	740	0.54%
Nucleus	Soteapan	3	4,248	3.13%
Nucleus Total		7	8,204	6.04%
Buffer	Catemaco	7	7,724	5.69%
Buffer	Mecayapan	7	6,004	4.42%
Buffer	Soteapan	7	7,068	5.20%
Buffer Total		21	20,796	15.31%
Influence	Catemaco	22	16,664	12.27%
Influence	Mecayapan	16	36,356	26.77%
Influence	Pajapan	4	17,656	13.00%
Influence	Soteapan	20	36,136	26.61%
Influence Total		62	106,812	78.65%
Total Study Area		90	135,812	100.00%

Source: PSSM (1995)

Household survey: design and sampling criteria
The broad objective of the survey was to collect information on a range of demographic, social and economic variables determining individual land users' decisions on management of natural resources in general, and conservation of biological resources in particular. Several indicators of the status of conservation were considered, the most important being the types of

land vegetation cover encountered in the study area at data collection time. The objective of the survey, and the choice of indicators of ecosystem status informed both the design of the questionnaires and the definition of sampling criteria.

The following criteria were adopted in determining the sample for the household survey. The population was divided in *clusters* corresponding to land tenure units (private properties and communities), which in turn were assigned to *strata* corresponding to zoning categories (that is, nucleus, buffer and influence zones), and to municipalities. A multi-stage sampling was conducted on the clustered, stratified holdings. The first stage was the definition of a sample of 47 clusters (land units). In the second stage, a random sub-sample of holdings was selected within the clusters selected in the first stage. In accordance with the broad objectives and choice of indicators described above, first stage sampling was determined with the following criteria. (a) Land units (in all the three zones) with no permanently residing population were not included in the sample; (b) all the (remaining) 17 land units located in the buffer zone were included in the sample;(c) to allocate remaining survey resources to the influence zone, it seemed sensible to use a "probability proportional to size" approach (Kish, 1989).

Sampling probabilities were made proportional to population. The assumption was that the larger the population, the larger the pressure on forest resources –intended as a proxy for a wider spectrum of biological resources– be those located in the community of residence or in neighbouring ones.[7] Table 4.2 summarises the main elements of the first stage sampling process.

The second stage sampling consisted of selecting random samples of holdings in each of the land units selected in the first stage. Once again, a broad principle that guided the allocation of survey resources in this stage was to give special consideration to the buffer zone. Subject to this overall priority, cost considerations (transport, accessibility, etc.) dictated the choice of the individual sub-sample sizes. The total number of heads of household interviewed was 531, with broad distribution over zones and municipios summarised in Table 4.3.

Estimation

Survey data was used to obtain *sample* means, totals, and proportions, as well as *estimators* of the same quantities for the *population* of the study area. In order to calculate population estimates, the following methodology is used in the rest of the chapter, unless otherwise indicated (Scheaffer, Mendenhall and Ott, 1986).

Table 4.2   First stage sampling: selection of land units

Zone	Municipio	Total units in study area	Total units with permanently residing population	Total units sampled	Percentage of population in sampled units
Buffer	Catemaco	7	4	4	1.65%
Buffer	Mecayapan	7	6	6	1.97%
Buffer	Soteapan	7	7	7	2.12%
Influence	Catemaco	22	15	5	1.58%
Influence	Mecayapan	16	16	8	25.21%
Influence	Pajapan	4	4	2	13.55%
Influence	Soteapan	20	20	15	21.94%
Total		83	72	47	68.03%

For the generic variable y, the notation y^k_{ij} indicates the observation coming from household i located in land unit (or cluster) j, which belongs to stratum k. There are seven strata (i.e., $k = 1...7$); the number of clusters in each stratum is indicated in Table 4.2. For stratum k, the number of clusters in the sample and in the population is, respectively, n^k and N^k; similarly, for cluster i, belonging to stratum k, the total number of household is m_i^k and M_i^k. The sample mean of variable y in cluster i, belonging to stratum k is:

$$\bar{y}_i^k = \frac{\sum_{j=1}^{m_i^k} y_{ij}^k}{m_i^k} \tag{4.1}$$

For stratum k, unbiased estimators of the populations mean, μ, and of the population total, τ, are given by:

$$\bar{\mu}^k = \frac{N^k}{M^k} \frac{\sum_{i=1}^{n_k} M_i^k \bar{y}_i^k}{n_k} \; ; \quad \bar{\tau}^k = M^k \bar{\mu}^k \qquad (4.2)$$

The estimator used for the proportion of the population with a given attribute is:

$$\hat{p}^k = \frac{\sum_{i=1}^{n_k} M_i^k \hat{p}_i^k}{M^k} \qquad (4.3)$$

where $\hat{p}_i^k$ is the proportion of households sampled in cluster i belonging to stratum k in possession of the given attribute.

Table 4.3   Second stage sampling

Zone	Municipio	Population	Sample
Buffer	Catemaco	976	56
Buffer	Mecayapan	1,164	36
Buffer	Soteapan	1,251	48
Influence	Catemaco	929	33
Influence	Mecayapan	14,867	110
Influence	Pajapan	7,991	30
Influence	Soteapan	12,941	218
Total		40,119	531

4.2 BIODIVERSITY RELEVANCE

4.2.1   Biogeographic significance of the area

Biological resources of Los Tuxtlas and the Sierra de Santa Marta have state, national and regional importance. In recent years, a very comprehensive assessment of the conservation priorities for the Latin American and

Caribbean region has been undertaken by a consortium of the World Bank, WWF and other agencies (Dinerstein, 1995). The study classifies the moist jungles of the Sierra, together with those in other parts of Mesoamerica (broad-leaved humid jungle ecoregion of Tehuantepec) as outstanding on the bioregional level (Central America) or level 1, which is an ecoregion of top regional priority. Therefore, these remnants of rain forest are a high priority for the conservation of regional biodiversity (Latin America and the Caribbean).

Other types of habitats represented in Santa Marta are classified as relevant for the conservation of biodiversity: the warm climate oak forests (Veracruz) and the savannas are classified as critical and important on the local level, with moderate priority on the regional scale. The mountain forests are classified as outstanding at the bioregional level.

The biodiversity significance of SSM stems mainly from its geological past: SSM has been the destination of intense migration of plants and animals. According to Toledo (1982), Los Tuxtlas and SSM maintained relatively stable climate conditions during the abrupt climatic changes of the Pleistocene. The region therefore provided a refuge for the tropical biota threatened by those changes. At present, Los Tuxtlas is regarded as the northernmost patch of tropical rain forest in the American continent (Dirzo & Garcia, 1992).

The agrobiodiversity of the SSM is also important. There is anecdotal evidence of a large range of varieties of maize and beans that have been selected and maintained by indigenous people in the past. Many of these traditional varieties are now disappearing because of marketing constraints, or changes in the dietary habits of local communities. An integrated strategy of biodiversity conservation for SSM should also include the protection of landraces and traditional varieties.

4.2.2 Biological wealth

Diversity of habitats
The coastal location, the orographic complexity, the isolation from other moist jungles, the extensive range of altitudes, and the succession of climate and vegetation bands, among other factors, make for a very wide variety of habitats, running from coastal, lake, and shoreline, to lowland and mountain forests, apart from the disturbed and agricultural areas.

The biota is rich in number and quality, owing to the concurrence of species of tropical and boreal origin and species that are native to the region and exist there alone (Ibarra-Manriquez and Sinaca Colin, 1995; Ramirez, 1984; Wendt, 1993). The Sierra de Santa Marta contains the widest variety of ecosystems, communities, and organisms typical of the Los Tuxtlas region and of the biogeographic province of the coastal plain of the Gulf of Mexico (Rzedowski, 1978). The Sierra has five life zones and three transitions, based on the Holdridge bioclimatic classification (1967).[8]

Plants

The Sierra exhibits significant plant biodiversity, mostly with neotropical affinity and a substantial component of isolated and residual mesoamerican and neartic elements, many of which are native. Some 1,300 species of vascular plants have been recorded (Ramirez, 1984) out of an estimated flora of over 2,000 species (Sousa and Vázquez-Torres, personal communication). These species belong to 143 families and 607 genera of vascular plants, which represent 66% and 31.4% of all families and genera reported for Veracruz. In Sierra de Santa Marta in particular, and in the Los Tuxtlas region in general, 26 of the 41 native species of trees growing over 18 meters high and present in the moist jungles of the Gulf and the Caribbean divide of Mexico are to be found (Wendt, 1993). This is the equivalent of 62% of the woody plants native to Mexico studied by that author. The destruction of habitats and over-exploitation, in some cases, threatens numerous species of plants including various species of *Chamaedorea*, some of which are native or rare such as *C. hooperiana*, *C. tuerckheimii*, and *C. tenella*.

Animals

The fauna is as rich as the flora. The bird population is one of the most varied in the country and includes 405 species, counting resident and migratory birds (Winker, Oehlenschlager et al., 1992), or 40% of the 1,010 species of birds recorded in Mexico. The birds in this region are rare owing to ecological isolation and special environmental factors (Edwards & Tashian, 1959; Andrle, 1964; Andrle, 1967). Five subspecies are found only in the region.

There are 102 species of mammals (Gonzalez Christensen, 1986), or 27% of the species recorded nationally, and 66% of those reported for Veracruz. Not including rodents and bats, 83% of the species have been traditionally used for food, medicine, hides, and other uses (Navarro, 1981). There are 43 species of amphibians (9 endemic to the region) and 109 species and subspecies of reptiles (11 endemic to the region). Together they account for 15.6% of the national herpetofauna, which is the richest in the world. In addition, 359 species of butterflies (Ross, 1967), 124 species of odonata (Gonzalez and Villeda C., 1980) and over 50 species of aquatic insects have been found in the different rivers and bodies of water (Bueno, 1980).

Endangered species of vertebrates

The most highly endangered species in Los Tuxtlas include animals with larger territorial requirements who may not be able to survive in small islands of forest. This is the case of species such as the jaguar (*Felis onca*), the puma (*F. concolor*), the wild boar (*Tayasu tajacu*), the ocelot (*Felis pardalis*), the spider monkey (*Ateles geoffroyi*), the paca (*Agouiti paca*), cabeza de viejo (*Eira barbara*), birds such as the royal pheasant (*Craz rubra*), the mountain hen (*Tinamu major*), and predator birds such as the crested eagle (*Spizaetus ornatus*) and the harpy eagle (*Harpya harpija*). The green iguana (*Iguana iguana*) and the boa constrictor are on CITES Appendix II as species endangered by illegal trade. A short summary of species recorded, endangered, and endemic is presented in Table 4.4.

Table 4.4   *Species recorded in the Los Tuxtlas region*

Zoological group	Number of species	Endangered species	Endemisms
Mammals (a,b)	102	19	2
Birds (c,d,e)	405	96	6
Reptiles (f)	109	23	17
Amphibians (f)	43	19	9
Lepidoptera (g)	359	?	5
Total	1015	157	39

Source: (a): Gonzalez Christensen (1986); (b): Navarro (1981); (c): Winker, Oehlenschlager et al. (1992); (d): Andrle (1967); (e): Ramos (1982); (f): Ramirez, Perez - Higareda G. et al. (1980); (g): Ross (1967).

Endangered ecosystems

By 1991, 59,276 hectares of jungles and forests had disappeared out of an original area of 96,640 hectares of wild vegetation existing in 1967 (61.3%). The most highly endangered ecosystems are those that have been most heavily deforested, and are generally found in low-lying and mid-mountainous areas. They include the moist jungles in low-lying zones (high and medium perennial jungles), mid-mountain mesophilic forests (virtually supplanted by coffee fields and pastures), the mangrove swamps, and the warm climate oak. Fires continue to be a threat to the remaining forested areas.

4.3   THE SOCIO-ECONOMIC ENVIRONMENT

This section presents and discusses information on the resident population's economic activities that directly or indirectly affect management of natural resources in the study area. Before we proceed to the data, a simple conceptual framework will be proposed. This will help organise and systematise the information, and introduce some of the themes that will be developed and elaborated upon in the modelling exercises of the following chapter. The framework follows conventional extensions of neo-classical microeconomic theory to households which are both consumption *and* production units (see for example Michael and Becker, 1973; Ellis, 1988).

Households have access to an endowment of factors of production: their total labour time *T*, capital goods, and the land area that they own, borrow, rent or use with the community's tacit or explicit consent (see section 4.3.2 and Annex 4.1 below for details on formal and informal land tenure arrangements). Accessible areas can be broken down into basic land use categories: cropland, pasture, primary or second growth forest.

It is assumed that households derive utility from use of natural (*N*) and man-made (*M*) goods: $u = u (N, M)$. The household is subject to a production constraint, which specifies technological possibilities for producing/ harvesting man-made and natural products out of land, labour and capital goods. The difference between own production and use of the various goods can be positive, in which case the superavit is sold on the market; or it can be negative, in which case the deficit is purchased in the market. The household is further subject to a time constraint, which limits the allocation of total time across labour on-farm, gathering of wild products, salaried employment off-farm, and leisure. Finally, the household is subject to a budget constraint:

$$p_m M^{Net} + p_N N^{Net} = wT_w + I \qquad (4.4)$$

where the *p* variables are price vectors, the *Net* superscripts indicate the difference between consumption and own production of the different types of goods, *w* is the wage rate, T_w is labour time sold off-farm, and *I* is income from other sources.

Based on this broad framework, the rest of the chapter is organised as follows. In sections 4.3.1 to 4.3.2 the human capital and land endowments of the study area will be discussed. Sections 4.3.3 and 4.3.4 present information on the activities that impinge on natural resources (primarily production/collection of domesticated/wild plants and animals); finally, section 4.3.5 discusses the evidence on non-farm employment and off-site sources of income.

4.3.1   Population

According to official census data, in 1995 a total of 57,804 people lived in the study area, distributed in 72 land tenure units (ejidos, ranching colonies, agrarian communities and private properties), belonging to four municipalities (Catemaco, Mecayapan, Pajapan and Soteapan). Between 1990 and 1995 an average demographic growth rate of 5.3% was recorded, which is more than twice the national rate (2.5%).

The population is composed for the most part of indigenous people (80%) of the ethnic groups "nahua" and "zoque-popoluca". The rest corresponds to "mestizo" populations of different origins. Indigenous people are especially concentrated in the southern portion of the study zone, with the nahuas located toward the southeast, in the municipalities of Pajapan and of Mecayapan, and the popolucas toward the southwest, in the municipality of Soteapan. The mestizos initially populated areas belonging to the Catemaco municipality (to the north-west of the SSM), and from there they have been expanding toward areas in Mecayapan and Soteapan. In some ejidos, mestizos and indigenous people interact in daily life and share commercial and productive activities, but strong cultural differences persist, most notably with respect to natural resources management. In particular, indigenous communities are typically more inclined towards traditional, integrated management options of natural resources, based on sustainable systems of shifting cultivation. In contrast, in mestizos communities a mentality of natural resource "mining" prevails, such that large tracts of forests have been cleared for the sake of (often short term) gains associated with land extensive livestock activities.

4.3.2   Land tenure

Much as in the rest of Mexico, land tenure in the Sierra de Santa Marta consists of private and communal arrangements ("ejidos" and agrarian communities). The present configuration of the system, and the current division of land across the various tenure categories, is the result of a long process of historical evolution unfolding from pre-Hispanic times, through the Mexican revolution of the early 1900s, to the constitutional and policy reforms of the 1990s. As illustrated with more detail in Annex 4.1, recent Mexican administrations have started a process of gradual transformation of the largely communal system which arose from the revolution, into a more private-property oriented system. The transition will entail parcelling of communal holding, regularisation of illegal and informal arrangements, and resolution of outstanding agrarian disputes. Social tensions may be produced to the extent that titling, parcelling and tenure regularisation will result in evictions. A resulting negative impact on forest cover and biodiversity may not be excluded a priori, as discussed in the rest of this section.

Table 4.5 provides a summary of the different types of land ownership encountered in the study area. As can be seen, communal arrangements are largely prevalent, amounting to over 70% of the area's size and to nearly 80% in terms of land tenure units.

Table 4.5   Types of land ownership

Category	Type of ownership	Land Units	Size (has)	% of total study area
Communal	Agrarian community	2	11,280	8.3%
Communal	Ejido	66	88,380	65.1%
Communal Total		68	99,660	73.4%
Private	Private Agrarian Colony	6	17,984	13.2%
Private	Private Property	12	14,952	11.0%
Private Total		18	32,936	24.3%
Other	Federal	1	152	0.1%
Other	Irregular	1	3,064	2.3%
Other Total		2	3,216	2.4%
Grand Total		88	135,812	100.0%

Source: PSSM (1995)

Area-wide data on parcelling, provided by the agrarian reform authorities, is reported in the first three columns of Table 4.6. This data, however, does not allow identification of communities where partial parcelling coexists with remaining communal spaces. More detailed information on parcelling processes and on the availability of communal spaces was obtained through the key informant's survey. As illustrated by Table 4.6, out of the 41 communities surveyed, approximately two thirds still have communal land, either because the parcelling process has not been completed (30% of the cases), or because it has not yet started (37% of the communities surveyed).

Table 4.6   Land parceling, various sources

Municipio	Area-wide data			Key informants survey sample			
	Land units	Un-parcelled	Parceled	Land units	Incompletely parcelled	Totally parcelled	Communal
Federal land	1	1		-	-	-	-
Catemaco	30	3	27	6	2	3	1
Mecayapan	25	6	19	13	5	6	2
Pajapan	3	1	2	1	0	1	0
Soteapan	29	17	12	21	5	4	12
Total	88	28	60	41	12	14	15

Source: PSSM (1995); GEF and PSSM (1995)

In connection with the discussion of ongoing land reform programs (see Annex 4.1), it is of interest to map the different categories of land users in SSM according to the type of title of access to land they have. In particular, it would be desirable to determine the share of the population that has informal, precarious or no access at all to land. This would be the set of peasants who are most likely to be affected by the implementation of tenure reforms, and whose migration/land use decisions may have a very significant impact on conservation of natural resources in the study area.

Figure 4.2 provides a tentative taxonomy of the different types of dwellers in the SSM according to the type of land unit, to the availability of communal or otherwise encroachable spaces, and to the existence of a formal title of access to land.

Physical Access to Land		Legal Access to land			No access to land
		Based on title	**Not basec on title**		
			Not based on contract	Based on contract	
Type of land unit — Private	No (perfectly monitored private property)	(1) Legitimate land owners	*(5) Peasants farming borrowed land*	*(9) Tenants, share-croppers*	*Land-less labou-rers*
	Yes (uncontrolled property)	(2) Legitimate land owners	*(6) Squatters, peasants farming borrowed land*	*(10) Tenants, share-croppers*	
Type of land unit — Social	No (parcelled commu-nities)	*(3) Ejidatarios, plus non-ejidatarios with purchased land*	*(7) Peasants farming borrowed land*	*(11) Tenants, share-croppers*	
	Yes (unparcelled or partially parcelled commu-nities)	*(4) Ejidatarios, plus non-ejidatarios with purchased land*	*(8) Peasants farming communal or borrowed land*	*(12) Tenants, share-croppers*	

Note: The scope of the terms "avecindados" and "anexantes" is indicated by the bold italic font in shaded cells

Source: own analysis

Figure 4.2   Taxonomy of land users

A first indication on the extent of actual and potential (i.e. precarious tenure) landlessness comes from the way in which farmers interviewed in the individual household survey defined themselves. However, as is indicated by the shaded area of Figure 4.2, the range of tenure arrangements that are covered by the terms "avecindados" or "anexantes" is a fairly large one. The table's taxonomy suggests that, even if *de jure* landless, "avecindados" do have *de facto* access to land in a number of ways. They may borrow land from relatives, rent it against cash payments or in return for provision of farm labour, or they may engage in share cropping arrangements.

In communities where parcelling processes have started, avecindado farmers may even have purchased individual plots. In this case, they will still not qualify as community land right holders (which excludes them from the community's various governance bodies), but they will have secure title on the purchased plot. In a few cases, avecindados are also present in private land units, like agrarian colonies or private properties. These may be farmers who have been excluded from land allocation during past processes of transition from social to private tenure; or they can be landless migrants from communal units. Because of this broad range of possibilities, measuring the extent of actual and potential landlessness in the study area is not an easy task. The exercise is further complicated by the fact that farmers may feel nervous about answering questions on informal land tenure arrangements, for fear that the information provided may be reported to their disadvantage to the agrarian reform authorities.[9]

Table 4.7 illustrates the range of different definitions that can be used, and the quite different results that can be consequently obtained. Columns (1) to (4) report area-wide estimates obtained from the household survey. These are calculated by multiplying the number of households in each stratum times the proportion of landless farmers obtained through application of Equation (4.3) (see page 102).

Column (1) refers to the percentage of interviewed farmers who defined themselves as "avecindado" or "anexante". It can be argued that this measure would unduly overestimate the extent of actual or potential landlessness, as many avecindados have in fact access to land, often in non-precarious ways (for instance when they buy a parcel of their own). Conversely, column (2), which adopts the most stringent criteria possible, i.e. counting in only farmers who have reported a size of zero for the parcel they have access to, is likely to underestimate landlessness (intended as factual but precarious access to land). The criterion of column (3) is looser, as it includes farmers who have reported non zero holdings, and yet claimed to neither have access to communal land, nor to possess their own plot.

Column (4) includes farmers who have just reported to have no privately owned land. The argument is that even if they have access to community land, this may be on the basis of a concession that the community has granted in the past, but can at any time revoke. This seems to be a plausible criterion, and has been adopted as a "best guess" estimate on the presence and distribution in the study area of actual and potential landless farmers.

Table 4.7   Landless population, various estimation criteria

Zone	Municipio	Stated "avecindados" (1)	Totally landless (2)	No ejido, no private land (3)	Best guess: No private land (4)
Buffer	Catemaco	18	0	0	7
	Mecayapan	27	10	16	27
	Soteapan	66	5	19	62
Buffer Total		111	15	35	96
Influence	Catemaco	214	79	103	214
	Mecayapan	607	14	312	600
	Pajapan	168	0	84	168
	Soteapan	1,639	54	391	1,412
Influence Total		2,628	147	890	2,393
Grand Total		2,739	162	925	2,489

Source: Own calculation based on GEF and PSSM (1995) and INEGI (1997)

4.3.3   Land use: agriculture, livestock and forest

Agricultural uses (including croplands and pasture) predominate in the study area, amounting to about 60% for the entire region, with a range of 2% to 71% moving from the nucleus to the influence zone (see Table 4.8). Total land with vegetation cover (including primary forest, second growth, degraded forests and fragments) accounts for about 36% of the study area.

The agriculture and livestock sector is by far the most important in the study area, both in terms of allocation of households' labour and in terms of contribution to household income. Industrial activity within SSM is limited to two small hydro-electric and water treatment plants which generate a very small number of jobs. Trade in agriculture and other natural products takes place mostly through intermediaries, so that the number of residents whose primary economic activity is related to commerce is practically negligible.

Agriculture: cropping patterns

Table 4.9 provides area-wide estimates of how agricultural land is allocated to a selected number of uses, across ZAUs. It is easy to see that pasture is by far the predominant use of agricultural spaces, accounting for over 65% of non-forested land. Maize, which is the second most significant use, is mostly cultivated for consumption within the farm household.[10]

Table 4.8   Land uses, zoning and municipios (hectares)

Zone	Municipio	Area	Main forest	Other forest (a)	Agriculture (b)	Other uses (c)
Nucleus		152	132	-	20	-
Nucleus	Catemaco	3,064	3,028	-	36	-
Nucleus	Mecayapan	740	740	-	-	-
Nucleus	Soteapan	4,248	3,884	260	104	-
Nucleus Total		8,204	7,784	260	160	-
Buffer	Catemaco	7,724	4,228	724	2,736	36
Buffer	Mecayapan	6,004	3,012	324	2,604	64
Buffer	Soteapan	7,068	3,868	397	2,751	52
Buffer Total		20,796	11,108	1,446	8,090	152
Influence	Catemaco	16,664	1,456	3,482	10,854	144
Influence	Mecayapan	36,356	3,156	6,925	25,751	524
Influence	Pajapan	17,656	1,216	1,058	14,998	384
Influence	Soteapan	36,136	1,940	8,532	25,088	576
Influence Total		106,812	7,768	19,997	76,691	1,628
Grand Total		135,812	26,660	21,702	84,942	1,780

Notes: (a): includes second growth, forest fragments and degraded forest; (b): Includes cropland and pasture; (c): mainly urban uses

Source: own calculations based on PSSM (1995)

Among cash crops, chilli and beans have some significance in a number of communities of the influence zone; coffee is also an important crop for the buffer zone, and for the communities of the influence zone with remaining forest cover (especially in the Soteapan municipality). A recent activity is plantation of Chamedor Palm in second growth forest as an alternative to the more labour-intensive (and ecologically disruptive) practice of harvesting wild populations from the nucleus and buffer zone; as can be seen from the table it is still very limited in geographical scope.

Conversion of formerly forested land to pasture is a pervasive feature of land use patterns throughout SSM. However, farms in the region differ markedly in terms of the modalities of livestock activities undertaken.

With the help of data presented in Table 4.10, one can attempt some categorization. Around two thirds of resident households are estimated not to own cattle (they may still have land under pasture, which they can rent for grazing to neighbouring cattle owners).

Table 4.9   *Cropping patterns, area-wide estimates in hectares*

		Maize	Beans	Palm	Coffee	Chilli	Other	Pasture (*)
Buffer	Catemaco	300.8	13.7	6.9	78.7	-	18.3	1,158.3
	Mecaya-pan	419.1	18.4	-	53.5	-	2.0	1,839.1
	Soteapan	502.2	51.3	20.1	167.1	4.0	0.5	2,058.0
Buffer Total		1,222.1	83.4	27.0	299.4	4.0	20.7	5,055.4
Influence	Catemaco	1,300.9	324.0	-	74.0	42.5	88.0	8,457.5
	Mecaya-pan	9,502.0	1,567.6	-	0.9	316.6	81.4	14,807.0
	Pajapan	3,849.3	11.6	23.3	-	-	567.8	13,759.9
	Soteapan	6,131.7	913.3	77.2	2,398.0	70.5	47.2	17,525.6
Influence Total		20,784.0	2,816.6	100.5	2,472.9	429.6	784.4	54,549.9
Grand Total		22,006.1	2,900.0	127.5	2,772.2	433.6	805.1	59,605.3

Note: (*) Calculated as difference between non forested area and estimated total cropland

Source: Own calculation based on GEF and PSSM (1995)

Approximately one fourth of the households is estimated to possess small to medium size herds (that is, 1 to 5 heads, and 6 to 20 heads, respectively). Large herds above 20 heads are concentrated in the hands of less than 10% of the households.

Livestock is the most important source of agricultural income; as a result, it is plausible that a significant portion of cattle-less households are mainly subsistence-oriented. For small and perhaps medium size ranchers, livestock is likely to have mainly the purpose of providing a means for investing family savings. For large rangers (and for some of the medium-size ones), ranching is a primarily commercial activity.

It is interesting to note that the Soteapan municipality features at the same time the highest cattlelessness rates and the lowest stocking rates (average number of cattle heads per hectare of pasture). This seems to suggest that in this part of the study area conversion to pasture has been at the same time highly inefficient and significantly inequitable.

Table 4.10   Cattle ranching: size and distribution of herds

Zone	Municipio	Total cattle	House-holds with no cattle	House-holds with small herds (1 to 5 heads)	House-holds with medium herds (6 to 20 heads)	House-holds with large herds (over 20 heads)
Buffer	Catemaco	858	57.2%	10.6%	29.0%	3.1%
	Mecayapan	2,144	33.0%	27.6%	10.3%	29.0%
	Soteapan	309	76.0%	16.8%	7.1%	0.0%
Buffer Total		3,311				
Influence	Catemaco	10,042	43.8%	15.0%	17.1%	23.9%
	Mecayapan	26,462	73.6%	12.6%	5.6%	8.2%
	Pajapan	16,175	40.7%	28.2%	22.7%	8.2%
	Soteapan	8,703	77.2%	12.6%	6.3%	3.9%
Influence Total		64,692				

Source: Own calculation based on PSSM - GEF (1995)

4.3.4   Uses of forest-related resources

In several communities of the study area, forest resources are an important asset for resident households, both in terms of direct use, and of income generation through sale of harvested products. Forested areas are a source of timber and non-timber products, of fuelwood, and are the habitat for wildlife used for both hunting and live-trapping.

Gathering of forest products

Several species of plants are collected for use in the preparation of drugs, as building material, textile fibers, or are sold for ornamental purposes. Gathering activities are not normally undertaken throughout the year, but only during a number of months in which climatic and other ecological conditions permit them. Many of the gatherers are concentrated in communities of the buffer and influence zones closer to areas with significant forest cover. For a sub-set of four plants with particular commercial importance, Table 4.11 provides area-wide estimates of the number of households engaged in gathering activities, the volume of extraction per annum, and of the value (based on 1995 prices) of the harvest. [11]

Apart from the case of Chocho (*Astrocarium Mexicanum*, an edible sprout) where gathering rates (i.e. percentage of households engaged in gathering) are estimated to exceed 30%, collection of several species is not so widespread in the entire area (with gathering rates ranging between 0.5 and 8%) and yet can be quite important for individual communities adjacent to forested areas with the necessary ecological and climatic conditions.

Collection of Chamedor Palm is one of the main channels of residents' interactions with the nucleus zone and with primary or second growth forested area of the buffer zone. For many households in the buffer zone with small or no cattle herds, Palm is also an important source of cash to support family incomes. At the same time, the lack of direct access to the end market (both national and international) forces gatherers to resort to intermediaries, who pay low farm-gate prices. For gatherers to meet their cash objectives, harvest rates often exceed regeneration rates; increasing evidence points to the resulting dwindling of wild populations of several palm species. Plantation of palms outside the nucleus zone has therefore repeatedly been proposed as a conservation strategy with double benefits: on the one hand, reducing the pressure on wild populations, and on the other, creating incentives for conserving primary and second growth forest which could otherwise be converted to pasture or agriculture.

Trapping of live animals

Trapping of live animals is also a significant activity in a small number of communities of the study area. Trapped animals, which include songbirds like Clarines, Tucans and Parrots, as well as monkeys and rare insects, are sold as mascots or captive specimens in towns inside and outside the study area.

Table 4.11   Gathering of non-timber forest products

Zone	Buffer	Influence	Total
Land units	17.0	55.0	72.0
House-holds	622.0	9,709.0	10,331.0
Sampled units	17.0	30.0	47.0
Sampled Hholds	140.0	391.0	531.0
Palm			
Gatherers	42.4	208.8	251.1
Extraction/ annum (gruesas) (*)	15,050.6	37,850.7	52,901.3
Value (1995 MexPes)	37,626.6	94,626.8	132,253.3
Chocho			
Gatherers	230.5	2,894.7	3,125.2
Extraction/ annum (000 Kg.)	1,135.9	3,567.1	4,703.0
Value (1995 MexPes)	NA	NA	NA
Bejucos			
Gatherers	28.0	245.5	273.5
Extraction/ annum (000)	2,045.0	275.5	2,320.5
Value (1995 MexPes)	NA	NA	NA
Ixtle			
Gatherers	17.1	71.7	88.8
Extraction/ annum (000 Kg).	1,090.8	1,122.0	2,212.8
Value (1995 MexPes)	NA	NA	NA
Other Species			
Species	11.0	12.0	
Gatherers	93.5	796.7	890.1

Note: (*) One "gruesa" is a bundle of 120 leaves of the plant

Source: own calculation based on PSSM - GEF (1995)

In many cases, this activity is conducted illegally as it infringes national regulations on endangered species protection. As a result, data provided by farmers interviewed, summarised by Table 4.12, is likely to underestimate of the actual extent of live animal trapping. In any event, based on sample information on community reporting trapping activities, it is estimated that between 350 and 400 households may be engaged in those practices. Because of the sensitivity of the topic, more detailed information on trapping such as number and species of animals captured, albeit available, is often not consistent; therefore, calculations on the proceeds from the sale of the catch has not been included in the table.

Table 4.12   Trapping of live animals

	Zone		
	Buffer	Influence	Total
Land units	17	55	72
Households	622	9,709	10,331
Sampled units	17	30	47
Sampled households	140	391	531
Units reporting trapping	5	9	14
Trappers in sample	9	14	23
Trappers in population (estimate)	57	323	380
Indicative annual revenues from sale of trapped animals (range or average, 1995 MexPes):			
Clarin			60 - 4,000
Tucan			3,000
Parrots			1,200 - 24,000

Source: own calculation based on PSSM - GEF (1995)

Hunting
Hunting in SSM is undertaken both for direct consumption and for re-sale to buyers outside the study area. The latter is increasing in importance in recent years due to higher demand for game meat from households and restaurants in urban areas adjacent the region. Main species hunted include birds (Faisán

real, Faisán gritón, Chachalacas, Palomas, Codorinces, ducks), reptiles (iguanas), monkeys, varieties of wild-boar (Tepezcuintle, Jabalí), deer (venado real, venado cola blanca), other mammals (armadillos, squirrels, serete, mazate, tejón, rabbits).

Table 4.13   Hunting, area wide estimates

	Zone		
	Buffer	Influence	Total
Total Population	3,400	55,573	58,973
Households	622	9709	10331
Land units	17	55	72
Sampled units	17	30	47
Sampled units with hunting reported	11	21	32
Percentage of household hunting	28.77%	20.85% (a)	
Kills/ household/ annum	12	8.56	
Kills/ annum	2,147	17,322	19,470

Notes: (a): Sample average

Source: own calculation based on PSSM - GEF (1995)

On the basis of survey information, it is estimated (see Table 4.13) that the percentage of households undertaking some hunting activities varies between 20 and 30% in the various zones of the region. Between 8 and 12 kills per household per annum are estimated, amounting to an approximate 20,000 kills per annum for the entire region.[12] Anecdotal evidence from both the household and key informant surveys suggests that because of past and current high harvest rates populations of several of the hunted species are declining.

4.3.5   Off-site employment, non farm income and migration patterns

There is a close relationship between the SSM and the main cities of the southern part of Veracruz state. The towns of Acayucan and Jaltipan are the main market for cash crops produced in the SSM, as well as for staple crops purchased by SSM's subsistence farmers unable to cover consumption needs with their own production. Perhaps even more importantly, SSM has been a significant provider of workforce to the industrial triangle of Coatzacoalcos, Minatitlán, and Cosoleacaque, one of the most important petrochemical zones in Veracruz and in fact in the whole of Mexico.

In the past, the income of many families of the Sierra used to depend on the level of economic activity of the oil district. For example, during the second half of the past decade, 44% of the salaried population of Pajapan were employed in the cities of the district: 29% in the construction and 15% in rural and urban services (Buckles, 1987).

Following a period in the 1980s of reduced activity of Veracruz's oil industry, measures of sectoral restructuring have been launched in the early 1990's. These measures also include the proposed sale of a number of petrochemical complexes in the southern district. As a result of the crisis and the following restructuring packages, unemployment in southern Veracruz has increased alarmingly. In the Cosoleacaque-Minatitlán-Coatzacoalcos corridor, which used to be the single most important source of employment of southern Veracruz, more than 50 thousand jobs have been lost; the city of Coatzacoalcos features the highest unemployment rate (9.8%) in the domestic trade and services sectors.

Another outlet that traditionally provided temporary employment opportunities to the SSM is given by the agricultural activities that require seasonal labour in neighboring localities. The Perla del Golfo colony receives annually, during the chilli agricultural cycle (April-June), a significant number of workers from the SSM (approximately 400 labourers). Seasonal employment to the Perla has traditionally been attractive due to the high wages paid: between 25 to 30 pesos per day, which compares well to the 10-15 pesos rate normally paid in the indigenous zones of Mecayapan, Soteapan and Pajapan. Another zone with some significant demand for farm labour is the zone of Chinameca and Tonalapa (neighboring localities of Mecayapan and Soteapan) during the papaya harvest between May and July. However, both of these temporary sources of employment are at present insufficient to absorb the excess labour supply of the SSM. In the wake of the crisis, the flow of seasonal workers toward Perla del Golfo has decreased, since payment of the formerly high wage rates can no longer be guaranteed.

In the face of Veracruz and Mexico's economic downturn, many former migrants from the Sierra de Santa Marta have been forced to return to their localities of origin, thereby increasing population densities and putting more pressure on land and natural resources. This is illustrated by the case of the Tatahuicapan community, where the number of avecindados rose from 900 to 1733 between 1991 and 1995, most likely due to the crisis-induced return migration from the oil district (Blanco, 1995, quoted in Cervigni and Ramirez, 1996).

Table 4.14   *Migration patterns and off-site employment*

Zone	Municipio	Land units	In migrant families, 1990-95	Out migrant families, 1990-95	Permanent off-site workers
Buffer	Catemaco	3	73	41	25
Buffer	Mecayapan	6	12	39	6
Buffer	Soteapan	7	8	21	
Influence	Catemaco	3	10	5	3
Influence	Mecayapan	7	25	18	49
Influence	Pajapan	1	10		
Influence	Soteapan	14	45	43	22
Total		41	183	167	105

Source: own calculations based on key informants survey (PSSM - GEF, 1995)

Table 4.14 summaries information gathered in a subset of 41 communities, through the key informant survey, on net regional migration flows and current permanent employment outside the study area. Despite some cases of positive out-migration, the general trend during the period 1990-95 has been one of return to rural areas; the prospects of permanent employment outside SSM are not encouraging, as highlighted by the last column of the table.

Table 4.15 provides area-wide estimates on the pattern of temporary off-site employment in SSM, as well as estimates of non-agricultural incomes. Household size averaged between 4.8 and 10 people, with average labour force (individuals older than 10 years) ranging between 3.2 and 6.5 people. An average of at most one person with temporary off-site employment was recorded, with average employment time reaching one year just in one case (the Catemaco portion of the influence zone).

Table 4.15   Off-site employment and non-farm income

Zone	Buffer			Influence			
Municipio	Cate-maco	Mecaya-pan	Sotea-pan	Cate-maco	Mecaya-pan	Pajapan	Sotea-pan
Household size	6.13	5.79	4.79	4.15	8.16	10.05	4.80
Family labour, pers./ h.hold (a)	4.00	4.09	3.07	2.89	5.94	6.53	3.20
Off-site workers (avg per h.hold)	0.85	0.63	0.14	1.08	0.47	0.16	0.28
Off-site workers (sum)	137	126	38	722	1,737	277	1,001
Months of work per annum	7.87	4.54	0.40	12	2.95	0.76	1.53
Family labour supplied off-site, (%) of total (b)	10.68%	7.75%	0.63%	21.57%	3.90%	1.13%	2.45%
Wage income/ h.hold (US$) (c)	1,063	567	72	1,044	475	271	223
Other non farm income/ house-hold (US$) (c)	97	133	53	166	56	147	51
Total non-farm income / house-hold (US$) (c)	1,160	700	125	1,210	532	417	275
Total non-farm income per capita (US$) (c, d)	189	121	26	291	65	41	57

Notes: (a): includes all family member older than 10 years; (b): given by months worked off-site divided by (12* family labour); (c): exchange rate used: 1US$=6.3 MexPes; (d): equals total non-farm income per household divided by average household size

Source: own calculations based on PSSM - GEF (1995)

The estimated total number of people with some temporary off-site employment is around 4,000, corresponding to less than 10% of the estimated economically active population. However, in terms of time, the ability of the regional economy to absorb SSM's labour supply is even lower.

Out of the total working time of the economically active population (EAP), a weighted average of less than 5% is used in temporary employment in the industry and services sectors of southern Veracruz's economy. It follows that over 95% of the EAP's working time is available for (sustainable or unsustainable) use of the region's natural resources.

The last four columns of Table 4.15 provide estimates of non-farm incomes obtained through salaried work or through other sources (mainly sale of artisanry items, handicrafts, etc.). Non-farm activities in the study area generate an estimated per capita income of only US$ 88 per annum (according to World Bank data, in 1994 per capita income in Mexico was around US$ 4,000).

The recovery of the regional economy is not likely to be immediate; in fact, it is plausible that higher regional unemployment rates will result from the prospective privatization of the petrochemical conglomerate of the industrial corridor Cosoleacaque-Minatitlán-Coatzacoalcos. Considering also the current population growth rates, it is not difficult to suppose that the pressure on natural resources and land in the SSM will be yet greater than what has been observed in 1995.

ANNEX 4.1: BACKGROUND ON MEXICO'S LAND TENURE SYSTEM[13]

Basic categories and parameters of land rights were defined in Article 27 of the 1917 Constitution, allowing three types of property: ejidos, small property, and communal property (comunidades Ejidos constitute a land grant for usufruct to a population group, and until a major constitutional reform in 1992, ejido land essentially belonged to the state and could not be sold. Small property is privately owned and is subject to size limits according to the quality of the land and type of crop or economic activity. Communal property is based on the historical rights of pre-Hispanic indigenous communities who have maintained their traditional communal property structure.

Land was not distributed to ejidos immediately after the 1917 Constitution and only began to proceed in 1930. In subsequent years land distribution would vary considerably between presidential periods. When first distributed in the 1940s, all ejido land was communal, but many ejidos have since opted to parcel part or all of their land to individual "ejidatarios" (community members). Thus, some ejidos have communal land only (about 7% of total ejidos in 1991), some have communal and parcelled land (65 %), and some are completely parcelled (28 %) (World Bank, 1994).

In 1992, in preparation for Mexico's joining in the North American Free Trade Agreement (NAFTA), major reforms of Constitution's article 27 and of the agrarian law were undertaken. The purpose was allowing the allocation of land among competing uses to become more responsive to international market forces. Under the new system, community members are allowed to gain title over land. Subject to some limitations spelled out in the new agrarian law, ejidatarios are permitted to sell and rent their land, pledge it as collateral and form associations with private investors.

In the intentions of its promoters, the reform will increase allocative efficiency in the agriculture, livestock and forestry sectors. Improved land property rights will result in more active land markets, which in turn will facilitate the allocation of the different types of land to their most profitable use; in particular, it is expected that inefficient, land-extensive cultivation of basic staple crops like maize and wheat will be replaced, possibly with the support of foreign investors, by crops with a clear climatic comparative advantage, like citrus fruits and other tropical produce.

In order to implement the constitutional and legislative reform, a major nation-wide land titling program has been launched in 1993: the PROCEDE (*Programa de Certificación de Derechos Ejidales y Titulación de Solares*

Urbanos, i.e. Program for Certification of Ejido Rights). PROCEDE is headed by the Minister for agrarian reform, with the National Institute for Statistics and Geography responsible for the preparation of maps and titles (World Bank, 1995). According to the World Bank, as of April 1995 only 20% of the ejidos included in PROCEDE's workplan obtained community level titles, and few individual land titles had been granted. It is likely that because of the ambitious goals of the program, the poor quality of baseline information, the high costs involved, and the need to resolve a large number of infra- and inter-ejido disputes, PROCEDE will proceed at a fairly slow pace.

One of the key social issues that have been raised concerns the impact of the program on the different tenure arrangements (including formal and informal ones) that have been developing since the beginning of the post-revolution land distribution process. Both in private and communal land units, formal land rights holders ("propietarios" in the former case and "ejidatarios" or "comuneros" in the latter) are by no means the only type of land dwellers. Along with genuinely landless salaried agricultural labourers, a significant proportion of the rural population does not possess either private or community land titles, and yet farms individual parcels of land by entering in contractual or informal arrangements (land rental, borrowing or sharecropping) with either private landlords or ejidos.

A broad term which describes this category of land users is "avecindados" (the other term sometimes used, "anexante", denotes titleless farmers whose parcel is in a community different from the one of residence). There are various reasons why a farmer may be an avecindado. Because the title of "ejidatario" is inherited by only one of the incumbent's children, in several communities many avecindados are non-inheriting sons of land rights holders; others are migrants from communities where opportunities for informal modes of access to land were limited. Even in the absence of contractual arrangements of a written or verbal nature, avecindados living in communal land units may also use common property land on the basis of the tacit or explicit consent of the ejido's authorities.

It is fair to expect that the overall social and economic impact of PROCEDE will depend on the way its implementation will affect the various situations of "de-facto" land use that can be encountered in rural Mexico. A strict application of the program, disregardful of informal tenure arrangements, may result in eviction of avecindados on a significant scale. This opens up a number of issues related to the social and economic costs of the likely resulting migration to urban areas, as well as questions about the capacity of some stagnant segments of the industry and services sector to absorb the incremental supply of unskilled labour. From the environmental point of view, one reason for concern may be that, as a result of PROCEDE, evicted peasants unwilling or unable to migrate to urban areas may be forced to clear, for subsistence agriculture, marginal forested land, currently not subject to parcelling processes under the agrarian law.

This may suggest some qualification to the conventional wisdom about the linkages between land tenure, deforestation and natural resource management in general. As is often argued in the literature,[14] lack of secure tenure is often a major cause of pressure on forests and other natural resources, so that titling programs are often regarded as essential components of strategies for encouraging sustainable use of natural resources. At the same time, it needs to be recognized that improving the security of tenure of one part of the population at the expense of "de-facto" users may, in the absence of mitigation measures, have the undesirable effects of actually increasing pressure on forests.[15]

NOTES

1. As explained in the preface, the Sierra de Santa Marta (SSM) was the subject of a case study on sustainable development and biodiversity conservation financed by the PRINCE program of the Global Environment Facility (GEF). The study was conducted between 1995 and 1996 in a partnership involving the GEF, the Proyecto Sierra de Santa Marta (PSSM), a local non-governmental organisation, and CIMMYT (Centro Internacional para el Mejoramiento del Maiz y Trigo), an international research centre on maize and wheat in the CGIAR network. See Cervigni and Ramirez (1996).

2. There is no single definition of the exact territorial extension of the Los Tuxtlas region. Several sources indicate the size of Los Tuxtlas as ranging around 250,000 hectares. Accepting this figure, one obtains that the study area makes for approximately half of the broader Los Tuxtlas.

3. Subsequent to the case study that forms the basis for this chapter and the following ones, the Mexican government has issued (in November of 1998) a decree that reclassifies the area as a biosphere reserve with a total extension of 155,122 has. The reserve thus redefined covers an area in part different from the study area of this research, as it includes the three additional municipalities of Angel Cabada, Santiago Tuxtla, and San Andrés Tuxtla. See Instituto Nacional de Ecología (2000) for more information.

4. The Proyecto Sierra de Santa Marta (PSSM), the local non-governmental organisation referred to in note 1, developed in the early 1990s a proposal for a

zoning of the region, in order to assist the implementation of its protected
status, formally decreed in the 1980s but for a long time not enforced in
practice. See Pare (1993).

5.   The Geographic Information System of the Proyecto Sierra de Santa Marta is
     based on maps at the 1:50,000 scale. Maps have been digitalized using a grid of
     200 metres -per side boxes (equivalent to 4 has per box). Land use data are
     based on interpretation of 1990 aerial photography and satellite images, and
     validated through ground truthing exercises. For further details, see Pare (1993).

6.   This fieldwork was undertaken as part of the case study mentioned in note 1.

7.   Fuelwood and a number of other forest products are often gathered in
     communities adjacent to the one of residence, especially if forest cover in the
     latter has been cleared.

8.   These are: very moist forest, moist subtropical forest, rain forest, very moist
     forest, subtropical low mountain rain forest.

9.   In the individual farmers survey, this factor affected in some cases the internal
     consistency of answers on the breakdown of individual holdings across the
     different tenure categories.

10. The average size of the area under maize in the various Zoning and
     Administrative Units (ZAUs) ranges between 0.15 and 8 has, with 2 has as a
     reasonable area-wide average. Given yields in the range of 1 to 2.5 tons/ ha,
     harvests barely exceed the consumption needs of the average household (4-6
     individuals) with a diet mainly based on corn.

11. Information on this last category is not complete.

12. Estimating the financial value of the harvest would necessitate a finer break
     down, over the different species, of the data on aggregate kills; this has not been
     attempted here.

13. This section draws, among other sources, on material discussed in reports of the
     World Bank (World Bank, 1994; World Bank, 1995).

14. See for example Pearce and Warford (1993)

15. This theme will be the subject of quantitative analysis in the modelling exercise
     of subsequent chapters of the book.

5. The process of land use change: modelling farm behaviour

The purpose of this chapter is to develop farm-level models of resource management decisions likely to result in biodiversity loss (land use change, over-harvesting of wild fauna and flora) in the Mexico case study area. The modelling exercise will be based on a brief historical overview of social and economic trends in the study area, as well as of policies that have had significant influence over time on natural resource management decisions.

5.1 THE PAST: OVERVIEW OF THE PROCESS OF LAND USE CHANGE

This section provides an historical analysis of the interaction between communities in the region and the environment, from the turn of the century to the 1990s. This information provides the background for the modelling exercise of section 5.3, which attempts to identify the economic processes likely to affect land use over the next decade.

5.1.1 First half of the century

The land use pattern that prevailed up to the mid-1950s resulted from a production system composed of three complementary activities: (a) agriculture (mainly staple crops), (b) hunting and gathering, and (c) small scale livestock (mainly hogs and poultry). In spatial terms, the system was based on tradition- and community-ruled access to four agro-ecological sub-systems: the primary forest (*monte*), the second growth forest - fallow land (*acahual*), the cropping area (*milpa*), and the farm orchard (*solar*). The main feature of the system was that none of the activities required elimination of the others to operate (Pare, 1993; Chevallier and Buckles, 1995).

Under the system, the main crops were maize and beans, but they were grown in association with more than ten other tuberous, gramineous, and fruit crops. The jungles and forests were additional sources of food, aside from providing products for other uses, such as construction. Popoluca and Nahua peasants sold coffee, loaf sugar, alcohol, and hogs on local markets. Hog farming was accompanied by maize production, needed for fattening and breeding the animals. Maize, in turn, formed part of a farming system (slash and burn) based on grasslands/second growth forest (*acahual*) and jungle.

5.1.2   Second half of the 20th century

The production system described above was dramatically altered by the adoption of extensive cattle ranching, which had been little practised until that time and in any case only for on-farm consumption or saving purposes. Extensive cattle farming moved into the primary forest and into areas used for farming and regeneration (*acahual*). Two stages can be distinguished in the development of cattle farming.

(a) The introduction of cattle, linked to the initial stages of communal land enclosures, but located in very specific areas and restricted to a small group of farmers, which was the case of the Tatahuicapan and Pajapan municipalities from 1950 to 1970. Land concentration led to serious political conflicts in the towns (Buckles, 1987; Velázquez, 1992) and undoubtedly caused a loosening of family ties since a number of family units had to abandon their places of birth.

(b) The expansion of cattle ranching, in the ensuing decades, to a larger number of farmers and communities, due, first, to the inception on a larger scale of communal land parcelling; and second, to more readily available bank loans.

Additional pressure was put on the traditional production system from the decade of the 1950s onwards by waves of domestic migration, caused both by unresolved land tenure conflicts in other Mexican states and by official colonisation policies. Newly arrived settlers began to cut down trees to establish their communities and clear fields for their crops. Many of them came from areas traditionally dedicated to cattle ranching, and so imported a livestock-oriented mentality, often with little concern for necessary adjustments to local ecological and marketing conditions. Nevertheless, deforestation was not devastating in the early days, since most of the new settlers did not have the means to expand ranching on a large scale.

5.1.3   The impact of government programs in the 1970s

Much as in several other developing countries, in the three or four decades following the middle of the century Mexico's economic policy was guided by a development model based on import substitution, stabilisation, and heavy government intervention in the basic sectors of the economy. Programs were launched in a number of areas with significant impacts on the management of the country's natural resources. As discussed below, the consequences on the present study area were profound.

Cattle ranching
The expansion of cattle ranching in the Mexican tropics[1] was massive during the decades of the 50s through the 80s. In the southern part of the state of Veracruz the number of heads of cattle grew from 206,000 in 1950 to about 2.3 million in 1986; the area under pasture increased from 430,000 to 1.1 million in the same period (Lazos, 1995).

Two public programs introduced in the mid-1970s marked a distinct new stage in the growth of cattle farming: the Livestock Trust for *ejidos* and the Comprehensive Rural Development Program (PIDER). Both provided subsidized credit for cattle raising. As described in detail for the Pajapan community by Chevallier and Buckles (1995), an indispensable ingredient for the rapid growth of pasture was the process of enclosure of communal spaces and of concentration of large extenses of land into the hands of relatively few politically influential *mestizos* ranchers.

As an interesting qualifications to the diagrammatic analysis of Chapter 2 (Section 2.2), the land conversion sequence started in many cases not with road building, but with the replacement of swidden agricultural production with pasture in communal spaces located in the fertile lowland areas. The displaced *milpa* production would then move into forested area uphill for a few years, that is, until yield drops and/or new enclosures would determine additional conversion to pasture, so that food crop production would be displaced even further in the forest.

The impact of enclosures and credit policies became visible by the mid-1970s. The forested area shrank from 96,640 hectares in 1967 to 60,857 hectares in 1976, i.e. 35,788 hectares of forests and jungle were lost in nine years (Ramirez, 1984). A land use model that would be difficult to reverse was becoming consolidated. The process of substitution of agriculture and forested land with pasture expanded as wealthier farmers began converting land, not only through use of subsidized credit, but also by investing their own resources. Once the land was turned into pasture, a complex web of social and economic interactions revolving around cattle started to develop: farmers would purchase their own cattle, obtain animals under sharecropping agreements, lease their pastures (or their herds) to ranchers in their communities or in neighbouring ones (Buckles, 1987; Chevallier & Buckles, 1995).

Coffee

As it did in other coffee-growing parts of the country, in the 1970s the Instituto Mexicano del Café (INMECAFE, Mexican Coffee Board) opened up coffee warehouses in the Sierra and provided credit and advisory services for the introduction of technological changes to boost productivity. Government support for coffee farming was maintained during the entire decade and almost all of the 1980s.

This support had socio-economic and ecological impacts of different kinds: (a) it promoted the cultivation of new varieties (*caturra mondonovo*) that were more productive but with higher fertiliser requirements; (b) it introduced the use of agro-chemicals that were later extended to corn; (c) in terms of marketing, it broke a regime of monopsony (in previous years there was one main buyer from Acayucan, who imposed coffee prices at will); (d) the expansion of coffee, fostered by favourable conditions on the international market, decreased the area dedicated to staple crop farming, with negative impacts on maize-based systems;[2] (e) on the other hand, the expansion of coffee growing had a beneficial impact on forest conservation to the extent that shaded coffee varieties were adopted.[3]

Forestry activities

In the 1970s and 1980s the Mexican government also intervened in the Sierra's forestry activities. Two episodes are of particular significance. The first concerns the use of non-timber products. The parastatal agency PROQUIVEMEZ promoted the exploitation of non-wood products which were in high demand in the decade of the sexual revolution. Mullein (*barbasco*) a root used to manufacture contraceptives, was greatly sought after by the pharmaceutical industry, just at the time when the government expanded its role into agriculture and other productive sectors. A government-owned company was established to sell mullein and the plant was harvested so heavily that it had almost disappeared by the end of the decade. In some communities in the sierra, such as Benigno Mendoza, the residents recall that it was thanks to mullein that they survived during the 1970s, when the jungle on much of their communal land was cut down to establish pasture (Pare, 1993).

The second episode concerns logging activities. In 1988 logging permits (773 hectares) were issued for two *ejidos* in the municipality of Mecayapan to supply a sawmill in Tatahuicapan. A large forested area was destroyed by harvesting timber in areas not covered by the permits. In particular, timber extraction quickly entered in conflict with conservation policies.

On April 28, 1980, the federal government responded to the concerns of academic institutions and declared the Sierra de Santa Marta to be a "protected forest and wildlife refuge zone".[4] However this act was not accompanied by measures to implement it. No campaign was promoted to inform the public that the area had been protected nor was any management plan prepared to regulate production activities inside the protected area.[5] Despite the decree and in the absence of adequate legislation, the forestry authorities allowed the sawmill that had been established in Tatahuicapan in 1979 to continue operating. It formally became the property of several *ejidos* in 1982 and continued to operate until 1989.

5.1.4   Recent agricultural and land use policies

In line with the changes in the global political and economic climate prevailing after the early 1980s, and prompted by a serious financial crisis in 1982, Mexico undertook a significant change in its macreconomic and development policies. A liberist model was chosen, of outward growth based on structural adjustment. Macroeconomic and monetary policies focused mainly on inflation control, higher interest rates to attract international capital, and cuts in public spending. One of the main objectives of these policies was to create the conditions permitting the integration of Mexico into the world market under the North American Free Trade Agreement with the United States and Canada, which will become effective at the end of 1993.

To pursue the objective of Mexico's integration in the global economy, a number of reforms of the productive sectors' legislation and policies were adopted, with significant repercussions on the incentive framework for the management of natural resources in the country in general and in the in Sierra de Santa Marta in particular. In what follows, some key policies will be briefly summarised in the areas of land tenure, agriculture, and livestock.

Land tenure
The salient features of the ongoing land tenure reform have already been described in Chapter 4 of the book, including the amendments to Article 27 of the Constitution and the introduction of a new agrarian law. As mentioned in that chapter, the main objective of the reform is to shift from a mainly communal system of rural land tenure to a system of individual property. The reform is implemented through the Ejidal Rights Certification and Urban Land Titling Program (PROCEDE), which is administered by a newly founded public agency, the Procuraduría Agraria (Office of the Agrarian Commissioner), which is responsible for issuing property titles.

It has been observed that in several communities of the study area, PROCEDE is likely to be the cause of inter-community and inter-family conflict, particularly conflicts between rightful claimants to the land, children inheriting rightful claim, children not inheriting rightful claim, and persons not entitled to any claim (*avecindados*).[6] The outcome of these disputes may be to induce evicted farmers to encroach into communal forested areas, which according to the law, are not subject to parcelling processes.[7]

Agriculture
In contrast to the high degree of public interventionism in the previous decades, the main thrust of the new policies is to open up Mexican agriculture as much as possible to market forces, and let them determine the optimal output and input mix, including cropping patterns, selection of production technologies and allocation of labour between the urban and rural sectors. This is accompanied by welfare programs and income support measures aimed at reducing the farmers' costs of adjustment and transition to the new equilibrium (and mitigate in the process the possible political costs of policies otherwise highly unpopular).

Maize production
A number of programs have had an impact on corn farming in Sierra de Santa Marta in recent years: the Programa de Apoyo al Campo (PROCAMPO), the corn fertiliser program (better known as "credito a la palabra"), land conservation programs involving the construction of living hedgerows and stone terraces, and the green manure program.

As part of the strategy to obtain admission into NAFTA, president Salinas' government had to change its farm subsidy policies, since the guaranteed prices for staples were higher than international prices. Mechanisms were established to compensate for the gradual lowering of corn prices and of subsidies for other staple crops (beans, wheat, rice, sorghum, soya, cotton, barley, sunflower and sesame) over the next 15 years. Unlike the earlier subsidy (guaranteed prices per ton), the new PROCAMPO subsidy mechanism, in its first stage, relates to area and not to production, and consists of providing direct support (in cash) to producers to compensate for their loss of income. It has had a significant impact in Sierra de Santa Marta in the last two years, both with regard to extension (9,065.35 hectares in the study area) and with regard to its role in reviving corn production, which in the past had been consistently unable to cover the region's needs.

Before PROCAMPO, Sierra de Santa Marta had faced a crisis in obtaining enough corn for on-farm consumption. However, the program also had an impact on deforestation of woodlands and on secondary growth (*acahual*). Although the program was not officially intended to open up new farming areas, many farmers cleared land to expand the area they habitually planted, which averaged a maximum of 1.5 to 2.5 hectares, so that they could become eligible for larger subsidies. The situation was compounded by the lack of supervision of the Ministry of Agriculture, owing to a shortage of personnel.

Among the initiatives to support farmers' income, the corn fertiliser program was established in 1988 to assist in marketing and production for on-farm consumption, under the responsibility of the Instituto Nacional Indigenista (INI) [National Indigenous People Institute]. The program worked with a revolving line of credit (at no interest)[8] as part of the Regional Solidarity Funds.[9] This program supported 83 producers with a total of 125 hectares in the study area in the last two years.

There have been other much smaller programs designed to address shrinking corn yield in the Sierra. The soil conservation and green manures programs were introduced on a small scale by the PSSM[10] (1992-1993). In 1994 a larger program was carried out in conjunction with the Department of Agricultural and Forestry Development of the State of Veracruz (SEDAP) and CIMMYT,[11] but the PSSM continued alone with the program in 1995.[12] The stone terraces program was promoted by SEDAP and implemented by the Shared Risk Trust (FIRCO). The green fertilisers and hedgerows programs[13] were carried out simultaneously with the stone terraces program[14] in the same region but with no co-ordination between the two.

In short, the technological programs to support corn production have gone off in two different directions. The "credito a la palabra" is based on a technological package of farm chemicals, whereas the hedgerows, green manures and stone terraces program foster soil conservation and improvement with a minimum of external inputs. This second group of programs promote a land-intensive, soil conservation oriented approach to yield and income support which is also in contrast with the subsidy policy (PROCAMPO) which, if not properly monitored, favours an increase in production based on an increase in area.

Coffee production

The coffee groves are distributed in a very complex association with other crops and forested land. In some cases it is difficult to detect the transition between the coffee fields and jungle or secondary vegetation (*acahual*). Coffee is also grown in vegetable gardens (*solares*) on the outskirts of urban areas. The lower and upper limits of altitude are 300-400 to 1,000-1,100 meters above sea level.

In the study area there have been fewer fires in the coffee-growing zone than in the livestock or corn-growing area, since farmers are interested in protecting the coffee crop because of its commercial value. Planting of other crops in the coffee fields has contributed to the conservation of biodiversity, with regard to both plants and animals.

As described in page 132, much of the development of coffee growing activities in the study area and in other parts of Mexico was linked to support provided to small holders by public agencies, in terms of technical assistance, extension, marketing and price buffering.

The major withdrawal of the government from many of the previous forms of support to the coffee sector, coupled with a sharp drop in international coffee prices at the end of the 1980s changed dramatically the conditions of production for many Mexican coffee growers.[15]

In the study area, the closure of the INMECAFE office in Acayucan when the institution was dissolved[16] strongly affected the coffee growers of the region. Advances against crops, coffee improvement programs, rust control programs, and all the technical advisory services that had extended to over 80% of the coffee-growing zone ceased. Since 1989, government assistance has been limited to specific aid for coffee zones that suffered heavy frost damage and to the transfer of the processing plants to producers. In 1991, responsibility for support for coffee growers with less than 2 hectares was transferred to the INI (National Indigenous People Institute), which became the administrator of the Regional Solidarity Funds. As of 1995, the coffee program provided support for 866 producers with 1,341.5 hectares in the study area.

Cattle ranching

The massive expansion of cattle ranching in the second half of this century transformed profoundly the landscape of the study area. As illustrated in Chapter 4, recent land use data suggest that pasture accounts for close to 50% of the entire study area.

Much of the transformation process was caused by a combination of credit policies, migration waves and social and political processes leading to enclosures and land concentration. As argued by scholars on the basis of extensive field evidence (Chevallier and Buckles, 1995), the conversion nearly always resulted in significant ecological damage, and rarely, if ever, in long lasting[17] financial returns to ranchers. In cases where the availability of communal land permitted it, ranching took place under land-extensive conditions, that is, with low stocking rates[18] (ratio between number of cattle heads and land under pasture). In cases where further extensive conversion were limited by geo-topographical or land tenure constraints, new pasture became more intensively grazed. However the more intensive land use was typically not followed by more intensive management, so that productivity, measured in terms of animal live weight, rapidly dropped.

Virtually all of the federal programs that provided strong financial incentives to ranchers have been discontinued, in the context of the broader policy of public disengagement from the agricultural sector. At the state level, there is some sign that policy makers have become aware in recent years of the ecological damage and economic inefficiency of the livestock policies of the past. Attempts to increase the land efficiency and productivity of cattle ranching have been made through the "intensification modules" of the Integrated Forest Development Program in Los Tuxtlas, funded by the State's government Secretary for Agriculture between 1990 and 1992; reforestation campaigns have been promoted repeatedly, albeit often haphazardly, to restore the soil and watershed protection function of the most severely degraded areas.[19]

While deprived of the public support obtained in the past, livestock activities may be revitalised by the financial crisis of the end of 1994. The devaluation of the peso increased the potential competitiveness of the low-input dual purpose[20] livestock system typical of tropical areas like the Sierra, both in absolute terms (lower export price of output) and more importantly, relative to the more intensive, high-input, import-dependent systems of the temperate zones of Mexico. Of course, in terms of sales to the domestic markets, this potential may not be realised until the stagnation of domestic income and consumption caused by the devaluation will be reabsorbed, so that the demand for income-elastic goods like meat can be restored to pre-devaluation levels. Furthermore, a significant number of ranchers who benefited in the past from subsidised public credit are now heavily indebted and in some cases insolvent, so that only a smaller number of financially stable ranchers may be able to seize the post-devaluation opportunities.

Assuming that, even in spite of the above financial and demand-side constraints, there may be a boost to tropical livestock production, two different effects on land-use pattern are possible. On the one hand, the increased competitiveness may result in further expansions of the pasture frontier wherever land tenure, geographical and topographical conditions allow it. On the other hand, large extension of under-utilised and poorly managed pasture offer significant opportunities for intensifying livestock operations and concentrating them in smaller areas, with the ensuing possibility of increasing regeneration areas under fallow so as to improve buffering around remaining forest. The significance of this option in the context of a conservation strategy for the region will be discussed later.

5.2   THE PRESENT

The previous sections of this chapter have reviewed the evolution of the policy context and of key social and economic processes in the study area over the last five decades. One key conclusion is that the region's traditional system of production and interaction with the ecosystem, by and large a legacy of pre-Hispanic times, has been profoundly altered in the second half of this century. The present situation retains few of the characteristics of the earlier system, in terms of appearance of the landscape, land use patterns, social organisation, cultural and religious customs (Chevallier & Buckles, 1995). The key determinants of the process of transformation have been identified in changes of the regional, national and international economic climate, policy interventions, shifts in the control of land and other natural resources among social and ethnic groups.

Which of the "old" causes of change are still likely to play a role, and which new ones are likely to emerge? This is the question addressed in qualitative terms in this section, and in quantitative terms in section 5.3 and subsections.

5.2.1   The legacy of the past

At the time the field work of the present research was undertaken, the Sierra appeared as a fairly impoverished region, both from the ecological and socio-economic point of view. Forest, at the midle of this century the dominant form of land cover, was restricted to about a third of the study area. This entails a greatly reduced habitat size for many of the species that make up the biological richness of the region, and in several cases it may eventually entail risk of extinction,[21] unless adequate measures are undertaken to ensure conservation of remaining forests, and improve the buffering function of lands surrounding them.

From the social and economic point of view, a population that is growing at about twice the national rate is among Mexico's poorest. The lack of access to basic services like water, sanitation, and electricity is particularly severe in the Sierra.[22] Agriculture in several communities provides the bare means of subsistence, with cash crop income limited by severe marketing and technological constraints and cattle-related wealth concentrated in the hands of relatively few ranchers. Opportunities for employment and income outside the rural sector have been declining with the crisis and pending restructuring of the Gulf of Mexico oil districts. As illustrated by the data of Chapter 4, non-farm yearly income amounts to about $80 per capita on average.[23]

5.2.2   The policy context

Like many of the marginal areas of rural Mexico, the Sierra de Santa Marta has received limited benefits from the interventionist policies of the past, and is experiencing high costs of adjustment to the new, more limited role played by federal and state governments in the productive sectors. To be sure, the process of transition to the new policy stance in the agriculture and social sectors is far from complete. The ultimate impact on areas like the Sierra will depend upon the modalities under which the reforms of land tenure, income and welfare support and agricultural pricing will be implemented.

In the case of land tenure, Chapter 4 discussed the significant presence in the region of farmers with insecure access to land or no access at all. These farmers also happen to be those who rely most heavily on the forest and other natural resources as a source of goods and services for direct use or for resale. The PROCEDE program is likely to improve the tenure security of farmers with rightful claims to land. However, its impact on *de jure* landless farmers is controversial, and, as discussed earlier, suggestions have been made that it can even lead to more pressure on natural resource use.

It is unclear the extent to which a more developed land market (one of the ultimate goals of programs like PROCEDE) can meet the demand for subsistence means of the region's poorest farmers. It is likely that in the short run many of them will have neither resources of their own nor adequate access to credit to purchase formal land rights. It is also likely that only a significant boost of the regional economy can generate employment opportunities for the evicted farmers, either via migration to the urban sector or through salaried work in rural areas.

Given the growing integration of Mexico into the global economy, the revitalisation of the economic activity in both the rural and urban sectors is clearly dependent upon general trends in the international economy, on which national policy makers have little or no influence. However, public policies may have a role to play in choosing measures to mitigate the social and economic impacts of local adjustments to new equilibria in the national and international markets. This need not be, as in the past, in the form of direct income support, nor of distortion of market prices. For example, technical, institutional and capacity barriers can be removed, which prevent access of small holders to markets for natural products, for which marginal tropical areas may have an agro-climatic and image-marketing comparative advantage. These issues will be discussed again in the next chapter.

5.2.3   How to predict biodiversity impacts for the future

Predicting future impacts of human activities on the study area's biological resources entails various steps: (a) an understanding of the forces that historically have driven the process; (b) identifying old and new forces which are likely to drive the process in the future; and (c) analytical tools which can establish quantitative relationships between driving forces and biodiversity impacts. Section 5.1 has addressed the first aspect, and sections 5.2.1 and 5.2.2 the second one.

The rest of this chapter will provide an analytical framework to estimate in the short to medium run the impact of economic activities on biodiversity conservation in the region. This exercise is challenging for a number of reasons. First, there is the complex issue of choosing a biodiversity objective function. What is the biodiversity that is to be protected, and correspondingly, what are the processes of loss that have to be analysed? Is the objective to conserve the remaining primary forests, or also other forms of vegetation cover (like second growth forest)? What types of land uses are to be considered a threat to biodiversity, and therefore included in the analysis of the process of loss?

The second problem concerns the choice of the "explanatory variables". In real life, the interaction of observable variables both within natural and socio-economic subsystems, and between them, can be of daunting complexity. There are various lessons that can be drawn on these issues from the brief review of the literature undertaken in Chapter 1:

(a) *Subject of analysis.* Few studies explain biodiversity loss *directly* (e.g. extinction, in the case of species diversity); instead, loss is explained *indirectly*, through the analysis of causes of processes (deforestation[24] and other forms of land use change, species over-exploitation) that are likely to affect biodiversity.
(b) *Land use processes investigated.* Many studies of land use change focus on loss of forest, with no clear indication of the type of forest being lost (primary, second-growth), and with no explicit considerations of forms of land use in between full development and full conservation of forests.
(c) *Theoretical basis.* Relatively few studies of deforestation have explicit micro-economic foundations that justify the choice of the explanatory variables selected.[25]
(d) *Data.* Relatively few studies use data at a disaggregated level (e.g., at the household, farm or municipal level).

With regard to these features, the contribution that this research intends to provide is based on the following elements:

(a) *Subject of analysis.* Biodiversity will be "proxied" by selected indicators of ecosystem status. It will be assumed that biodiversity conservation will be affected by (a) Intensive extraction of plants and animals from natural or semi-natural areas (negative impact); (b) conversion to agriculture uses and pasture of areas with significant vegetation cover (primary and second growth forest, shaded coffee groves) (negative impact); (c) size of currently perturbed areas devoted to vegetation regeneration (positive impact). These indicators could then be aggregated in different objective functions.
(b) *Land uses investigated.* The models developed will generate predictions of a broader set of land use options (not just forest cover): these include primary and second growth forest, coffee groves, pasture.

(c) *Theoretical basis.* Pprojections of land use and resource extraction are based on a microeconomic model of household behaviour. Two categories of farmers will be studied, whose resource allocation decisions are likely to have an impact on the biodiversity objectives identified above. The first group includes newly formed households and evicted farmers (these are likely to generate "new" pressure on biodiversity). The second group includes already established farmers ("existing" sources of pressure).

(d) *Data.* Model projections are base on micro-level data (at the farm and municipality levels).

5.3   PROSPECTS FOR THE FUTURE: MODELLING FARM-LEVEL DECISIONS

This section summarises the key elements, assumptions, and results, of a set of three linear programming models developed to analyse and predict decisions made by local resource users with likely impacts on the conservation or depletion of biological resources in the study area. Further details are illustrated in annexes: Annex 5.1 discusses the conceptual basis and relevant background literature for the models; Annex 5.2, Annex 5.3 and Annex 5.4 contain technical material on profit margins, parameter selection, and land constraints.

The approach proposed here uses a multi-period linear programming with "safety-first" constraints along the lines proposed originally by Low (1974). The farm household is assumed to minimise the weighted sum of deviations from survival targets, and of the net present value of its income, subject to technical production constraints, financial constraints (access to credit, availability of own assets), time constraints, and survival constraints.

This set-up is expressed formally as follows. In each time period t, x^t_i denotes the level of the generic i ($i=1,...,n$) activity variable selected by the farm household: e.g., labour supplied on-farm, area planted with maize, natural products extracted from the wild, etc. The p_i variables denote prices of the corresponding x_i variables. The farm's objective function is:

$$Min\left[\sum_{t=1}^{T} w_t \Delta_t^{(-)} - \hat{w} \sum_{t=1}^{T} \sum_{i=1}^{n} \frac{\bar{c}_i x_i^t}{(1+r)^{t-1}} \right] \qquad (5.1)$$

The second term in (5.1) is the net present value of the farm's income, in which $\bar{c}_i$ is the expected[26] net profit margin on activity x_i, and r is the discount rate. The w coefficients are weights reflecting the farms' set of priority among its different goals: w_t are single period weights, and $\hat{w}$ is the weight attached to long term income. The first term in (5.1), which is the weighted sum of deviations from survival targets, requires some explanation based on the illustration of the household's constraints.

The farm faces different sets of constraints. The first set refers to the technical requirements for resource use:

$$\sum_{i=1}^{n} a_{ji} x_i^t \leq b_j; \ j = 1,...,m; \ t = 1,...,T \tag{5.2}$$

where a_{ji} is the technical requirement of input j for undertaking activity x_i, and b_j is the total amount of input j available to the farm[27]. (Resource constraints are in general assumed to be time-invariant, unless otherwise indicated). A second set of constraints reflects the maxi-min, safety-first criterion, whereby the farm selects activity levels in a way that will leave it with enough resources to meet a given subsistence level:

$$\sum_{i=1}^{n} f_i^{ht} x_i^t \geq V_t; \ h = 1,...,H; t = 1,...T + 1 \tag{5.3}$$

where f_i^{ht} is a cash flow coefficient[28] for activity x_i^t. V_t is the minimum value of the cash flow over the relevant set of states of nature $\{1,..., H\}$: each state of nature is defined by different combinations of randomly determined variables, such as input or output prices, etc.[29] This set of constraints ensures that under the optimal choice of x_i^t, the cash flow will be equal to V_t in the worst case, and larger than that in all other states of nature. In the "safety-first" literature, V_t is typically a survival level of consumption. To avoid limiting unduly the feasibility region of the model, while retaining realism in representing the household's survival strategy, it was decided to model attainment of survival objectives as a process with two logically distinct steps. In the first step, the farm household meets absolutely basic subsistence objectives, related primarily to nutrition. It is assumed that for a given subset of basic commodities, ($i_0 = 1, ..., n_0$) the farm will select levels no smaller than the predefined survival levels, $x_{i_0}^0$:

$$x_{i_0}^t \geq x_{i_0}^0; i_0 = 1,...,n_0; t = 1,...,T; \sum_{i_0=1}^{n_0} p_{i_0} x_{i_0}^t = S^0 \qquad (5.4)$$

The survival levels are defined on the basis of World Bank's measures of the extreme poverty line (World Bank, 1996a), and of dietary habits prevailing in the region.[30] The second part of the household survival strategy is attainment of a complementary basket of basic goods (clothing, shelter, etc.). This is modelled not as a fixed constraint, but as a deviation from a target, that the household attempts to minimise. The deviations employed in (5.1), $\Delta_t^{(\cdot)}$, are given by:

$$\Delta_t^{(-)} = S_1 - V_t \qquad (5.5)$$

where S_1 is the difference between moderate, S, and extreme poverty line, S_0:

$$S_1 = S - S_0; \quad S_0 = \sum_{i_0=1}^{n_0} p_{i_0} x_{i_0}^t; t = 1,...,T \qquad (5.6)$$

Combining (5.1), (5.5) and (5.4), it follows that the farm seeks to minimise the deviation from the moderate poverty line, subject to the constraint of at least meeting the extreme poverty line.[31]

On the basis of this general framework, three models are specified, with the purpose of analysing the behaviour of three distinct groups of resource users: (a) newly formed farm households; (b) evicted farm households; (c) existing farms with land constraints. Key features of the models are summarised in Table 5.1

Sources of data and parameter selection
For all three models, information on crop margins, input coefficients and other variables was obtained through field work undertaken in the summer - autumn of 1995 in the context of the case study described in Chapter 4 (Cervigni and Ramirez, 1996). All prices originally denominated in Mexican Pesos are converted into US$ dollars using the exchange rate of 6.3 MexPes per dollar, prevailing at data collection time. The analysis does not allow for inflation, so all prices and values are to be considered as expressed in constant 1995 US dollars.

Table 5.1   Key features of the linear programming model

	Objective	Decision Variables	Constraints
House-hold well-being	Minimise weighted sum of (a) deviations from survival targets, (b) expected net present value of income		Subsistence consumption of basic staple food (maize and beans)
Allocation of time		Permanent migration to urban areas, temporary employment off-farm, gathering products from the wild, work on farm, hiring labour	Yearly labour budget, "management constraint" on hired labour
Land use, forest product extraction		Areas under maize, beans, coffee, pasture (own use or rented); leaves of Chamedor Palm extracted from primary forest	*Newly formed households*: Land clearing requirements of new crop areas; fallow requirements; no disinvestment for perennial crops *Existing households*: same as above, plus fixed total area under use (see Figure 5.3 in Annex 5.1)
Financial resources		Short term and long term credit, cash carry-over from one period to the next	Own funds available, credit limits, interest rate, end-of-period replenishment of initial own funds

Annex 5.3 lists the values of the parameters used in formulating the model's objective function and constraints, as well as providing additional explanatory remarks.

Size of the models and solution algorithm
The basic model devised to analyse newly formed farms (see section 5.3.1) had 70 variables with 108 constraints. This size changed to allow for variations in the number of random variables, and the inclusion of additional land constraints in the case of the existing farm model, as illustrated in the following sections. The complete model, including the full linear programming tableau is provided in Cervigni (1998). The model was set up in *Excel* 5.0 for Windows; solutions were found by applying *Excel*'s Solver package.

5.3.1   First model: newly formed farms' decisions

Purpose of the model
The model of this section purports to describe the land use decisions of newly formed farms, with special emphasis given to farms located in areas with remaining communal land under primary or secondary forest cover. It is assumed that a new (subsistence) household is formed every time a male individual reaches the adult age, which on the basis of local customs, is considered to be 18 years.

Decision variables and constraints
A first group of decision variables refers to the allocation of time. These include work on-farm, temporary off-farm employment,[32] hiring additional labour to complement the family workforce, gathering plants and animals from natural or semi-natural areas. In terms of the latter activity, collection of Chamedor Palm has been explicitly included in the analysis, given the availability of detailed data on price and quantities of labour and other input requirements.[33]

A second group of decision variables concerns the household's financial management. These include the level of short term and long-term (i.e., repayable at the end of the time horizon considered in the analysis) credit, as well as the amount of cash that the farm transfers from one year to the other.

Finally, there is a group of decision variables concerning land use and conversion decisions. The farm household will require a certain amount of land for setting up basic staple crops (maize, beans) production,[34] plus possibly some additional cash crop or livestock activities. The demand for land of the new subsistence-farming households can be met in several different ways. Land can be inherited from parents and relatives, borrowed from friends and family, purchased, rented, farmed under share cropping arrangements. However, in communities with remaining unparcelled land, use of communal spaces is often the first choice in terms of convenience and cost. It is assumed that the only communal land available for maize production is under either secondary or primary forest cover. The former is likely to be converted first because of lower access and conversion costs. Primary forest starts to be converted only when all second growth forest has already been converted.

In the present model it is assumed that where communal land is available, newly formed farms do not face a land constraint in their decision making. Rather than constraints, land conversion and uses are decision variables. Total land that will be converted to agricultural use is therefore the result of the various decisions taken by the farm with respect to land to be used for staple and cash crops production and for pasture. The newly formed farm faces labour, subsistence, cash flow and credit constraints, as described in section 5.3.

Results: baseline case

Table 5.2[35] reports some key results of the LP model run for the baseline case. In a scenario of poor employment prospects, variable coffee prices, limited and expensive access to credit, full attainment of the moderate poverty line will not be possible. In fact, for level of own funds below the cut-off level of $45, no feasible solution to the model could be found: that is, farms with an initial endowment of wealth below $45 may not even be able to reach the extreme poverty line. This is indicative that alternative survival strategies may be adopted: for farms located in proximity of wilderness areas, these may consist of extraction of additional natural products on top of Chamedor Palm (which in the baseline case accounts for over 60% of the household's labour use on average).

Duality properties of linear programming can give an indication of the conditions under which the farm household can profitably undertake an extra activity. At an optimum, the total opportunity cost[36] of producing a unit of a given product must be equal to the unit profit margin for that good.

Assuming that extractive activities require labour as the only input, in any time period the minimum level of profit margins (per unit of labour) required for profitable production is given simply by the shadow wage rate for that time period. For the baseline case, this implies that the new extractive activity's profit margin must be at least of $2.1, $.0.3 and $0.2 for periods one to three, respectively.[37]

For households with own resources in excess of the minimum level, subsistence is guaranteed by conversion of land to agriculture uses for about 5 has, and extraction of Chamedor Palm over an area that can be estimated to cover around 10 has.[38] No conversion to pasture occurs, neither for the household's own use nor for rental purposes.

Table 5.2   *New households: baseline case*

	Initial values	Year 1	Year 2	Year 3	Total
Minimum level of own funds (US$)	45.0				
Objective function (US$)					910.32
Deviation from moderate poverty line		63%	63%	38%	.
NPV of gross expected margin (US$)					2,091.17
Pasture (has)		0.0	0.0	0.0	.
Rented pasture (has)		0.0	0.0	1.5	.
Milpa (has)		5.1	5.1	0.7	.
Total incremental land clearance (has)		5.1	0.0	0.0	5.1
Coffee (has)		0.0	0.0	0.0	.
Extraction of Chamedor Palm (*gruesas*: bundles of 120 leaves)		766	3,582	4,640	8,989
Off-farm employment (days)		87.07	0	0	87
Short term credit (US$)		137.53	200.00	0	338
Long term credit (US$)		62.47			62

Off-site employment
As explained in detail in Annex 5.3, the demand for off-site labour is modelled as a random variable. What happens if the employment prospects off-site improve? This is can be assessed by running the model with more

optimistic values for the high and low levels of labour demand. If the farm household expects to be able to find employment off-site between 40% and 60% of the time, its subsistence prospects improve in the way illustrated by Table 5.3

Table 5.3   New households: improved employment prospects

	Initial values	Year 1	Year 2	Year 3	Total
Minimum level of own funds (US$)	0.1	.	.	.	
Objective function (US$)		.	.	.	779.38
Deviation from moderate poverty line		57%	63%	0%	.
NPV of gross expected margin (US$)		.	.	.	1,506
Pasture (has)		0.0	0.0	0.0	
Rented pasture (has)		0.0	0.0	0.0	
Milpa (has)		0.7	0.7	0.7	
Total incremental land clearance (has)		0.7	0.0	0.0	0.7
Coffee (has)		0.0	0.0	0.0	
Extraction of Chamedor Palm (*gruesas*: bundles of 120 leaves)		(0)	1,780	0	1,780
Off-farm employment (days)		272	268	444	984
Short term credit (US$)		29.99	-	0	30
Long term credit (US$)		-	.	.	0

No minimum level of initial wealth is required to obtain a feasible solution. With respect to the baseline case, both the use of land for agriculture and the extraction of Chamedor Palm decrease substantially; the household's level of indebtedness also decreases, as labour income substitutes borrowed funds in meeting cash flow constraints.

Credit

Another set of interesting results can be derived by modifying the parameters representing farmers' access to credit. Table 5.4 lists the results of the model under a hypothetical scenario in which subsistence farmers may obtain credit at substantially lower borrowing rates and higher credit limits: these have been set, for heuristic purposes, at levels of 20% and $500, respectively.[39]

Table 5.4   New households: improved access to credit

	Initial Values	Year 1	Year 2	Year 3	Total
Minimum level of own funds (US$)	0.0	.	.	.	
Objective function (US$)		.	.	.	125.27
Deviation from moderate poverty line		49%	63%	0%	.
NPV of gross expected margin (US$)		.	.	.	9,426
Pasture (has)		0.0	0.0	0.0	.
Rented pasture (has)		0.0	3.3	3.3	.
Milpa (has)		0.7	0.7	0.7	.
Total incremental land clearance (has)		0.7	3.3	0.0	4.0
Coffee (has)		0.0	0.0	0.0	.
Extraction of Chamedor Palm (*gruesas*: bundles of 120 leaves)		2,754	8,134	4,491	15,380
Off-farm employment (days)		-	0	0	0
Short term credit (US$)		-	500	500	1,000
Long term credit (US$)		500	.	.	500

The objective of this exercise is purely illustrative, so that issues related to provision of collateral, moral hazard and risk of default have not been addressed. The impact on household welfare is clear: the objective function improves over 110% with respect to the baseline case, in period 3 the target level of the moderate poverty line is achieved. Furthermore, a low or even zero level of initial endowment does not preclude attainment of financial equilibrium and subsistence objectives. However, in the absence of specific incentives and/or changes in the relative prices of outputs, improved credit results in increased extraction of natural resources, while the pressure on land conversion does not disappear. About 4 has of land are cleared for *milpa* but mainly for rented pasture; the average extraction rate of palm increases to over 5,000 *gruesas* per year, which amounts to over 15 has of forested area being brought under extractive pressure.

Coffee
An example in which improved credit conditions, rather than encouraging conversion, results in use of forested areas for shaded coffee production is illustrated in Table 5.5. This assumes an initial wealth endowment of $100 and an 8% weight[40] attributed to the expected income objective. Credit terms are the same as the previous example; what varies are the improved marketing prospects for coffee sales. In the baseline case, the price of coffee is assumed to be affected by a "shock" varying between 0 and 50%; here the range of variation of the price shock is assumed to be only 0-10%. About half a hectare of land under secondary forest is turned into coffee production; sensitivity analysis shows that the size of the coffee plot grows with the initial endowment of funds. *Milpa* area is reduced to a minimum, while extraction of Palm is lower than the previous case, but still higher than in the baseline.

Conclusions on the newly formed household model
The model suggests that newly formed farms with little financial resources of their own and limited (and expensive) access to credit, critically depend on intensive use of natural resources for their survival. Intensity of extraction of forest products and expansion of the agriculture frontier are quite sensitive to availability of off-farm employment opportunities; biodiversity-friendly uses of forested area like shaded coffee are unlikely in the absence of favourable conditions of access to credit and final output markets. Using information on the vegetation cover and population's demographic structure, it is possible to construct aggregate projections of agriculture expansion and extractive pressure for the region's different administrative and zoning units. This exercise will be undertaken in the next chapter.

Table 5.5   New households: improved coffee prospects

	Initial values	Year 1	Year 2	Year 3	Total
Assumed level of own funds (US$)	100.0				
Weight of expected income objective					8%
Objective function (US$)					135.91
Deviation from moderate poverty line		63%	63%	63%	
NPV of gross expected margin (US$)					11,111
Pasture (has)		0.0	0.0	0.0	.
Rented pasture (has)		0.0	0.0	0.0	.
Milpa (has)		0.7	0.7	0.7	.
Total increm. land clearance (has)		0.7	0.0	0.0	0.7
Coffee (has)		0.4	0.4	0.4	.
Extraction of Chamedor Palm (*gruesas*: bundles of 120 leaves)		2,476	6,796	4,327	13599.7
Off-farm employment (days)		-	0	0	0.0
Short term credit (US$)		-	500	500	1000.0
Long term credit (US$)		500	.	.	500.0

5.3.2   Second model: evicted farmers

In addition to newly formed households, an extra source of pressure on natural resources is likely to come from those farmers with no formal title to land, who may be evicted as a result of title regularisation programs (see Annex 4.1 on the PROCEDE program).

These households will find themselves in conditions similar to young farmers: they may face the choice of finding salaried employment in the region or in the urban sector, or encroaching, wherever possible, in forested spaces not subject to parcelling processes. Family sizes are likely to be larger than newly formed households, so that per-household demand for staple crops and farmland will also be larger. For those households who have enough own cash resources, an additional option may be to purchase parcels entering the land market as a result of the titling program.

Because of these similarities, the case of evicted farmers is studied here by simply running the newly formed farms model, with a larger family size (four instead of two adults). Not surprisingly, as shown in Table 5.6, baseline total incremental land clearance and Chamedor Palm extraction will both be higher than in the case of newly formed households. The minimum level of own funds required to ensure feasibility of the model is also considerably higher ($300).

Much as in the case of the newly formed households, improved prospects of off-site employment will also impact evicted farmers' resource allocation. If the probability of finding employment, instead of averaging 25%, ranges between 25 and 75%, then over 50% on average of households' time is allocated to non-farm employment; land clearing for agricultural purposes decreases from 10 to 1.3 has; extraction of Chamedor Palm also decreases, from 6,000 to about 1,200 *gruesas* per year on average. The next chapter will analyse the role of evicted households in determining pressure on land use and resource extraction.

5.3.3   Third model: existing farms with land constraints

This model intends to represent resource allocation decisions in situations where encroachment in communal areas is not an option. This will be the case for households with a plot of land of their own, located in communities with little or no availability of communal spaces. As was described in Chapter 4, a typical individual holding of land consists of areas under *milpa* mainly for domestic production of staple crops, of areas under pastures, and possibly of remaining patches of primary forest and of second growth vegetation.

From the point of view of impact on biological resources, it is important to analyse the conditions under which the household will be induced to change the allocation of land from current uses entailing vegetation cover (primary forest - *monte*, second growth forest - *acahual*, shaded coffee) to uses that require land clearing (maize-based farm land - *milpa*, pasture).

It is also important to explore the reverse process, that is, to analyse the conditions under which the household may cease using cleared areas of land.

Table 5.6   *Evicted farmers: baseline and high employment cases*

	Baseline Case				High Empl. Case			
	Year 1	Year 2	Year 3	Total*	Year 1	Year 2	Year3	Total*
Minimum level of own funds (US$)				300				0
Objective function (US$)				1,391				1,406
Deviation from mod.poverty line	63%	49%	0%		57%	63%	0%	
NPV of gross expected margin (US$)				0.00				0.00
Pasture (has)	0.0	0.0	0.0		0.0	0.0	0.0	
Rented pasture (has)	0.0	0.0	2.9		0.0	0.0	0.0	
Milpa (has)	10.2	10.2	1.3		1.3	1.3	1.3	
Total incremental land clearance (has)	10.2	0.0	0.0	10.2	1.3	0.0	0.0	1.3
Coffee (has)	0.0	0.0	0.0		0.0	0.0	0.0	
Extraction of Chamedor Palm (*gruesas*: bundles of 120 leaves)	2,170	7,164	8,983	18,317	(0)	3,559	0	3,559
Off-farm employment (days)	111	-	-	111	544	536	888	1,968
Short term credit (US$)	87	53	-	140	60	-	0	60
Long term credit (US$)	113			113	-			-

Note: * in the case of minimum level of own funds, the number refers to initial and not total value

As will be discussed in detail in the final chapter, liberation of land currently under pasture may have an important function to play in the context of an integral strategy of biodiversity conservation and sustainable use. Land released from grazing may be left idle to allow for nutrient re-storing and regeneration of the vegetation cover; subsequently, it could be used for agriculture, or, in more advanced stages of the regeneration process, to help forming corridors between forest fragments.

The introduction of a fixed amount of land in the basic set-up of section 5.3 entails the definition of a new set of constraints on land use, and of transitions from one type of use to another. These are illustrated in detail in Annex 5.4. The model's other basic characteristics (objective function, treatment of risk, types of decision variables) are the same as the newly formed households model. A brief discussion explaining the specific choice of a few key parameters follows.

(a) The number of adults is set at 4, and the overall family size (including children below the minimum working age) is at 6. These figures are broadly consistent with average family sizes in different parts of the study area as discussed in Chapter 4.

(b) Extraction of Chamedor Palm is still included in the model, but is contingent upon patches of primary forest being present in the household's parcel. That is, no extraction from communal areas takes place.

(c) The number of random parameters was lowered from 4 to 3: beans, coffee, and the wage rate. The matrix of land use transition entails a significant number of additional constraints, so that a reduction in the number of the cash crops was necessary to keep the model within manageable limits. As Palm extraction is likely to play a minor role in the income of households described by this model, it seemed reasonable not to include its price in the group of parameters subject to random variation.

(d) Farmland and cattle herds may be used as collateral for credit. Therefore, households owning these assets are likely to have access to better credit conditions than newly formed households. Following again the analysis of the above mentioned study on rural financial markets (World Bank, 1995), it is assumed that households being described in this model have access to credit from the "formal" sector (banks, chartered non-banks and other registered institutions) as opposed to newly formed households who were assumed to have access only to the "informal" credit sector (friends and relatives, moneylenders).

(e) Based on the data presented in Chapter 4, an initial allocation of land was used for a paradigm household with a total holding of 28 has. The assumed break-down of uses is reported in Table 5.7.

Table 5.7   Paradigm farm, assumed initial allocation of land

Land use	Has
Maize	2.0
Beans	0.5
Monte	5.0
Pasture	15.0
Coffee	1.5
Acahual	4.0
Total	28.0

Results

In a baseline scenario, settled farms are unlikely to be a major source of land use change. As illustrated by Table 5.8, the model suggests a total of 1.30 has of land clearance, which is used for increasing rented pasture (assuming a probability of demand for pasture land of 50%). *Milpa* production requires on average 4 has of land; household labour is partly allocated to non-farm activities: collection of forest products (an average of 1,140 *gruesas* per year, corresponding to about 10% of total working time), and temporary employment off-site (average of 500 days per year, about 40% of total household labour).

Improved prospects for cattle ranching

As discussed towards the end of section 5.1.4, cattle ranching activities in areas like the Sierra face a situation of crisis in the present, but of potential expansion in the future. The drop in incomes that followed the 1994 devaluation has been depressing demand for meat; the elimination of a number of subsidies has left several ranchers in a situation of heavy indebtedness. At the same time, the devaluation may help raise competitiveness, in the medium to long run, assuming easier access to export markets under NAFTA. When income starts picking up again, will this put pressure on the forest margins?

Chapter 6 will analyse the impact of income growth on ranching via increases in the demand for meat and dairy products. To assess the land use impacts at the farm level, one needs to hypothesise the adjustment mechanism. If income growth induces an increase in the demand for livestock products, their prices are likely to increase in the short run, that is, until herd sizes adjust to the new levels of demand; prices may rise even more if the market share of low-input ranching increases at the expense of the devaluation-penalised high inputs ranching from other parts of the country.

Table 5.8   Settled farms, baseline case

	Initial Value	Year 1	Year 2	Year 3	Total
Minimum level of own funds (US$)	0				
Objective function (US$)					(1,288)
NPV of gross expected margin (US$)					8,451
Pasture (has)		15.00	16.44	15.00	15.48
Rented pasture (has)		0	1.44	0	
Milpa (has)		2.56	5.06	6.50	4.70
Total incremental land clearance (has)		0.00	1.44	(0.00)	1.44
Coffee (has)		1.5	1.5	1.5	1.50
Extraction of Chamedor Palm (*gruesas*: bundles of 120 leaves)		340	2,752	340	1,144
Off-farm employment (days)		501	367	652	507
Short term credit (US$)		0	565	2,000	855
Long term credit (US$)					272

Note: Table assumes a stocking rate of 0.8 Animal Units (AU) per hectare

The impact on land use of higher demand for livestock products is estimated here by assuming, as in Table 5.9, a short-run increase in prices (and thus, for given costs, of prospective profit margins).

Table 5.9   *Settled farms, improved livestock prospects*

	Initial Value	Year 1	Year 2	Year 3	Total
Minimum level of own funds (US$)					
Objective function (US$)					(124)
NPV of gross expected margin (US$)					12,076
Pasture (has)	15.00	18.25	18.25	17.17	
Rented pasture (has)	-	3.25	3.25		
Milpa (has)	0.75	3.25	3.25	2.42	
Total incremen. land clearance (has)	0.00	3.25		3.25	
Coffee (has)	1.50	1.50	1.50	1.50	
Extraction of Chamedor Palm (*gruesas*: bundles of 120 leaves)	340	2,752	340	1,144	
Off-farm employment (days)	501	251	719	491	
Short term credit (US$)	0	555	2,000	852	
Long term credit (US$)				993	

Note: The table assumes a 100% probability of renting pasture, and an increase in livestock prices of 60%

For the farm studied here,[41] a 60% increase in the output price of beef and dairy[42] generates the results presented in Table 5.9: total land clearing more than doubles with respect to the baseline case, raising to 3.25 has per household: the cleared area is used for increased pasture (for rental, rather than direct use by the farm).

Options for regenerating pasture lands
As discussed in Chapter 4, in several areas of the Sierra ranching is a very land-extensive activity, that has been quickly displacing other forms of land use such as agriculture and forests. How could the land use intensity of pasture be reduced, so as to make more space available for agriculture or

vegetation regeneration? An option that can be explored within the present model (see Table 5.10) refers to the discussion in Chapter 2 of compensation mechanisms for foregone uses of land.

Table 5.10   Settled farms with compensation for foregone land use

	Initial value	Year 1	Year 2	Year 3	Total
Minimum level of own funds (US$)	0				
Objective function (US$)					(686)
NPV of gross expected margin (US$)					10,599
Pasture (has)		15.00	8.13	2.34	8.49
Rented pasture (has)		-	0.63	2.34	
Milpa (has)		(0.00)	2.50	9.37	3.96
Total increm. land clearance (has)		-	0.63	1.09	1.72
Coffee (has)		1.50	1.50	1.50	1.50
Extraction of Chamedor Palm (*gruesas*: bundles of 120 leaves)		340	2,752	266	1,119
Off-farm employment (days)		501	492	538	510
Short term credit (US$)		263.86	0	2,000	755
Long term credit (US$)					270
Idle pasture land		0.0	7.5	7.5	
Acahual (has)		4.0	3.4	3.4	
Rent for idle land (US$/ ha)					100

What would be the payment (provided through arrangements like tradable development rights or franchise agreements) that might induce the farm studied here to leave pasture land idle? It turns out that for rents below $100 per hectare, no land is set aside for regeneration. Table 5.10 illustrates the farm's allocation of land for that value of the rental payment. Much as for the case of new and evicted households, the results of the LP model for existing households will be used, in next chapter, to construct aggregate projections of land use.

ANNEX 5.1:   CONCEPTUAL BACKGROUND OF THE LINEAR PROGRAMMING MODELS

Peasant farming and economic theory

It is often argued by scholars of various social sciences that a proper understanding of the behaviour of farmers living in marginal areas of the developing world, such as the present study area, requires a distinct set of conceptual and analytical tools. In the social sciences, peasant and/or subsistence farming is the subject of a voluminous literature (Ellis, 1988; Dasgupta, 1993; Wharton, 1969; Clark & Haswell, 1970).

One fundamental issue under debate is the identification of the special features that distinguish the peasant household from other social and economic forms of rural organisation for production or consumption, and that therefore warrant the adoption of a special methodology of analysis. In economic terms, various features have been highlighted as the main characterising element of the peasant household, including the primary orientation towards subsistence, the attitude towards risk, the degree of insulation from markets for labour, credit and insurance.

One of the key features that has been highlighted is the simultaneous decision making on consumption and production. The standard analysis of the economic behaviour of households with this characteristic is provided by the literature on agricultural household models (Singh, Squire, and Strauss, 1986; Barnum & Squire, 1979). A simplified account of the basic approach of these models, adapted to the issues addressed in the present context, can be provided in the following terms.

The farm household maximises a utility function the arguments of which are goods only available on the market, m, and natural goods,[43] n, which can be either purchased or produced/gathered directly on-farm: $u = u(m, n)$. Goods of the n type thus include both agricultural products and plants and animals harvested from the wild. The on-farm production of natural goods is N; for the time being, production of N is assumed to be a function of labour only: $N = f(L)$.

The farm is subject to a time and budget constraint, which can be summarised as follows:

$$p_n(n-N) + p_m m = a + w(T - L) \qquad (5.7)$$

where a is exogenous income or wealth endowment, T is total household working time, L is labour used in the production of on-farm goods N, w is the wage rate, and p_m and p_n are prices of market and on-farm produced goods, respectively. Depending on whether T is larger or smaller than L, the farm can be a net supplier or hirer of labour; and similarly, depending on whether n is larger or smaller than N, it can be a net buyer or seller of natural goods. In summary, the farm maximises utility through its choice of n, m and L subject to budget, time and technology constraints.

First order conditions for this problem are:

$$\frac{\partial u}{\partial m} - \lambda p_m = 0;$$

$$\frac{\partial u}{\partial n} - \lambda p_n = 0; \qquad (5.8)$$

$$\lambda \left(p_n \frac{df}{dL} - w \right) = 0;$$

$$p_n(n-N) + p_m m = a + w(T-L)$$

The first three conditions are of course the standard utility and profit maximising conditions of conventional microeconomic theory, and the fourth condition reiterates the budget constraint.

One of the fundamental results of the agricultural household literature is the so-called independence of production from consumption decisions. Labour use and production are only determined by the profit maximising condition of (5.8); once the production decisions are taken, these determine the household's total income. Optimal consumption is then decided on the basis of the resulting budget constraint.

This point is illustrated in Figure 5.1. Optimal labour use L^* is identified by the tangency between the production function and a line with slope w/p_n. This determines optimal production of N, which in turn, together with the initial endowment of the household's time and exogenous income, fixes the position of the budget line in the space of consumption goods. For illustration, in Figure 5.1 the budget line is located at $budg^1$. Optimal consumption is then achieved by selecting the bundle (m^*, n^*). N^*-n^* happens to be positive in this example, and so has the interpretation of a marketed surplus of natural good production. Should it be negative, it would be a net purchase.

The critical element that ensures the separability of the production and consumption decisions is the existence of complete markets for labour and goods.[44] In general, the profit maximising level of production can be attained only if all the relevant inputs and outputs can be bought and sold as required, subject to economic and technology constraints only, and not to quantity constraints on hiring and selling which would prevail with imperfect access to markets. Under complete markets, utility maximisation follows income maximisation, which can be thus assumed as the main objective of the farm household. Farm's income is linear in output prices and quantities; this therefore justifies the use in the following sections of linear programming as an appropriate modelling technique of farm behaviour.[45]

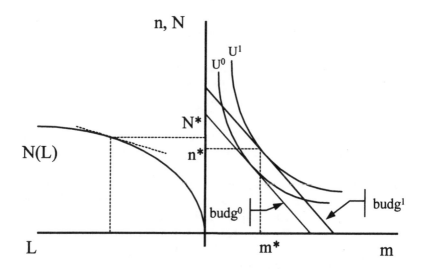

Figure 5.1   Equilibrium of the agricultural household

Survival Strategies and Risk

Some important qualifications need to be added to the assumption on (simple) income maximisation. There may well be cases in which (low) values of the initial endowments result in low values of the disposable income, which in turn result in very low levels of utility. In Figure 5.1, let us define U^0 as the minimum level of utility consistent with survival; all situations where the budget line falls short of *budg*^{0} entail that the farm household puts its own survival in jeopardy. Survival may also be at stake when risk is introduced in the analysis. If the profit margin of N falls below the level expected at the time when production decisions are made, the budget line may fall, possibly below the minimum income level. In Figure 5.2 the effects of a drop in p_n are illustrated. There is an "expenditure" effect, whereby at the original level of income more of good n can be purchased; this translates graphically into an upward shift of the budget line, in the direction indicated by *budg'*. However, the lower farmgate price of N reduces the farm's available income, pulling the budget line downwards; if the income effect dominates the expenditure effect, the net result will be a reduction in the available income, possibly below the survival level, as exemplified by *budg''*.

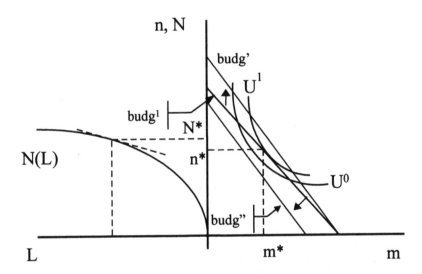

Figure 5.2   Agricultural household and survival objectives

What are the strategies that the farm household is likely to pursue to avoid survival-endangering situations? Two options will be considered and developed in the rest of the analysis. The first refers to the range of activities undertake by the farm household. There is a potentially large number of activities that the household can engage in to supplement income from food crops or livestock. For farms located in proximity of towns or other trading points these can consist of handicrafts production, small scale food processing (cheese, sweets) and so forth. In communities with more immediate access to forest and semi-wild areas, a broad range of natural products potentially may be extracted, which are valuable both for sale and direct consumption.[46] Regarding the second case, data on natural goods production and harvesting is unlikely to be exhaustive, be it in the present study area or elsewhere. As a result, optimal production and consumption decisions resulting in level of income and utility below survival can be interpreted as *prima facie* evidence that additional, unrecorded production/ gathering of natural goods may be taking place. The analysis can then illustrate the magnitude of the profit margin parameters of the unrecorded natural goods, which would be necessary to guarantee achievement of minimum income levels (for an example, see page 147 and note 36).

The second direction that can be pursued is to incorporate explicitly in the model risk related to profit margins.[47] This, in turn, can be done, either using the expected utility framework, or, which is the approach pursued here, adopting a safety-first criterion (Roy, 1952; Boussard & Petit, 1967; Low, 1974).[48] In what follows, an adaptation of Low's framework will be proposed. In Low's original model, the farm household maximises the expected total income subject to the constraint of satisfying a subsistence requirement under the most adverse state of nature.[49] Formally, the farm's problem is:

$$\underset{N}{Max}\ \bar{p}_n N\ s.t.$$

$$p_n^h N + a = w(L - T) + S;\ h = 1,2,...,H \tag{5.9}$$

where $\bar{p}_n$ is a vector of expected margins for goods N, h is an index of the H states of nature identified by the farm, so that $p^h{}_n$ is the price vector prevailing in the generic state of nature j, and S is the cost of the survival bundle of goods.[50] In the present analysis, Low's original model has been modified as follows:

Time horizon. Modelling farm households' impact on the ecosystem requires introducing in the analysis perennial crops and conversion of agriculture to pasture. The relevant time horizon for planning is therefore assumed to be 10 years. However, to make the model more manageable and decrease computation time, the linear programming tableaux actually used only go as far as three years. For most crops or activities considered, yields or returns stabilise after the third year. As a result, margins for year three incorporate the stream of benefits for years 3-10, discounted at the selected rate. That is to say, given original margins for year three c_3, the margin actually used in the tableau, $\hat{c}_3$, is given by the equation:

$$\hat{c}_3 = \sum_{k=3}^{10} \frac{c_k}{(1+r)^{k-3+1}}(1+r) \tag{5.10}$$

where r is the discount rate. It is in fact easy to show (see Annex 4.1) that in general, the net present value of a series of T margins can be obtained by summing, up until a given cut-off year τ, the discounted values of the original margins, and for year τ, the discounted value of a "corrected" margin $\hat{c}_\tau$, which is the capitalised net present value of the margins from τ to T.

Objective function. One problem with the problem specification of (5.9) is that if S is large relative to the maximum attainable income, there may be no choice of N that satisfies the survival constraints. An alternative option is to express subsistence as a *goal* from which the farm household wishes to deviate as little as possible. The introduction of a multi-year time horizon requires that the farm tries *each year* to deviate as little as possible from its goal. This leads to a problem of multiple goal programming,[51] whereby the farm minimises the weighted sum of deviations from set goals. The advantage of allowing for multiple goals is that income maximisation objectives can be introduced along with survival requirements.

Subsistence requirements. When the analysis allows for multiple periods, there is a difference between the final income and the year to year cash flow. Clearly the latter has direct bearing on the farm's subsistence prospects, as in every period the farm needs to have enough cash to purchase S. Therefore the single income requirement has been replaced by a yearly cash flow requirement.

States of nature. In principle, risk affects the entire set of elements characterising the farm's decision-making problem. Technical input coefficients and overall resource availability may be affected by adverse climatic and environmental conditions; profit margins may be affected by output prices fluctuations. To keep the problem within manageable dimensions, it is assumed that different states of nature are defined only by different values taken on by the prices of key outputs. In particular, it is assumed that these prices can take on, with equal probability, a "low" and a "high" value (these have been determined on the basis of unsystematic time series evidence from the field). If q is the number of output prices subject to random variation between a low and a high value, the total number of states of nature is $H=2^q$.

ANNEX 5.2: DERIVING "CORRECTED" PROFIT MARGINS

Given a series of profit margins with a generic term c_i for time i ($i=1, 2, \ldots$ T), it is always possible to decompose the present value of the series in two components, one including the margins accruing before the generic time τ, and one including the subsequent ones:

$$\sum_{i=1}^{T} \frac{c_i}{(1+r)^i} = \sum_{i=1}^{\tau-1} \frac{c_i}{(1+r)^i} + \sum_{j=\tau}^{T} \frac{c_j}{(1+r)^j} \tag{5.11}$$

The second summation in the RHS is equivalent to a "corrected" margin, $\hat{c}_\tau$, which solves the equation:

$$\sum_{i=1}^{\tau-1} \frac{c_i}{(1+r)^i} + \frac{\hat{c}_\tau}{(1+r)^\tau} = \sum_{i=1}^{T} \frac{c_i}{(1+r)^i} \tag{5.12}$$

From this, it is straightforward to obtain the value of $\hat{c}_\tau$ actually used in the model:

$$\frac{\hat{c}_\tau}{(1+r)^\tau} = (1+r) \sum_{k=\tau}^{T} \frac{c_k}{(1+r)^{k-\tau+1}} \frac{1}{(1+r)^\tau} \tag{5.13}$$

ANNEX 5.3:   PARAMETER SELECTION

This annex provides a list (see Table 5.11) of the values selected for the parameters of the baseline case in the newly formed farms model (section 5.3.1), as well as explanatory remarks on selected parameters. For the other models, variations of parameters from the values presented here are discussed in the corresponding sections of the main text.

Table 5.11   Parameters for linear programming model

Name	Base Value	Units	High	Low
Discount rate	15%			
Working days per adult	300	Working days per year		
Maize per adult per year	800	Kg		
Beans per adult per year	260	Kg		
Commuting cost	25%	Percentage of time lost in commuting to urban jobs		
Time horizon after project	10	Years		
Baseline stocking rate	1.48	Animal unit/ ha		
Cow weight	400	Kg		
Yearly working days	300			
Duration LT credit	10	Years		
Children per adult	0.5			
Child cash subsistence	0.3	In percent of adults cash needs		
Exchange rate	6.30	MexPes/ US$		
Farmgate price of maize	0.13	US$/ Kg		
Retail price of maize	0.13	US$/ Kg		
Retail price of beans	0.51	US$/ Kg		
Farmgate price of beans	0.51	US$/ Kg	1	0.01
Wage (rural)	2.38	US$/ Day		
Wage (urban)	3.17	US$/ Day		
Price of organic coffee	0.68	US$/ Kg		
Price of traditional coffee	0.52	US$/ Kg		
Subsistence consumption of maize per adult	1840	Kg/ year		
Subsistence consumption of beans per adult	598	Kg/ year		

Table 5.11   Continued

Name	Base Value	Units	High	Low
Family labour	600	Work days per year		
Family size	3.0	Number of individuals		
Family subsistence cash	1,495	US$/ year		
Milk price	0.14	US$/ Liter		
Cow price	0.71	US$/ Kg		
Bull price	0.76	US$/ Kg		
Weaner price	0.71	US$/ Kg		
Stocking rate	1.48	Animal unit/ ha		
Employment rate	25%		20%	5%
Borrowing rate	200%			
Credit limit	200	US$		
Farmgate price of wild Chamedor Palm	3	MexPes/ gruesa	100%	0
Variation to coffee price	0%		0	0.5
Initial value of wealth (own funds)	35	US$		
Adults per family	2.0			
Cash subsistence per adult	650	US$/ year		
Contingent parameters	4			
Demand for rented pasture	20%	Probability of pasture being requested for rental		

Family size. The number of adults (and thus workers) per family was set at 2, which is consistent with the objective of modelling a newly formed household. It is assumed that the newly formed household already has a child.

Subsistence consumption. Total staple crops and cash requirement of the two-adults, one child household is then determined on the basis of field information relative to per capita annual consumption of maize and beans, and of the above mentioned World Bank figures on minimum subsistence expenditure.

Random variables. The number of output prices subject to random variation was set at 4. This represents a compromise between realism and model size. On the one hand, the need for adequately representing the highly uncertain environment in which subsistence farmers operate would dictate that as many prices as possible should be considered random. On the other hand, the dimensions of the model are significantly affected by the number of random output prices: even in the simple case considered here of variables with only two possible values - high price, low price -, adding one extra random variable to n pre-existing variables adds 2^n constraints. With four random prices, the dimensions of the model are of 70 variables in 108 constraints.

In the baseline case, the four following prices were included as random: Chamedor palm, beans, coffee, and the wage rate. The latter requires some additional explanation. From the household's point of view, the amount of labour that can be committed to temporary off-farm employment needs to be known at the beginning of the agricultural annual cycle. However, the demand for labour in the urban area is not known in advance, and so can be considered random from the farm household's standpoint. If p is the percentage of total household time T for which there will be demand in the off-farm sector, total revenues from non farm labour will be wpT where w is the wage rate. Therefore, the farm's revenue per unit of time is wp (that is, the farm will be able to obtain employment - remunerated at rate w -, p percent of the time). Different values of p will represent different levels of expected demand for labour. If the two (high, p^h, and low, p^l) levels of demand for labour are expected, returns from labour will vary between wp^h, and wp^l .

Weights in the objective function. Subject to the constraint of adding up to 1, many combinations of the four[52] weights included in (5.1) are possible. However, a plausible description of subsistence farming restricts considerably the range of possible choices. As will be discussed in the rest of the section, in a fairly wide range of financial (credit, own resources) and profit margins parameters, the model's solution suggests that the farm household will not be able to eliminate the deviation of net cash flow from subsistence targets. In this range, it is quite unlikely that farmers will be concerned about the net present value of their activities over the entire time horizon considered. Rather, they will be more concerned about period to period survival. It is therefore assumed that $\overline{w}$ will start having non zero values only when the farm has enough own resources to meet survival objectives. As for the other weights, it is assumed that the underachievement variables have weights of 0.8, 0.1 and 0.1, respectively. This captures the idea that the farm attaches a high premium to immediate (next period) subsistence: the higher the chances of meeting subsistence targets initially, the better the prospects for enduring worse times later.

Livestock parameters. Costs from, and returns to, livestock activities were derived through adjustment of FAO herd projections prepared in the context of the already mentioned GEF-funded case study. A key parameter in the calculation of the benefit stream from ranching is the stocking rate, i.e. the per hectare carrying capacity (in number of head of cattle) of pasture land. The stocking rate will be positively affected by accessibility and by the pasture's age and management: newly opened pasture areas with good access are likely to have higher rates than areas that are poorly accessible and/ or where little or no investment has been made in measures to counteract overgrazing. A baseline stocking rate value for areas recently converted from forest was set to 1.4 Animal Units/Ha.

Pasture land's rental value. It is assumed that this is an annuity equivalent to the net present value of cattle ranching[53] over a 10 year time horizon. However, the actual returns to pasture land put on the rental market will depend upon the existence of a demand for such land. Any given hectare of newly converted pasture will have a chance of being rented if there are ranchers in reasonable proximity with excess cattle (either because they have purchased new cattle, or because existing pastures have been overgrazed). On top of geographical and ecological factors, the demand for rented pasture is also affected by financial variables: a rancher with cattle in excess of his pasture's carrying capacity may not be able to rent land if previously contracted debts[54] force him to liquidate part of his herd. In analogy with the treatment of the demand for off-farm labour, a parameter, r, has been introduced in the analysis to describe the probability that a particular hectare of pasture will be requested for rent.

ANNEX 5.4:   EXISTING FARMS WITH LAND CONSTRAINTS

The introduction of a fixed amount of land in the basic set-up of section 5.3 entails the definition of a new set of constraints on land use, and of transitions from one type of use to another. Figure 5.3 provides the basic conceptual framework to develop those constraints. The column headings refer to stocks of different types of land at the generic time t. The row headings refer to land stocks of at time $t+1$. The "yes" cell intersections identify those transitions from one stock type to another which are included in the model.[55] These transitions, as illustrated by the legend, can be of four types: (a) maintenance of land uses entailing no vegetation cover (*milpa* land under maize or beans, pasture); (b) maintenance of land uses entailing vegetation cover (primary and secondary forest, coffee groves, *milpa* area under fallow); (c) conversion; (d) regeneration. So for example, land that was under primary forest in time t can turn into farm land (maize, beans) in time $t+1$ through conversion; land that was under pasture in time t can be reclaimed for regeneration in time $t+1$, to start a process which will eventually result (either naturally or supported by human intervention) in formation of second growth forest.[56]

The matrix provides the conceptual basis for the specification of a number of land use constraints in the LP model. These are reported in the last four rows and last column of the matrix. The flows which deplete or accrete stocks are defined in the fourth and third to last rows; for example, deforestation at time $t+1$ is the difference between Monte at times t and $t+1$: $ForestClear_{t+1} = M_t - M_{t+1}$. The last two rows express constraints about the total uses of flows and of stocks. So, for example, in flow terms, forest land cleared in time $t+1$ must be turned in one or more of the following uses: maize, beans, new pasture, rented pasture: $ForestClear_{t+1} \geq Mz_{t+1} + B_{t+1} + NewPasture_{t+1} + R_{t+1}$. In terms of stocks, forested land in time t must be devoted to one or more of the following uses in time $t+1$: forested land, maize, beans, new pasture: $M_t \geq M_{t+1} + Mz_{t+1} + B_{t+1} + NP_{t+1}$.

The last column formulates constraints about the sources of stocks at time $t+1$ in terms of stocks of land types at time t. For example, pasture rented in time $t+1$ must not exceed the sum of already cleared areas (maize, beans and pasture at time t) plus the sum of newly cleared areas (primary and secondary forest, coffee groves cleared at time $t+1$): $R_{t+1} \leq P_t + B_t + Mz_t + ForestClear_{t+1} + AcahualClear_{t+1} + CoffeeClear_{t+1}$.

USES (time $t+1$)	Sources (time t)							Total sources
	Monte (M_t)	Acahual (A_t)	Coffee (C_t)	Maize (Mz_t)	Beans (B_t)	Pasture (P_t)	Idle Pasture (IP_t)	
Monte (M_{t+1})	Yes	No	No	No	No	No	No	$M_{t+1} \leq M_t$
Aca-hual (*Milpa*)	No	Yes	Yes	Yes	Yes	No	No	$AM_{t+1} \leq A_t + C_t + Mz_t + B_t + P_t$
Aca-hual (non *milpa*)	No	Yes	Yes	Yes	Yes	No	Yes	$Anm_{t+1} \leq A_t + C_t + Mz_t + B_t + P_t$
Coffee (C_{t+1})	No	Yes	Yes	No	No	No	No	$C_{t+1} \leq C_t + A_t$
Maize (Mz_{t+1})	Yes	Yes	Yes	Yes	Yes	No	No	$Mz_{t+1} \leq Mz_t + B_t + FC_{t+1} + AC_{t+1} + CC_{t+1}$
Beans (B_{t+1})	Yes	Yes	Yes	Yes	Yes	No	No	$B_{t+1} \leq Mz_t + B_t + FC_{t+1} + AC_{t+1} + CC_{t+1}$
Pasture (P_{t+1})	Yes	Yes	Yes	No	Yes	Yes	No	$P_{t+1} \leq Mz_t + B_t + P_t$
Rented Pasture (R_{t+1})	Yes	Yes	Yes	Yes	Yes	Yes	No	$R_{t+1} \leq P_t + B_t + Mz_t + FC_{t+1} + AC_{t+1} + CC_{t+1}$
New Pasture (NP_{t+1})	No	No	Yes	Yes	Yes	No	No	$NP_{t+1} \leq FC_{t+1} + AC_{t+1} + CC_{t+1}$
Idle Pasture (IP_{t+1})	No	No	No	No	No	Yes	Yes	$IP_{t+1} \leq IP_t + P_t$
Total								

Continued overleaf

	Sources (time t)						
Accretion of stocks			$NC_{t+1} \leq A_t$	$NP_{t+1} \leq Monte\ Clear_{t+1} + AC_{t+1} + CC_{t+1}$			
Depletion of stocks	$FC_{t+1} + M_{t+1} = M_t$	$AC_{t+1} + AM_{t+1} = A_t$	$CC_{t+1} + C_{t+1} = C_t$				$IP_{t+1} = P_t - P_{t+1}$
Total uses of stocks	$M_t \geq M_{t+1} + Mz_{t+1} + B_{t+1} + P_{t+1}$	$A_t \geq Anm_{t+1} + AM_{t+1} + C_{t+1} + Mz_{t+1} + B_{t+1} + P_{t+1}$	$C_t \geq Anm_{t+1} + AM_{t+1} + C_{t+1} + Mz_{t+1} + B_{t+1} + P_{t+1}$	$Mz_t = AM_{t+1} + Anm_{t+1} + Mz_{t+1} + B_{t+1} + P_{t+1}$	$B_t \geq AM_{t+1} + Anm_{t+1} + Mz_{t+1} + B_{t+1} + P_{t+1}$	$P_t \geq Anm_{t+1} + P_{t+1} + R_{t+1}$	
Total uses of flows	$FC_{t+1} \geq Mz_{t+1} + B_{t+1} + NP_{t+1} + R_{t+1}$	$AC_{t+1} \geq NC_{t+1} + Mz_{t+1} + B_{t+1} + NP_{t+1} + R_{t+1}$	$CC_{t+1} \geq Mz_{t+1} + B_{t+1} + NP_{t+1} + R_{t+1}$				

Legend:

Meaning of Shadings:

No change, no conservation of vegetation	Conversion
No change, plus conservation of vegetation	Regeneration

Meaning of Symbols:

A:	*Acahual*	FC:	Forest Clearance
AC:	*Acahual* Clearance	IP:	Idle Pasture
AM:	*Acahual* (Milpa)	M:	Monte
Anm:	*Acahual* (non milpa)	Mz:	Maize
B:	Beans	NC:	New Coffee
C:	Coffee	NP:	New Pasture
CC:	Coffee Clearance	P:	Pasture

Figure 5.3   Transition matrix for land uses

NOTES

1. On the impact of cattle ranching on deforestation in Mexico and Latin America in general, see Toledo (1992).
2. In particular, fallow decreased in duration or was eliminated altogether. To compensate, farmers began to use part of the fertilisers provided by INMECAFE for the coffee plantations on their *Milpa* areas.
3. The large numbers of existing coffee varieties can be grouped in two main types: shaded and unshaded coffee. Shaded coffee refers to a management technique whereby coffee is grown under shade trees of species found in tropical forests; unshaded coffee is grown in cleared-up areas. The first type is normally compatible with the conservation of an ecosystem that retains many edaphic, biological and ecological characteristics of natural ecosystems. The second type of management entails a much higher degree of natural habitat modifications and homogenisation. See Nestel (1995) for a discussion of the economics of coffee growing in Mexico, and of the ecological implications of different varieties.
4. As mentioned in Chapter 4, after 1980 two new reclassification and delimitation decrees were issued, in 1988 and in 1998.
5. Misinterpretations of the objectives of the decree resulted, as an effect of the lack of adequate information. Local communities thought that the government would expropriate all forested areas, and decided to clear them faster, while the better organised ejidos went to court to oppose the decree establishing the protected area.
6. Subject to the semantic qualifications discussed in Chapter 4, a*vecindados* have no possibility of becoming *ejidatarios* and do not own the land. They normally rent or borrow land from *ejidatarios* or work with relatives who possess land.
7. Agrarian Act, Article 59: "By law, the allocation of parcels in forests or tropical jungles shall be void".
8. The program supports producers with technological packages of farm chemicals.
9. The National Solidarity Program (PRONASOL) was established during the Salinas government (1988-1994) as the linchpin of the new social policy to combat extreme poverty. Its chief characteristic was that the projects were targeted to the production of goods for sale, thus providing income and making it possible to recover loans, with the surplus used to maintain a revolving fund to guarantee the continuity of the program.
10. PSSM: Proyecto Sierra de Santa Marta, a local non-governmental organisation.
11. CIMMYT: Centro Internacional para el Mejoramiento del Maiz y Trigo, an international research centre on maize and wheat in the CGIAR network.
12. In the first two years of the program, the PSSM covered 38 communities and about 2,200 farmers. In 1994 SEDAP carried out a soil conservation program together with the PSSM in the Los Tuxtlas and Santa Marta region.

Administrative problems with the timely delivery of financial resources and the quality of the foodstuffs provided under the program were such that the PSSM decided to return to its normal scale of work and SEDAP did not continue the program in the region.

13. The shelterbelts are a sort of natural terrace obtained by planting the legume *cocuite* (*Glyricidia sepium*) between the rows of corn to help retain the soil.

14. This technique consists of placing stones at intervals that are theoretically defined based on the grade and contour planting.

15. There is field evidence that in the early 1990s, as a result of the crisis, many coffee groves were either abandoned or converted to other uses.

16. As a result of the new policies of the Salinas government, INMECAFE's coffee processing installations were transferred to producers, with no prior training. The transfer led to serious difficulties since the farmers had never managed a warehouse or a processing plant.

17. Under certain ecological and financial conditions, relatively high levels of short-lasting profitability may make financial sense from the point of view of the individual rancher. This will be the case if nutrients stored in the soil and vegetation of land turned into pasture can be mined quickly enough, so that the initial investment cost can be recouped, and the end-of-period value of the herd can be reinvested elsewhere in the economy, before overgrazing and poor management result in productivity decline. For a discussion of a similar process in the context of the Brazilian Amazon, see Schneider (1995).

18. Evidence on low stocking rates in several ecological and administrative units of the Sierra was presented in Chapter 4, on the basis of survey data.

19. For example, the government of the State of Veracruz has promoted in the mid 1990's a program of groundwater recharge and runoff control. This was based on the construction of "mini-catchment" tanks ("tinas ciegas") and subsequent reforestation, to be applied to the higher slopes of the San Martin Pajapan volcano (which is located in the nucleus zone of the study area). The original plan was to apply the scheme to 2,000 has. Due to budget constraints, the construction of the mini-catchments could be carried out only on 180 has.

20. There are two main livestock farming models in the sierra: dual-purpose (that is, dairy and beef products) and fattening, beef-only. Dual-purpose farming is widely found in the north, northwest, west, and central parts of the sierra, with beef-only mainly located in the south, in the old Indian towns of Pajapan, Tatahuicapan, Mecayapan, and Soteapan, and in some nearby ejidos.

21. The literature on the critical size of ecosystem and on minimum viable population is extensive: see for example Soulé (1987); Shafer (1990); Burgess and Sharpe (1981); Harrys and Silva-Lopez (1992). Rodriguez Luna, Cortés Ortiz et al. (1995) and Silva-Lopez (1987) discuss minimum viable populations for selected monkey species in Los Tuxtlas, the broader region to which the present study area belongs.

22. Application of the UNESCO methodology for the estimation of the degree of marginalization suggests that nearly 80% of the communities are to be found in the last (i.e., the worst) two deciles of the distribution of access to the above services (Cervigni and Ramirez, 1996).

23. Nation-wide per capita income for Mexico was US$3,320 for 1995.

24. Two recent studies of deforestation in Mexico are of particular relevance here. Deininger and Minten (1996) use disaggregated, municipality-level data to estimate the demand for land to be deforested on the basis of an agricultural household-type model. They find that physio-geographic factors, poverty, and government policies have distinct effects on deforestation. On the last two variables, they also argue that the recently adopted, NAFTA-induced, package of trade liberalisation and elimination of government interventions in agriculture, may result in increasing poverty of marginal farmers, who may not be able to benefit in the short run from increased opportunities linked to more open export markets, and are therefore likely to put additional pressure on forest and natural resources in rural areas.

   A similar conclusion is also reached by Barbier and Burgess (1996), who estimate the increase in agricultural area and livestock numbers (a plausible proxy for deforestation) as a function of a range of price, income and policy variables. Barbier and Burgess argue that ongoing removal of input and output subsidies in agriculture may, on the one hand, reduce incentives for conversion, but, on the other hand, may make poorer farmers worse off and induce them to migrate to the agricultural frontier. In order to mitigate pressure on forests the authors therefore suggest complementing the broader liberalisation policies with a program of investments in land improvement for existing cultivation on rain-fed areas.

25. Of the 146 models of deforestation reviewed by Kaimowitz and Angelsen (1998) some 20% are based on hypothesis on the behaviour of individual actors involved in deforestation processes (households and firms).

26. The model allows for random variation of certain variables over a "low" and a "high" state of nature. See below and Annex 5.1 for details.

27. Labour budgets fall in this category; these require that in any given time period, the sum of labour used by the different production activities does not exceed the total household's work time. The latter is given by the number of family members times an assumed annual working time of 300 days per individual minus the amount of labour hired outside the household. Hired labour is further limited by a "management constraint", whereby the total amount of hired labour must not exceed a given proportion of the household's own labour. It may not be realistic to expect that small producers have the time and managerial resources to supervise hired labour in excess of, say, 50% of their own working time.

   Another important group of resource constraints refers to the farm household's access to credit. It is assumed that this would be quite limited on account of the significant degree of overall imperfection of Mexico's rural credit markets (World Bank, 1995b). Because of the likely inability of new households to offer collateral to formal financial institutions, it is assumed that they may only have limited access to credit from moneylenders and/or friends or relatives. The conditions are likely to be quite unfavourable, in terms of low credit limits, short repayment periods and very high interest rates. The actual parameters used in the analysis have been borrowed from the World Bank's study on rural financial markets in Mexico referred to above.

28. This will be positive for inflows like wage income, receipt from sale of products, credit obtained, cash carried forward from previous years, and own funds. It will be negative for outflows like payment of fixed or variable factors, wage payments for hired labour, repayment of credit's interest and principal, cash carry forward to following years.

29. With only two states of nature per random variable (see note 26), the total number of cash flow constraints will be 2^q $(T+1)$, with q being the number of random variables. That is, the number of cash flow constraints equals the total number of states of nature times the number of time periods plus the end-of period cash flow constraint.

30. Given dietary habits prevailing in the study area, it is assumed that survival nutrition may be provided by consumption of maize and beans, the region's (and Mexico's) main sources of carbohydrates and proteins, respectively. Fieldwork information suggests an approximate ratio maize/ beans of 3 to 1 (in physical terms). At 1995 prices, a diet of 800 kg of maize and 260 kg of beans per adult per year yields a value for S^0 close to the World Bank figure.

31. In the models, the original World Bank poverty lines have been inflation-adjusted as appropriate.

32. Depending on the conditions of the local economy, members of households may decide to migrate to the urban sector to seek year-long employment in the oil district. This possibility will be included in the aggregate model of Chapter 6.

33. Other gatherings of natural products may take place; see below for an analysis of the conditions under which this may happen.

34. A variety of other crops are farmed at a lower scale in the region, including squash, chilli, papaya, zapote, watermelon.

35. A few remarks on this result table, as well as in the following ones. Lower values of the objective function correspond to higher level of farms' well-being (the LP problem is a minimisation one); area under *milpa* includes plots of staple crops (maize and beans) as well as fallow land.

36. Formally, the total opportunity cost of engaging in activity i is given by

$$\sum_{j=1}^{m} a_{ij} y_j$$, where y_j is the shadow value of the j-th resource constraint.

37. Detailed estimation of margins (per unit of labour) of gathering and hunting activities has not been attempted. However, evidence presented in Chapter 4 (e.g. section 4.3.4) suggests that several plant (including Ixtle and Chocho) and animal

species (like Parrots and Tucans) are good candidates for harvesting margins in the range of $0.5 - $2 per unit of labour.

38. Assuming 9,000 plants/ha, 4 leaves per plant, and noting that 1 *gruesa* = 120 leaves.

39. As indicated in Annex 5.3, the baseline values are $200 for the credit limit, and 200% for the borrowing rate. The latter captures the notion that households without access to formal credit channels are subject to conditions imposed by money lenders, who often charge usury rates.

40. This is the minimum weight resulting in non-zero values of coffee area.

41. The level of price increase needed to trigger a land use response is likely to depend, among other factors, on the stocking rate of the farm's pasture. In ranches with higher stocking rates than the level considered here (0.8 AU/ha)., land use responses are likely to be generated by lower increase in output prices.

42. It is plausible that improved prospects for ranching would also be reflected in the market for rented pasture; the analysis therefore assumes that the farm would be able to rent pasture, if it wished to do so, with probability equal to one.

43. This formulation of the farm's objective does not include two sets of goods that are often explicitly analysed by the agricultural household literature: leisure, and z-goods, that is, goods that are produced and consu"nsmed on-farm only. The reason for the first exclusion is that it is assumed that in conditions of near subsistence, leisure time coincides with resting time, in turn determined on the basis of customs and of physical needs. Concerning z-goods, detailed modelling of household conversion of m and n goods into final consumption goods is a very data-intensive exercise that the data collected for the present research can not adequately cater for.

44. For analyses of cases where the decisions are interdependent, see Nakajima (1969); Ellis (1988)

45. Linear programming is also particularly suited to the analysis of decisions of the "some or none" type (Dorfman, Samuelson and Solow, 1958), which are particularly pertinent in an agricultural household context (e.g. cropping patterns).

46. Lists and inventories of valuable forest and other natural products abound. For a recent thorough economic analysis of natural resources use in rural Zimbabwe, see Cavendish (1997).

47. The literature on the appropriate treatment of risk in agriculture is vast (see for example Roumasset, Boussard, and Singh (1979) for a classical collection of papers).

48. In the standard expected utility framework, farmers are assumed to maximise the expected value of a utility function that adequately represents their attitudes towards risk, subject to a priori information on probability structures of uncertain events. Quite apart from the substantial information requirement in terms of mean and dispersion of the variables identified as stochastic, it has been argued that the expected utility framework may not necessarily capture the behaviour of poor farmers who may be exposed to the risk of starvation and who may have very few

resources to fall back on in case of disastrous outcomes. If there is a non-zero chance that survival is at stake, it might be little consolation to the farmer that such a chance is being minimised. The farmer may be more interested in strategies that allow for survival in worst-case scenarios, no matter how unlikely they are. This is the justification behind some game theory-type models (McInerney, 1969), and safety-first approaches (Roy, 1952; Boussard and Petit, 1967; Low, 1974) that have been put forward in the literature.

49. This represents a significant departure from the standard expected utility paradigm: the maximum expected income is likely to be larger than the maximum expected income subject to the survival requirement. Therefore, the farm gives up some of the maximum income attainable to provide against ruin.

50. For the sake of simplicity, the internal composition of the survival bundle has been assumed fixed; in case of a change in the relative prices of the components, the farm is assumed not to substitute cheaper components for dearer ones.

51. On multiple goal programming, see Hazell and Norton (1986); Romero and Rehman (1984); Bouzaher and Mendoza (1987); Barnett, Blake et al. (1982).

52. Considering equation (5.1), the four weights are given (as T=3), by three weights for the under-achievements, plus one for the expected present value of total returns.

53. Including the value of the herd remaining at the end of the period considered.

54. See section 5.1.4 for a brief discussion of the financial difficulties of some of the region's ranchers.

55. The "No" cells refer to transitions which are prevented either by irreversibility (e.g. regeneration of primary forest) or by technical reasons (e.g. use of grazing areas for crop production requires some preliminary repletion of soil's nutrient contents, and clearing, so that the transition from pasture to *milpa* is assumed to be possible only via an intermediate transition to *acahual*).

56. The time required for the transition from fallow land to second growth varies depending on a variety of climatic, altitudinal and edaphic factors. Furthermore, regeneration time will depend also on the definition of "second growth": later stages of the natural succession process will clearly require longer time than earlier ones. So the critical time will depend on the succession stage of interest for the particular management problem at hand. Based on evidence from tropical south east Asia, Banerjee (1995) reports appearance of pioneer species after five years of fallow, while longer time (over 15 years) is necessary for a richer mosaic of species. It is also interesting that restoration of species diversity can be significantly accelerated and facilitated by human interventions, mainly trough plantation (Parrotta, 1993; Lugo, Parrotta et al., 1993).

6. Land use changes: model predictions and policy design

6.1   A MODEL FOR AGGREGATING FARM DECISIONS OVER SPACE AND TIME

The model proposed here simulates changes over time in a selected number of key *stocks* and *flows*, based on the farm-level resource allocation and land use choices analysed in the previous chapter. The model, which is constructed using the dynamic modelling software *Stella 5.0* for *Windows* (HPS, 1997), consists of three broad sectors: (a) Households and Land Tenure, (b) Land Use, and (c) Off-site economy (see Figure 6.1).

In sector (a), the processes are modelled, of formation of new households, and of allocation of land among existing and new households given tenure rules. Based on decisions taken in sector (a), sector (b) describes the processes of transition of land among different uses, as well as the extraction of natural resources from the wild. The off-site economy (sector c) is the market for goods produced in the study area, as well as for labour not employed in agricultural and harvesting activities.

To improve realism, most of the variables and parameters included in the model are arrayed in one or both of two dimensions of variability. The first dimension refers to the Zoning and Administrative Units (ZAUs): there are seven of them, according to the categorisation of Chapter 4. The second dimension is the household type (HT): the model distinguishes among i) new households (who are assumed to have no land of their own), ii) existing households with no secure tenure, iii) existing households with secure tenure. The model consists of a set of equations describing the relationships between stocks and flows. Stock/ flow relationships are also represented visually by diagrams, like the one in Figure 6.2 for the household sector. Each icon in diagrams like this represents an equation,[1] or the initial value of a variable. In the following sections, the basic structure of the model will be discussed, and some of the key equations will be presented. Further details of the model are contained in Annex 6.1 to Annex 6.4.

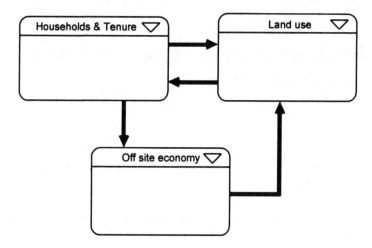

Figure 6.1   Building blocks of the simulation model

6.1.1   The household sector

At the beginning of the simulation,[2] there is a stock of "settlers", that is, households who have rightful or *de facto*[3] access to land. As time goes by, a stock of "space seekers" is generated; *inflows* to this stock are given by:

(a) the process of new household formation: a new household is formed every time a male individual reaches adult age (18 years). Annex 6.1 illustrates the procedure to obtain estimates of the yearly numbers of new adults based on official data on the age structure of the male and female population;

(b) the process of eviction of existing settlers with no formal title to land. Land titling programs (such as PROCEDE currently under way in Mexico) are likely to result in eviction of farmers who are not in possession of a valid *ejidatario* title and who do not own private land.

Households *flow out* of the space seekers stock through several different channels:

(c) Migration. Migration is assumed to depend on the demand for regular (i.e., non-temporary) work in the oil district; this, in turn, is a function of the region's income, and will be modelled in sections 6.1.2 and A6.1.3, which describe the off-site economy sector.

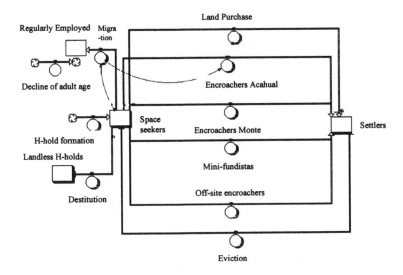

Note: for visual simplicity, the diagram reproduces all stocks and flows, but not all the converters that link them

Figure 6.2   Household sector: basic stock and flow structure

(d) Land purchase. It is assumed that a fraction (estimated as 15% based on survey data) of the evicted households will flow from the space seekers to the settlers stock through land purchases.
(e) Encroachment in communal secondary forest (*acahual*) or primary forest (*monte*) in the community of residence; and encroachment in primary forest areas outside the community of origin;
(f) Use of existing agricultural space via reduction in the average parcel size (*minifundio*). In communities with scarcity of communal land, households looking for land tend to establish themselves in spaces already under agricultural production, which is rented (often against

payment in kind of labour or crops) or borrowed from friends and relatives. It is assumed that in communities where the average *milpa* size has dropped below a critical threshold of 2 has, *minifundio* will no longer be a settlement option.

(g) Destitution. Where no settlement option is available, households will flow out of the space seekers pool and will add to the stock of landless farmers. These destitute households will only be able to support themselves through temporary employment, and through extraction of natural products from forested areas in the buffer and nucleus zones.

Equation box 6.1 summarises, at the generic time *t*, the balance of flows to, and from, the space seekers stock:

Equation box 6.1

Space_Seekers[Zone,Hhold_type](t) =
Space_Seekers[Zone,Hhold_type](t - dt) +
(Hhold_formation[Zone,Hhold_type] + Eviction[Zone,Hhold_type] -
Encroachers_Acahual[Zone,Hhold_type] -
Minifundistas[Zone,Hhold_type] -
Encroachers_Monte[Zone,Hhold_type] -
Off_site_encroachers[Zone,Hhold_type] - Destitution[Zone,Hhold_type] -
Land_Purchasers[Zone,Hhold_type] - Migration[Zone,Hhold_type]) * dt

---

Outflows (d) to (f) entail increases in the *Settlers* stock; however, only outflows in (e) entail land use changes:

Equation box 6.2

Settlers[Zone,Hhold_type](t) = Settlers[Zone,Hhold_type](t - dt) +
(Encroachers_Acahual[Zone,Hhold_type] +
Minifundistas[Zone,Hhold_type] +
Encroachers_Monte[Zone,Hhold_type] +
Off_site_encroachers[Zone,Hhold_type] +
Land_Purchasers[Zone,Hhold_type] - Eviction[Zone,Hhold_type]) * dt

---

Outflow (c) increases the stock of permanent workers in the off-site economy, whereas outflow (g) increases the stock of landless households:

Equation box 6.3

$$Landless\_Hholds[Zone,Hhold\_type](t) = Landless\_Hholds$$
$$[Zone,Hhold\_type](t - dt) + (Destitution[Zone,Hhold\_type]) * dt$$

Let us look in some more detail at the determination of the flows of farmers encroaching into forest land, inside or outside the community of origin.

Encroaching into forest land

Some farmers in the space seekers group will not have the option of migrating, of purchasing land, or of settling on existing farm land. To avoid the risk of starvation, they are likely to try and settle in community forested areas. The process of encroachment into communal forested land will depend on (a) the land use and conversion options available, (b) the relative attractiveness of the various options, and (c), given constraints on the overall area of the different land types, the way in which a given land use option will be adjudicated to different household types competing for it. These elements are analysed by means of a sequential decision tree (depicted in Figure 6.3). At every "node" of the tree, households will select the settlement options with lower conversion cost (secondary forest is less expensive to convert to agriculture than primary forest), subject to the physical availability of the option selected, and to the absence of competing claims of households with higher seniority of residence. If either of these conditions is not met, the household will move to the next preferred option in the decision tree. If all options are exhausted, households will flow out of the space seekers pool and will add to the stock of landless farmers. Further details of the process are illustrated in Annex 6.1.

6.1.2 The off-site economy sector

This sector is the market for goods and services not exchanged within the household sector, bur rather supplied for external purchase or hiring. In this model there are three main types of transaction between the rural household sector and the rest of the region's economy: (a) the sale of forest products (Chamedor Palm) (b) the sale of livestock products (milk and beef), and (c) the supply of labour. However, in order to concentrate the subsequent policy analysis on a limited number of key parameters, attention will be focused on the last two variables (livestock and labour supply). The Chamedor Palm market will be described in a simplified manner, assuming constant farm-gate price and continuous market clearing.

The off-site economy sector is the "gate" through which the national and global economies affect productive activities and natural resource use in the Sierra. As will be discussed in this section, aggregate production and income in the southern Gulf of Mexico oil district are assumed to determine the demand for products and service exported by the Sierra. Output in the oil district is clearly responsive to the overall volume of activity of Mexico's economy, which in turn, in a context of growing integration in the global markets, is affected by the world economy. Considering the objective of this research, the linkages between regional, national and global economy, albeit important, will not be addressed here. Variations in regional income growth will be treated as exogenous, and studied by means of parametric shifts in the growth rate coefficient.

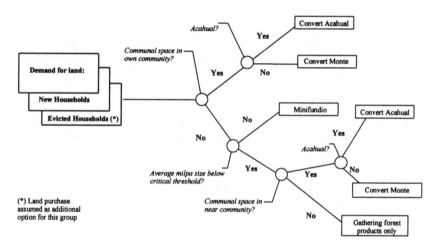

Figure 6.3   Decision tree for land conversion and use

Labour markets
The model divides the labour market of the oil district (municipalities of Acayucan, Coatzacoalcos, Cosoleacaque, and Minatitlan) in two segments: one is the market for temporary or seasonal labour, and the other one is permanent employment. In both cases, the demand for labour is projected using 1994 baseline data for employment and value of production, and

assuming exponential growth of income, with a parametrically varying "technical progress" coefficient, capturing possible substitutions of labour with other inputs that may prevail under proposed restructuring of the oil district.

The supply of seasonal labour is given by the previous chapter's estimates of households' labour supply response (lagged one period) to changes in the probability of finding employment. The latter, in turn, is given by the ratio between demand and supply of labour. Supply of permanent labour (and hence migration) is simply determined by the corresponding excess demand: at any point in time, farmers in the "space seekers" stock will migrate to the off-site economy in quantities sufficient to cover the employment gap. The distribution of migration across ZAUs will be proportional to their respective weight in the space-seekers pool.

Markets for livestock products
The off-site sector consumes livestock products (milk, meat) supplied by the study region. In the absence of detailed information on the demand for individual livestock products, the number of heads of cattle was used as the actual dependent variable.

It is assumed that cattle herds adjust to variation in demand for livestock products.[4] Given an underlying demand function, the model assumes that cattle numbers adjust to changes in income via an elasticity coefficient. A baseline value for the elasticity coefficient was borrowed from the literature on pasture-induced deforestation in Mexico (Barbier and Burgess, 1996); increases in demand for cattle in excess of the existing stock are given by the livestock demand's income elasticity, times the increase in income. To capture the possibility that meat's budget share first grows and then stabilises as income grows, the model uses a logistic growth function of the income elasticity of cattle numbers, from the initial to a plateau value (see Annex 6.3 for details).

6.1.3   The land use sector

This sector of the model studies the variation over time of a selected number of stocks of land uses: primary forest or *monte*, secondary forest or *acahual*, farm land or *milpa*, and pasture. In addition, it also examines the impact of human activities on the stock of a resource extracted from forested areas, Chamedor Palm. As visualised in Figure 6.4, conversion and/or regeneration flows link the various stocks. For example, forest conversion determines the decrease of the *monte* or *acahual* stocks, as well as the corresponding increase of the *milpa* or pasture stocks; conversely, regeneration flows determine increases in the stock of *acahual* at the expenses of pasture land.

The household sector (see sections 6.1.1 and A6.1.2) estimates the number of households projected to change land use (from forested land – primary or secondary– to agriculture). The land use sector translates household data into impacts onto the various categories of land use, across the different ZAUs: that is, it turns *household flows* into *land use flows* (and therefore, impacts on land use stocks). For example, based on the number of households projected to turn second growth (*acahual*) forest into farmland, the land use sector estimates, at every point in time, the conversion of *acahual* into *milpa* as the dot product, across ZAUs, of the number of a*cahual* encroachers, times the individual hectare requirements for the newly formed and existing (evicted) household types. The latter per-household conversion figures are obtained from the linear programming model of Chapter 5.

Concerning the conversion of forested land into pasture, the model, based on the results of Chapter 5, focuses only on conversions undertaken by already established farm households onto private (and not communal) lands. In this model, conversion of land from other uses to pasture may take place either to support a fixed herd when overgrazing leads to declining productivity in existing grazing lands; or to enable herd expansion, which takes place to meet increases in the demand for livestock products. In turn, demand for livestock products (proxied by cattle numbers) is determined in the off-site economy sector, as explained in sections 6.1.2 and A6.1.3.

Extraction of forest products

This sector of the model projects the impacts on Chamedor Palm populations of extraction undertaken by inhabitants of the study region. Palm populations are hypothesised to follow a logistic growth pattern, with carrying capacity determined by plant density (as observed in the field) and area of habitat suitable for reproduction. Aggregate extraction of Palm results from the per-household extraction figures generated by the linear programming model of Chapter 5, and from the numbers of residents with access to zones suitable for Palm growth.

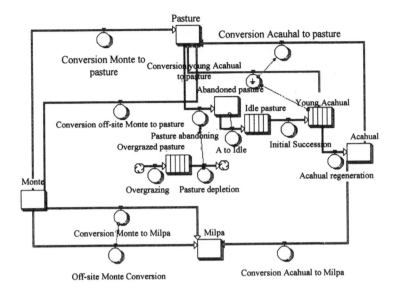

Figure 6.4   The land use sector

6.2   RESULTS

Based on the equations illustrated in the previous sections, the model simulates the behaviour over time of several stocks and flows in the household, land use and off-site economy sector. The results depend on assumptions on several parameters, related to the overall state of the regional economy, the demand for the study area's agriculture and forest products, farming technology, tenure adjustments, and to the ecosystem's ability to recover from perturbations. Section 6.2.1 presents, for illustrative purposes, results related to a reference, or baseline case. Section 6.2.2 analyses how results are affected by changes in key exogenous and policy-controlled parameters.

6.2.1   Reference case

A reference case is presented in this section, with the purpose of both illustrating the kind of diagrammatic results generated by the model, and of providing a benchmark for the subsequent sensitivity analysis. The reference case is based on the assumption of zero income growth in the off-site economy sector (a pessimistic extrapolation of the situation prevailing at data collection time). A first set of results refers to changes in the various stocks of population inside and outside the study area. Figure 6.5 displays the behaviour of the stock of permanent migrants to, and temporary workers in, the urban area; the stock of settlers in the study area, and the stock of landless farmers.

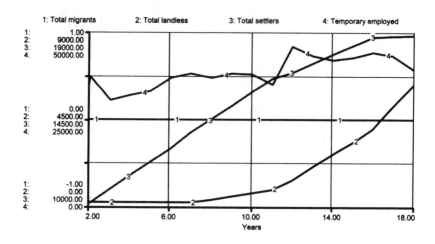

Note: Units: temporary employment in days of work per annum; other variables in number of people

Figure 6.5   Reference case: migration, settlers and landlessness

If income is constant, there will be no opportunities for new permanent employment (and hence migration), there will be stagnating or declining chances of temporary employment, and increasing numbers of destitute households. Therefore, in Figure 6.5 the number of settlers grows, but so does (and at an increasing rate) the stock of landless households. Given declining employment opportunities on the temporary job market, the supply of temporary labour stagnates. The lack of income growth has clear implications on land use patterns. Figure 6.6 illustrates some of the most significant trends.

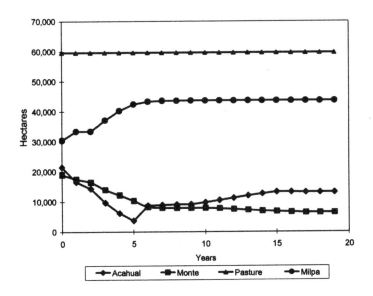

Figure 6.6   Reference case: land use (Has)

While pasture land is stationary (no additional demand for livestock products), farm land increases significantly at the expense of both secondary and primary forest, in order to accommodate the subsistence needs of a growing number of aspiring settlers with no alternative income sources. The reason why *milpa* stabilizes before year 10 of the simulation is not that the demand for land decreases, but rather that communal spaces are being exhausted, as illustrated by Figure 6.7. Both primary and second growth forest in communal land shrink towards rapid exhaustion to meet space seekers' demand for land.

Changes in private forest are driven by the need of maintaining pasture for a stationary cattle herd. As described in section 6.1.3 and in Annex 6.4, the rate of nutrient accumulation and of transition to mature *acahual*, as well as the speed of the overgrazing process, determine the feature of the process. If secondary succession is rapid enough, and overgrazing slow enough, the impact on primary forests may be limited. (Annex 6.4 provides a more detailed description of the pasture rotation cycle, through the stages of pasture idling, formation of young and mature second growth vegetation, and further conversions to pasture).

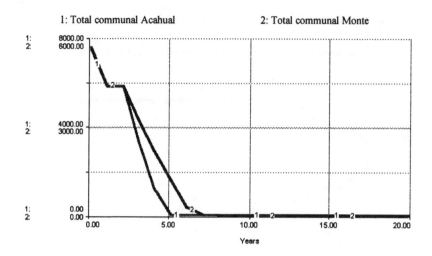

Figure 6.7   Reference case: forest in communal areas (Has)

In Figure 6.8, which assumes nutrient storing time (T_n) and regeneration time (T_r) of 2 and 3 years respectively (see Annex 6.4 for definitions of T_n and T_r), after an initial drop due to the replacement of pre-existing overgrazed land, a*cahual* picks up again around the initial level; primary forest tends to stabilize at about 70% of the initial level.

However, if regeneration is slow and/or overgrazing fast, *monte* can quickly be depleted: with T_n=3, T_r=4 and an average duration of the overgrazing process of seven years, the entire stock of private *Monte* is cleared after 15 years (not shown in Figure 6.8).

The high dependency of the region's households (especially those without secure land tenure) on natural resources, in the absence of other income sources, has clear impacts on Chamedor Palm populations. Figure 6.9 plots the behavior of the habitat's carrying capacity, and of the total stock of Palm (both are measured in *gruesas* – a *gruesa* is a bunch of 120 leaves). As primary forest shrinks, carrying capacity drops to the level that can be supported by the nucleus zone (due to poor access, the nucleus zone is assumed unaffected by deforestation); the Palm stock, however, is exhausted much earlier because of excessive extraction. Sensitivity analysis indicates that, other things being equal, depletion occurs for all coefficients of Palm growth below 1.7.

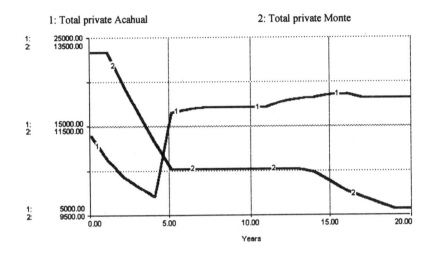

Figure 6.8   Reference case: forest in private land (Has)

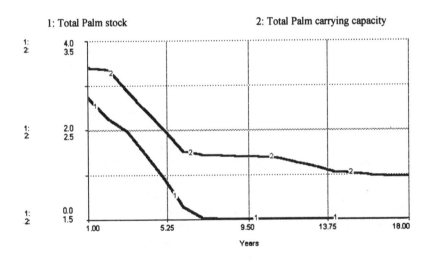

Figure 6.9   Reference case: palm extraction (million gruesas)

6.2.2   Variations in exogenous parameters

Most of the above results are likely to be affected by changes in the various parameters of the model. Given the purposes of this research, the ensuing analysis will concentrate on changes in:

(a) two exogenous parameters: (a1) the rate of growth of the regional income, r, and (a2) the regeneration time of second growth forest, T_r, intended as a measure of the ecosystem's ability to recover from human-induced perturbations (see Annex 6.4 for details on the process of secondary forest regeneration and the role of T_r);

(b) one "semi-exogenous" parameter, i.e. a parameter which may be partially affected by local policy makers (see ensuing discussion, section 6.3): the rate of change of the marginal (value) product of labour ρ, defined in (6.4), page 215.

(c) two parameters capturing effects of local policy making choices: (b1) the percentage of "wealthy *avecindados*" i.e., the percentage of households without secure title that have enough means to access land markets, therefore avoiding eviction; and (b2) the availability of technology for intensifying farming practices (see section 6.3 for details).

Variations in (a) and (b) will be studied in this section; section 6.3 will extend the analysis to variations in (c). Different sets of results can be obtained, depending on the value taken on by the various parameters. To keep the analysis simple, only a relatively small number of scenarios are considered, based on the assumption that each parameter can only take "low" and "high" values heuristically determined. The total number of scenarios is $H=2^q$, where q is the number of parameters that are allowed to vary.

In order to compare results of this section with results obtained under different policy interventions (section 6.3), it is necessary to select key features of the land use change process, and aggregate them into a single index, representing the "desirability" –in terms of likely impacts on human welfare– of changes prevailing in the various scenarios. A given policy may then be deemed "successful" in terms of addressing land use change concerns if it can increase the index under the various scenarios considered. Let us see how such an index may be constructed.

As discussed in Chapter 1, much of the debate on "deforestation" is motivated by its possible impacts on the ability of the ecosystem to deliver services affecting human welfare. The underlying argument is that land under some uses (typically forested land) is better suited to deliver eco-services than land under other uses; so a reduction in the area of forested land will decrease the provision of ecological services. However, size of perturbations may not be the only thing that matters. The ability of any given type of land to deliver eco-services may also be affected by the frequency of shocks. For example, an area under secondary forest may be periodically cleared for agriculture; even though vegetation may be able to regenerate in between clearances, some species residing in the area my suffer if the time between one shock and the other is too short.

Ideally, then, the impacts on human welfare of a change in the pattern of land use, would need to be assessed on the basis of the *size* and *frequency* of disturbances, and on some measure of how much, say, a large disturbance in one form of land use may be compensated for by stability in another form of land use. It seems reasonable to have such an index depend positively on conservation of the various forms of vegetation cover, and negatively on the frequency and magnitude of changes in land use.

Furthermore, changes in different stocks of land use will affect the index differently, as there will be some types of vegetation cover (e.g., primary forest) that will contribute more than others to the maintenance of the overall ecosystem stability and to the provision of ecological services.

It has to be noted that different environmental management objectives will be represented by different selections of land uses (and associated size and frequency of change), and different coefficients of substitution of one land type for another. For example, if the management objective is the sustainability of agricultural production, changes in the various types of farm and pasture land are likely to be included in the index; substitution of some form of forested land with some forms of farm land may be associated, through appropriate choice of the function's parameters, with constant or increasing levels of the utility index.

It is assumed here that the primary concern of an "environmental planner" is conservation of the various forms of forest cover. A simple index of utility of such an environmental planner is defined here, which increases in the end-of-simulation areas under primary (m_T) and secondary (a_T) forest cover (relative to their respective initial values), and decreases in the variability over time of those areas (proxied by the relative variance – the coefficient of variation squared). A simple Cobb-Douglas form is used:

$$U = \left(\frac{m_T}{\left(\sigma_M / \overline{M}\right)^2}\right)^{\alpha} \left(\frac{a_T}{\left(\sigma_A / \overline{A}\right)^2}\right)^{1-\alpha} \tag{6.1}$$

where σ_M, σ_A, $\overline{M}$ and $\overline{A}$ are standard deviation and average, respectively, for the stocks of *monte* (primary forest) and *acahual* (secondary forest). The premium attached to large size and low variability in primary forest is captured in the simulation by a value of α of 0.8.

Table 6.1 summarises the impacts on land and resource use in the eight scenarios given by a binary variation in the three parameters r (the rate of regional income growth), ρ (the rate of growth of the marginal product of labour) and T_r (*acahual* regeneration time). Case A is associated with the highest value of the utility index (highest end-of simulation stocks of primary forest and Chamedor Palm), case H with the lowest one (total depletion of primary forest). These two cases indicate that land use impacts tend to be stronger when income growth is slow (less opportunities for off-farm employment), and when the agro-ecosystem recovers more slowly (at any point in time, less fallow land will be ready for conversion to farming, which increases encroachment on primary forest).

The scenarios comprised between A and H give us an idea of the interplay of the exogenous parameters in determining impacts on land use patterns. A fast rate of ecosystem regeneration may partially compensate for slow growth in income (cases B and C); at the same time, higher income growth may also lead to significant land use impacts (case G) when labour-replacing technical progress ($\rho = 5\%$) decreases employment opportunities for unskilled labour.

An important observation concerns the process of land idling. Table 6.1 suggest that at mid-simulation time idle land amounts to a considerable 20-30% of farm land, and 15% of pasture land. This points to the potential for investments in soil conservation and improvement; these can prevent excess land abandonment, thereby providing a significant alternative to forest conversion to farmers seeking land for subsistence cultivation.

6.3   POLICY IMPLICATIONS

This section will explore two sets of options that local policy makers may pursue to reduce pressure on primary and second growth vegetation cover in the study area.

Intensifying agricultural activities

A first set of options refers to improvement in farming practices that would reduce the amount of land for given output. It is widely recognised that one of the key factors of loss of forested areas induced by swidden agriculture is the low productivity per hectare of key staple crops sowed by subsistence farmers in rain fed land (Southgate, 1991; Southgate, 1995; Barbier & Burgess, 1996).

Table 6.1   Impacts on land use of parameter changes

		A	B	C	D	E	F	G	H
r		5.0%	1.5%	1.5%	5.0%	5.0%	1.5%	5.0%	1.5%
T_r		2	2	2	4	2	4	4	4
ρ		1.0%	1.0%	5.0%	1.0%	5.0%	5.0%	5.0%	1.0%
Stocks	*Units*								
Acahual (*t*=0)	Has	21.4	21.4	21.4	21.4	21.4	21.4	21.4	21.4
Acahual (*t*=10)	Has	14.7	7.0	7.0	15.0	7.2	7.8	7.5	7.8
Acahual Final	Has	15.0	11.9	11.9	18.5	10.8	15.6	14.3	15.6
Monte t=0)	Has	18.8	18.8	18.8	18.8	18.8	18.8	18.8	18.8
Monte (*t*=10)	Has	12.9	8.0	7.9	6.5	7.2	1.0	0.8	1.2
Monte Final	Has	9.1	6.2	6.2	3.8	5.4	0	0	0
Idle (*t*=0)	Has	0	0	0	0	0	0	0	0
Idle (*t*=10)	Has	9.9	9.9	9.9	9.9	9.9	9.9	9.9	9.9
Idle Final	Has	8.1	7.8	7.8	7.5	8.1	7.4	7.5	7.4
Palm (*t*=0)	*Gruesas*	3.3	3.3	3.3	3.3	3.3	3.3	3.3	3.3
Palm (*t*=10)	*Gruesas*	0.0	0.0	0.01	0.2	0.01	0	0	0
Palm Final	*Gruesas*	0.3	0	0	0	0	0	0	0
Rel. Variance *Acahual*		0.03	0.20	0.20	0.02	0.21	0.14	0.15	0.14
Rel. Variance *Monte*		0.08	0.26	0.26	0.45	0.32	1.69	1.75	1.66
"Utility"		7.44	1.51	1.49	1.11	1.09	0.001	0.001	0.00

Note: Units in the table are thousands of hectares and million of gruesas

If credit, information or capacity constraints prevent access to productivity-raising technology, total yields can only be increased by increasing cultivated areas. In the Sierra de Santa Marta, a detailed analysis of constraints to, and opportunities for, intensifying maize-based systems has recently been provided by Buckles and Erenstein (1996). According to these authors, current patterns of maize cultivation are characterised by relatively large size of total crop area per household, and relatively long fallow times. Sustainable intensification of the current system would be achieved through a combination of technologies that increase fertility (green manures and fertilisers) and that ensure better conservation of existing fertility (green manures, shelter belts and live barriers in contour lines).

Based on this combination, it would be possible to reduce (in an equilibrium that would follow a transition period of one to three years) fallow time to just one year, and decrease total crop area to 33% or 50% of the original parcel size, depending on whether the intensification technology is applied to the buffer or the influence zone. Financial analysis suggest that the intensification package is attractive from the farmer's point of view. Buckles and Erenstein obtain such a result in the analysis of a farm undertaking maize cultivation only; Cervigni develops (Cervigni and Ramirez, 1996) multi-crop farm budget models,[5] and finds that, provided there is appropriate access to credit and training, adoption of the proposed alternative technologies and cropping patterns would yield NPVs between US$ 70-300 per household per hectare, with benefit cost ratios well in excess of 2.

The joint effect of the intensification package described by Buckles and Erenstein (small farmed area per household, shorter fallow time) is captured in this model by setting $T_n = 2$, reducing by 50% the minimum *milpa* size,[6] and by reducing by 50% the per-type-of household coefficients of forest conversion to agricultural area referred to in section 6.1.3.

Mitigating land tenure pressures
Another important area for policy is likely to be land tenure. Newly formed households and farmers who may be evicted as a result of the PROCEDE program are unlikely to have access to own resources or to credit to purchase farm land.

A first role for public policy would be facilitating settlements of disputes on land that, as a result of eviction, would be returned to the community, or to owners who may not have exercised their rights in many years. Under criteria of transparency and equity, farmers who have been using land for a long enough period of time without formal rights may be granted legal tenure title.

A further possibility would be to explore a program of credit (perhaps based on a revolving fund structure), which would support farmers without tenure in renting or purchasing land with some vegetation cover from larger farmers, in exchange for their commitment to dedicate part of the land to agroforestry or other uses with beneficial effects on biological resources. The program may be co-funded by the State government and/or by the Municipal water commission, in recognition of the soil conservation and watershed benefits of agroforestry uses.

This group of policies is captured in the model by an increase (from 15% to 50%) in the percentage of title-less farmers that leave the space-seekers pool as they find settlement options other than encroaching on forested land.

Introducing two additional parameters in the simulation brings the total number of possible scenarios to 2^5 i.e. to 32. Instead of expanding Table 6.1 to add the new scenarios, Table 6.2 summarises the impacts of the individual or joint adoption of farming and tenure policies in terms of comparison with results that would prevail in each of the eight scenarios identified by Table 6.1. In particular, Table 6.2 reports the improvement in the utility of the "environmental planner", as defined in equation (6.1); and the prevention, in percentage terms, of losses in areas under *monte* that would have prevailed in the eight scenarios described in section 6.2.2 and summarised by Table 6.1 (*P* stands for the percentage of wealthy *avecindados*, and $I =1$ means that the agriculture intensification package is being applied).

It can be seen that the joint adoption of farming intensification and tenure policies have a marked impact in both increasing the utility of the environmental planner (the ratio of alternative to baseline utility exceeds 2 in 17 out of 24 cases),[7] and in contributing to significant savings of areas under primary forest. The combined use of the two policies tends to be more effective than the adoption of either agriculture technology or tenure policy in isolation; however, tenure policy alone may lead to modest improvements in the conservation of the vegetation cover. Policies also are the most effective when they are undertaken in conditions of high income growth and slow labour-replacing technical progress; for example, when $r=5\%$, $\rho=1.5\%$, and $I=1$, the end-of-simulation value of primary forest ranges between 10,000 and 15,000 has, which, compared to the relevant reference value (Scenarios A and D), amounts to prevention of forest loss ranging between 27% and 41%.

The sensitivity of the results on assumptions about technical progress points to a further area of intervention for local policy makers concerned with conservation of natural resources in the study area. As it is likely that the oil district will be affected by processes of industrial reorganisation and modernisation that may lead to lay-offs (especially in a context of stagnating or declining oil prices), it will be important to create opportunities, especially through capacity building and training programs, for non-farm employment outside of the oil sector; for example, in the handicraft, food processing or tourism sectors. That way, landless farmers may be able to take advantage of income opportunities generated by the growth of the regional economy, rather than being left at a comparative disadvantage with the more skilled labour force in the urban areas.

Table 6.2   Agriculture technology, tenure policies and land use

	Ratio of "Utilities"			Avoided "Monte" loss		
Scenarios (columns of Table 6.1)	$P = 50\%$, $I = 1$	$P = 15\%$, $I = 1$	$P = 50\%$, $I = 0$	$P = 50\%$, $I = 1$	$P = 15\%$, $I = 1$	$P = 50\%$, $I = 0$
A	17.91	9.87	1.88	32.5%	26.6%	10.1%
B	7.30	7.63	0.05	19.5%	19.5%	0.0%
C	6.63	6.24	-	28.6%	28.8%	0.0%
D	71.31	17.79	1.74	40.8%	34.9%	10.1%
E	8.18	7.99	-	22.4%	22.4%	0.0%
F	1,941.78	1,850.52	-	33.4%	33.4%	0.0%
G	1,631.65	1,574.54	-	30.7%	30.7%	0.0%
H	18,439.4	17,584.3	11.68	33.5%	33.4%	0.0%

6.4   CONCLUSIONS

6.4.1   Conclusions on the land use change model

The last two chapters have proposed an application of computer based modelling of dynamic systems to original household survey data from a biosphere reserve in the Mexican tropics to predict land use changes over a 15-20 years time horizon.

In general, the model suggests that processes of conversion of forested land to productive uses (agriculture, pasture) are likely to continue over the medium to long term. However, the magnitude of the process is likely to be significantly affected by a number of parameters, some of exogenous nature, some under the potential control of local policy makers.

In terms of the former, land use changes are likely to be of larger size and frequency when non-farm employment opportunities are scarcer (either because regional income grows slowly, or because technical progress reduces the demand for unskilled labour), and when ecosystems recover slowly from perturbations. A fast rate of ecosystem regeneration may partially compensate for slow growth in income, and may be able to attenuate land use impacts; on the other hand, labour-replacing technical progress and slow ecosystem recovery can cancel out the potentially positive effects of income growth.

Policy makers may have opportunities for mitigating the land use impacts of growing demand for farm and pasture land by promoting land-saving agriculture techniques, by offering alternatives to encroachment to title-less farmers evicted as a result of tenure regularisation programs, and by investing in training and capacity building programs to facilitate the entry of unskilled labour in employment markets outside the agriculture sector.

This model permits estimation of land use impacts of different courses of policy action. This is an important element of decision making, but by no means the only one. To fully assess the social value of each policy option further research would be needed, in two main areas. The first refers to the full costing of the design and implementation of the various policy options under scrutiny.

The second area concerns the detailed specification of a utility function of the land use patterns estimated to prevail as a result of the various policies, under scenarios defined by different combinations of the exogenous parameters. Such a utility function would take into account the full range of substitution possibilities among land uses (and possibly ecological thresholds) in the provision of ecological services, as well as trade-offs between size and stability of various land types.

Another question to be incorporated in a revised utility function concerns the private trade-offs between alternative land uses. Preliminary indications coming from the farm budget models (Cervigni & Ramirez, 1996; Cervigni, 1998) referred to earlier (section 6.3) suggest that in a number of situations farmers might be better off with alternative, low-intensity land uses, than with the baseline cropping patterns. The augmented utility function would need to incorporate in a systematic way private opportunity costs of switching from one type of land use to another.

6.4.2   General conclusions

This book has defined the biodiversity problem, explored in theory and in practice the causes of land use change, and discussed policy and management options for supporting the conservation and sustainable use of biodiversity through mobilisation of local, national, and international resources. This final section draws some brief conclusions to broaden to a more general setting the findings of the Mexico case study, and to identify directions for future research.

The area analysed in the Mexico case study is representative of a number of other situations frequently occurring in much of the developing world. That is, areas containing important remnants of pristine ecosystems, along with larger tracts of landscape subject for a number of years (sometimes decades) to human intervention and transformation for productive use. At the same time, transformation of the original ecosystems has occurred – in Sierra Santa Marta as in other similar regions – in a spatially significant manner, but not yet in a pervasive one; and it has occurred in relatively recent times, so that options are still open, both for conservation of the remaining patches of pristine ecosystems, and for natural or man-induced regeneration of the areas transformed or degraded.

Prevailing social and economic conditions include strong demographic pressure, limited income and employment opportunities in the vicinity, and land tenure conflicts which make it difficult for conservation agencies to negotiate land use restrictions.

In the context of this research, key questions to address for the many areas in the world typified by SSM include:

* What explains the process of land use change?
* Does land use change result in biodiversity loss?
* What policy options are available to mitigate the potentially negative effects of land use change?

Explaining the process of land use change
A first point regards the analysis of the process of loss. In the same way that there is no single explanation for development, there is no single explanation for land use change, and there is no single strategy for mitigating the adverse impacts of land use change on biodiversity.

The Mexico case study has documented that multiple factors collude in determining pressure on forest margins, vegetation cover, and resource extraction; these factors include income growth, tenure, access to outputs and credit markets. Some factors may have ambiguous impacts: income growth, for example, both alleviates land pressures related to subsistence farming, and increases conversion to pasture via increasing demand for livestock products.

Because of these ambiguous impacts, and because the relative significance of other factors varies according to the initial conditions and the historical evolution of social and economic systems, there is a clear need for micro-level analysis of the causation process. These may provide local and national decision makers with situation-specific policy indications to address a problem that is, by nature, location-specific: any given ecosystem of particular significance in terms of its genetic, species and community diversity exists in a well-defined geographical location. Basing policy decisions on averages of effects across locations may not be appropriate, if the objective is to conserve individual ecosystems, and not their net sum.

Land use change and biodiversity loss
A second point concerns the definition of the biodiversity problem, and in particular the linkage between land use change and biodiversity loss. As discussed in the first chapter, the problem of saving or losing biodiversity is often portrayed as a dichotomous choice between leaving land in a "pristine state", or converting it irretrievably to a fully developed state for productive purposes. In fact, the actual situation faced by land users in real life is significantly different. First, the amount of land which is in true "pristine" conditions is considerably limited by the widespread presence of human intervention of some sort in the near or remote past. [8]

Secondly, the range of choices open to land users is broader than the simple "conserve" versus "develop": in fact, there is an almost continuous spectrum of land uses with varying degrees of impact on the ecosystem, and varying likelihood of threatening the survival of species or genetic diversity. Thirdly, it is not only the one-time intervention on the landscape that determines the fate of biological resources residing therein; but rather the dynamic sequence of decisions taken over time, after the initial land use change. Natural regeneration of original vegetation may follow an initial perturbation of the habitat, so long as productive activities undertaken after the first transformation are not incompatible with the re-establishment of the indigenous species and biotic communities. Second growth forest may prevail in areas initially converted from primary forest to agriculture; shaded coffee may replace wild vegetation in areas of forest partially cleared for productive purposes.

It follows that more accurate predictions of the biodiversity impacts of land use change processes should be based on more complete information on the characteristics (e.g., type, extension, duration of the change) of those processes. To exemplify the point, the model developed in this book proposes a simple approach, based on the size and frequency of the perturbation, and analyses how exogenous and policy choices may possibly affect them over time. Clearly, the approach proposed should be considered as a first approximation in the direction of interdisciplinary research, and more work is needed to specify more precise "objective functions" of a "biodiversity conscious" land planner. Section 6.4.3 develops the point further.

Policy options

In Sierra de Santa Marta, and in the many other similar areas in Mexico and elsewhere, biodiversity is "in the balance" between further conversion (and possibly loss), and sustainable management. In areas like Sierra de Santa Marta, prevailing social and economic conditions are such that outright protection through restricted use would be very costly or plainly impossible. Because of the heterogeneous nature of the landscape (including a mix of pristine, transformed and degraded areas), and because of the complexity of the social and economic context, a diversified strategy appears necessary to tilt the balance in the direction of sustainable management. For the areas better preserved, it would appear sensible to pursue an approach of minimising human interference with biological and ecological processes, by purchasing land whenever possible, or alternatively, providing compensation to land owners on a recurrent basis. In both cases, mechanisms are necessary[9] to permit transfer of capital (on a one-time only or on a recurrent basis) from private and public donors to landowners, in exchange for restriction on use. Because of the potential high costs involved and limited funding available, selectivity is key: funding should be restricted to areas with minimum degree of human perturbation, clear tenure title, low likelihood of outside invasion.

In SSM as in other similar cases, an equally if not more important challenge is however to manage biodiversity *outside* of pristine areas, that is, in the large tracts of land subject to a significant degree of human transformation. For those areas, it appears that the strategy would entail promoting biodiversity-friendly production (including the selection of inputs and technologies with limited impacts on the ecosystem, as well as choice of outputs compatible with the original ecological mosaic – e.g., shaded coffee, non timber forest products, etc.)

Finally, for both pristine areas and the productive landscape, sustainable biodiversity management is clearly crucially linked to the number of resource users that depend on biological resources either for direct use (own consumption) or for transformation and sale to intermediate and final output markets. This points to the importance of co-ordinating biodiversity with local and regional policies for broad-based (i.e. industry, trade, service-based) growth of income and employment: for a given rate of population growth, larger opportunities outside the rural sector are likely to decrease dependency on the use of biological resources and hence threats of excessive habitat modification (both land conversion and over-exploitation of biological resources from the wild).

6.4.3 Directions for future research

Inspection of the literature suggests that the interactions between social and economic systems on the one hand, and ecosystem functioning and health on the other, are poorly understood (Perrings et al., 1994; Barbier, Burgess, and Folke, 1994; Costanza, 1991; Perrings and Pearce, 1994). This defines a broad agenda for future research.

The call for national and international actions to correct market, government and institutional failures in the management of biodiversity, is justified by the argument that by preserving adequate levels of the diversity traits of natural systems, human welfare can be sustained in a lasting manner.

At the same time, there is no definitive understanding of: (a) the relationship between human activities and diversity; and (b) the relationship between diversity and welfare generating properties of natural systems. As a result, the management implications of the generic call for biodiversity conservation are far from clear. There are several important parameters affecting relevant decision making processes.

These are related, among others, to discounting (i.e. trading off present versus future welfare), local and international conservation preferences, infra-national and international redistribution parameters, probabilistic structures relating human activities to welfare via their impact on diversity. Depending on assumptions made about those parameters, alternative management options of natural and semi-natural systems can be justified.

At the policy level, recent studies of international agencies (e.g. World Bank, 1996; Srivastava, Smith, and Forno, 1996; Smith, 1996) as well as recent decisions of the Conference of the Parties (COP) of the Biodiversity Convention suggest that international policy makers are increasingly moving away from traditional paradigms of conservation based on the maintenance of large, undisturbed protected areas. Indeed, COP's emphasis on sustainable use and agrobiodiversity suggest that increasing importance for the biodiversity cause is being attached to management options that entail various degrees of natural habitat modification.

In the extreme, one can argue that in fact any management option can be justified ex post by an appropriate choice of parameters reflecting underlying probabilistic and value judgement assumptions. If this was the case, policy and management decisions would be the result of an essentially political process, where proponents of alternative courses of actions would try to influence decision makers through a partisan use of the scarce information available.

This state of affairs suggests that there are still important roles applied research can play. First, it can reduce the uncertainty surrounding preferences, probabilities and other key parameters of the decision-making problem. Second, even when information on the decision parameters is not yet available, applied research can elucidate the terms of some critical trade offs. For instance, it can clarify the social and economic processes whereby human activities modify ecosystems and presumably their diversity. In the same way, applied research can shed some light on the impact of alternative management options on natural systems, and on their social and economic costs and benefits.

ANNEX 6.1 THE COMPLETE STOCK AND FLOW MODEL

This annex complements with additional details and clarifications the description of the simulation model provided in the main text of the chapter.

A6.1.1 The household sector: inflows to the space seekers stock

Formation of new households

Based on field evidence, it is assumed that a new household is formed every time a male individual reaches adult age (18 years). To obtain estimates on the yearly numbers of new adults, the following procedure was used. Official data on the age structure of the male and female population was available for a subset of 17 communities of the Mecayapan and Soteapan municipalities (2 in the buffer and 15 in the influence zone).

Age classes were of one year intervals for the youngest ages (up to 15 years), and of wider (two to four years) intervals for the remaining classes. Through linear interpolation of the non-unit intervals, it was possible to construct a year-by-year cumulative age distribution function of the population. This distribution did not exhibit substantial variation over the subset of the 17 sampled communities.

An average of the percentage distribution of ages was therefore used, weighted by the size of the total (male and female) population relative to the total of the 17 land units sampled. The result is indicated by the function FDISTRIB(.) reported in Equation box 6.4, which maps into number of new adults the flow of time, and the consequent decrease of the 1995 adult age (for example, individuals who were 16 years old in 1995 will be 18 in 1997, that is, in year 2 of the simulation)[10].

Equation box 6.4

Hhold_formation[Zone,Hhold_type] =
Dummy_New_Hholds[Hhold_type] * People_per_Hhold[Zone] *
(delay(Average_men_age_structure,1)-Average_men_age_structure)*
INT(Proportion_of_men[Zone] * (INIT(Settlers[Zone,Existing_NoTitle]) +
INIT(Settlers[Zone,Existing_Title])))

Average_men_age_structure = FDISTRIB(Decline_of_Adult_age)

Figure 6.10 displays, as an example, the process of household formation in one of the seven ZAUs, the Influence zone in the Soteapan Municipality.

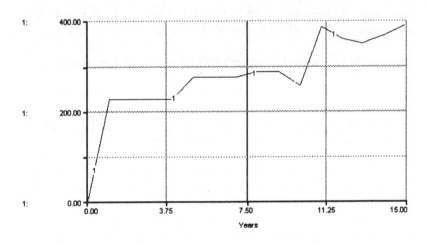

Figure 6.10   Formation of new households

Eviction

As discussed above, application of PROCEDE, the land titling program currently under way in Mexico, is likely to result in eviction of farmers who are not in possession of a valid *ejidatario* title and who do not own private land. Assuming that no mitigating measure will be in place, displaced farmers will be forced to join the pool of space seekers. The rate at which this will happen depends upon the implementation modalities of the land-titling program. For simplicity, it will be assumed here that displacement of title-less farmers will be evenly distributed over the time horizon of the simulation, starting from the second year:

Equation box 6.5

Eviction[Zone,Hhold_type] = IF(time<2) then 0 else
Dummy_avencid[Hhold_type] * INIT(Settlers[Zone,Hhold_type]) /
(STOPTIME-1)

A6.1.2   Outflows from the space seekers stock

Migration
As discussed earlier, some of the inhabitants of the study area tend to migrate
to the municipalities of the oil district. Migration is assumed to depend on the
demand for regular (i.e., non-temporary) work in the oil district; this, in turn,
is a function of the region's income, and will be modelled in section A6.1.3,
which describes the off-site economy sector.

Land purchase
Some of the households forming the space seekers pool may in fact benefit
from the revitalisation of the land market which should follow the titling
regularisation process. Farmers with necessary resources may purchase land
instead of encroaching into remaining communal areas. It is plausible that
land purchases will be more likely among established households, who might
have had more saving opportunities in the past than newly formed
households. It is assumed that a fraction (estimated as 15% on the basis of
survey data) of the evicted households will flow from the space seekers to the
settlers stock through land purchases.

Equation box 6.6

Land_Purchasers[Zone,Hhold_type] =
INT(Delay(Eviction[Zone,Existing_NoTitle], 1) * Percent_wealthy_avenc)

Searching land for subsistence farming
The linear programming models of Chapter 5 provided indications on the size
of the agricultural area which will be needed by new and evicted households
pursuing survival strategies, with no access to land of their own. In that
model it is illustrated that the size of the area converted depends on a number
of factors, including access to credit, family size, and employment prospects.
The last two variables are explicitly included in this model: family size varies
across household types, and the determination of the employment probability
is included in the off-site economy sector of the model, as explained below
(section A6.1.3).

The impact on land use (and thus ecosystem condition) depends on the
way the demand of space seekers for land will be met. This, in turn, depends
on (a) the land use and conversion options available, (b) the relative
attractiveness of the various options, and (c), given constraints on the overall

area of the different land types, the way in which a given land use option will be adjudicated to different household types competing for it.

Based on the existing literature (Paré et al., 1993) on field observations, and on a priori judgment, this model proposes a conceptual framework addressing these three issues. This is summarised by the decision tree depicted in Figure 6.3.

Both types of space seekers, newly formed and evicted households, will be faced with a number of options to meet their demand for land.[11] This model assumes that both groups will follow the same decision path, which dictates the land use options chosen at each of six decision nodes illustrated in Figure 6.3 on page 186, as a function of the "state of nature" prevailing at that node. When land of a given type is not sufficient to meet the demand of the entire space seekers group, it is assumed that evicted farmers will have priority over new households. Given that evicted farmers have by definition more "seniority of residence" in the community, this may not be an implausible assumption.[12]

Let us now elaborate on the various steps of the assumed sequential decision making process. The first option will be use of encroachable spaces[13] to establish *milpa*-type subsistence agriculture.

Because of lower cost, conversion of communal second growth (*acahual*) vegetation will be preferred to conversion of primary forest (*monte*), which it is assumed will start only upon complete conversion of the first type of land. The number of households encroaching into *acahual* areas will be:

Equation box 6.7

Encroachers_Acahual[Zone,Hhold_type] =
IF(Encroachable_Acahual[Zone]> (Space_Seekers[Zone,New] *
Milpa_size[New] + Space_Seekers[Zone,Existing_NoTitle] +
Milpa_size[Existing_NoTitle]))

THEN

INT(Dummy_non_settled[Hhold_type] *
Space_Seekers[Zone,Hhold_type]) ELSE

Dummy_avencid[Hhold_type] * Int(Encroachable_Acahual
[Zone]/ Milpa_size[Existing_NoTitle])

At any given time and in any given zoning unit, if space allows it,[14] all space seekers will settle in remaining encroachable *acahual*. Otherwise, the above mentioned rule will apply, which benefits evicted households: only a certain number of evicted farmers will encroach in *acahual* areas. This number is given by the encroachable land under second growth divided by the per-household farm area; the latter is obtained from the linear programming model of Chapter 5.

Space seekers who don't manage to settle down in *acahual* land (*Non_acahual_encr*) are likely to follow the next option in the decision tree of Figure 6.3, that is conversion of *monte* areas:

Equation box 6.8

Encroachers_Monte[Zone,Hhold_type] = IF(Encroachable_Monte[Zone]
> (Non_acahual_encr[Zone,New] * Milpa_size[New] +
Non_acahual_encr[Zone,Existing_NoTitle] * Milpa_size[Existing_NoTitle]
+ Non_acahual_encr[Zone,Existing_Title] * Milpa_size[Existing_Title]))

THEN Non_acahual_encr[Zone,Hhold_type]

ELSE Dummy_avencid[Hhold_type] * INT(Encroachable_Monte
[Zone]/ Milpa_size[Existing_NoTitle])

The number of encroachers in primary forest will be equal to the number of non-*acahual* encroachers, if there is sufficient communal *monte* area; otherwise, much as in the case of encroachment in second growth areas, priority will be given to evicted farmers.

Sharing farm land with existing households ("minifundio")

Field observations suggest that in communities with little remaining encroachable land, households in search of areas for farming tend to establish themselves in spaces already under agricultural production, which is rented (often against payment in kind of labour or crops) or borrowed from friends and relatives. This process, known locally as m*inifundio*, entails an increase in settlement density, and correspondingly a decrease in the average parcel size. The m*inifundio* is a short-term response to land scarcity, based on family and community-based exchange and support mechanisms. The m*inifundio* is unlikely to be sustainable in the medium to long term unless improvements in fertility conservation techniques prevent the decreases of yields per hectare eventually resulting from smaller crop areas and shorter fallow periods.[15] It is assumed that in communities where the average *milpa* size has dropped below critical thresholds,[16] *minifundio* will no longer be a settlement option. Otherwise, all space seekers who did not manage to encroach in communal forest (primary or second growth), will turn into "minifundistas".

Equation box 6.9

Minifundistas[Zone,Hhold_type] =
IF(Non_monte_encr[Zone,Hhold_type] = 0) *THEN 0*
ELSE IF(Avg_Milpa_Size[Zone] < *Minimum_Milpa_Size)*
THEN 0 ELSE Non_monte_encr[Zone,Hhold_type]

Encroachment in communal land outside the community of origin
In cases where encroachment in communal areas is not possible and settlement density is too high, space seekers may turn to other nearby communities to meet their demand for land. Precise modelling of inter-community migration would require a great deal of information on resettlement and transport costs, patterns of relative land fertility and so forth. In the present context, it is assumed that (a) space seekers coming from land units with a land deficit will be evenly distributed across land units with remaining land availability; (b) outsiders will only encroach in *monte* areas; and (c) land sharing (*minifundio*) outside of the community of origin will not take place (it is likely that kin-based support mechanisms will be less common outside the community of origin).

Equation box 6.10

Off_site_encroachers[Zone,Hhold_type] =
IF(Non_minifund[Zone,Hhold_type] =0) *THEN 0*
ELSE IF(Non_minifund[Zone,New] * *Milpa_size[New]* +
Non_minifund[Zone,Existing_NoTitle] * *Milpa_size[Existing_NoTitle]* +
Non_minifund[Zone,Existing_Title] * *Milpa_size[Existing_Title])*<
Total_encr_monte

THEN Non_minifund[Zone,Hhold_type] ELSE
Dummy_avencid[Hhold_type] *
INT(Total_encr_monte/ Milpa_size[Existing_NoTitle])

The demand for encroachment outside the community of residence is given by all those households that have not been able to settle down as minifundistas (and, by implication, who were not able to encroach in communal forested areas). The supply of potential settlement space will be given by the sum of remaining encroachable *monte* areas in all the ZAUs of the study area. If that area is smaller than the dot product of non-minifundistas, times *milpa* sizes, across the different household types, only evicted farmers will be able to encroach in primary forest located outside the community of origin.

Landless households
Where no settlement option is available, households will flow out of the space seekers pool and will add to the stock of landless farmers.[17] These destitute households will only be able to support themselves through temporary employment, and through extraction of natural products from forested areas in the buffer and nucleus zone.

Equation box 6.11

Marginalization[Zone,Hhold_type] = Non_minifund[Zone,Hhold_type] - Off_site_encroachers[Zone,Hhold_type]

A6.1.3   The off-site economy sector

This sector is the market for goods and services not exchanged within the household sector, but rather supplied for external purchase or hiring. In this model there are three main types of transaction between the rural household sector and the rest of the region's economy: (a) the sale of forest products (Chamedor Palm) (b) the sale of livestock products (milk and beef), and (c) and the supply of labour.

However, in order to concentrate the subsequent policy analysis on a limited number of key parameters, the attention will be focused on the last two variables (livestock and labour supply), leaving aside explicit modelling of the Chamedor Palm market[18].

The off-site economy sector is the "gate" through which the national and global economies affect productive activities and natural resource use in the Sierra. As it will be discussed in this section, aggregate production and income in the southern Gulf of Mexico oil district are assumed to determine the demand for products and serviced exported by the Sierra. Output in the oil district is clearly responsive to the overall volume of activity of Mexico's economy, which in turn, in a context of growing integration in the global markets, is affected by the world economy. Based on the objective this research, the linkages between regional, national and global economy, albeit important, will not be addressed here.

Labour markets
The accuracy of modelling labour markets is constrained by the fact that during field work it was possible to collect only a limited amount of information on the urban sector and its labour market.

Households of the study area may supply labour to the off-site economy in two ways: permanent migration and temporary employment. Equilibrium in both markets is achieved through adjustments in the quantities supplied; wages are assumed constant and equal to the marginal products of labour. Let us look at the way demands for temporary and regular labour are determined.

The starting point is the assumption of a simple production function for the aggregate output, Y, of the trade, manufacture, mining and services industries, whereby production is a function of regular labour, L^R, non-regular or unskilled labour, L^{NR}, and capital, K:

$$Y = f(L^R, L^{NR}, K) \qquad (6.2)$$

Data on 1994 employment of regular and non-regular labour and on value of aggregate production was obtained from the Economic Census for that year (INEGI, 1994; INEGI, 1997). The data is available at the municipio level of aggregation; so that information was collected on the four municipalities which provide most of employment opportunities in the region: Acayucan, Coatzacoalcos, Cosoleacaque, and Minatitlan.

For each labour type (regular, non regular), the ratio, y_L , between the value of production Y, and labour input, L, gives the average value of product of that labour type: $y_L = Y/L$. At any point in time, the demand for each labour type is simply the product of the value of output, times the reciprocal of the average value product of labour. For example, assuming a simple exponential growth of income, demand for labour at time t is (r is income's growth rate):

$$L_t = \frac{Y_0 e^{rt}}{y_t^L}$$

(6.3)

The actual value of the demand for labour depends on the assumed behaviour of the average (value) product of labour, which in turn depends on assumptions on technical progress. Assumptions on technical progress are important in the context of the present study area: the various reorganization plans being formulated for the oil district suggest that labour intensity of production in a number of firms of the manufacture and service sectors may decrease, with important consequences for overall employment patterns in the region.

With no technical progress, the average product of labour stays the same, which amounts to dropping the time subscript in (6.3): labour demand always grows (and at a constant rate) when production grows. With technical progress that substitutes the selected labour type with other inputs, the correspondence between increase in production and increase in labour hiring no longer always holds.

One simple way of describing the impact of technical progress on the demand for labour is to express the average (value) product as an exponential function of production increase:

$$y_t^L = y_0^L e^{\rho (Y-Y_0)}$$

(6.4)

where y_0^L is the initial value of the average value product of labour, Y_0 is the initial level of income, and ρ is a rate of growth parameter. If $\rho=0$, there is no technical progress, and the average product of labour is constant along the production's expansion path. If $\rho >0$, the average product of labour for given level of output increases with production. Whether the actual demand for labour will in fact increase depends on whether the "income" effect associated with the increase in production prevails over the "substitution" effect (less labour necessary per any level of output). The two possibilities are addressed in the model's simulation through appropriate choice of the technical change parameters in a scenario analysis (see section 6.2).

Initial values of the demand for labour and average labour product are obtained from INEGI data, as explained in detail in Annex 6.2. The equations for the demand for labour are thus:

Equation box 6.12

Perm_labour_demand = Income/ Avg_labour_product[Perm]

Temp_Labour_demand = Income/ Avg_labour_product[Temp]

The equation(s) for the average value product of labour (which reiterates (6.4)) is:

Equation box 6.13

Avg_labour_product[Labour_type] =
Initial_Avg_labour_product[Labour_type] *
Exp(Change_of_labour_demand[Labour_type] * (Income_billion_N$ -
INIT(Income_billion_N$)))

So much for the demand for labour; let us now turn to the determination of the equilibrium quantities in the two segments of the labour market.

Temporary employment. As discussed in the linear programming model mentioned earlier, a given portion of the total household's time will be supplied in the labour market of the urban sector for temporary employment. The actual amount of the household's labour supplied will respond to the perceived probability of finding employment.

This probability, in turn, will also affect household's decisions concerning agricultural land and natural product extraction: the subsistence constraint will be met by a combination, on the one hand, of use of natural resources obtained from the wild and from agriculture, and, on the other hand, of cash income earned through temporary employment. Higher employment chances will decrease farm land size and natural products extraction. It is assumed that the probability of finding temporary employment is simply the ratio between the demand and the supply for temporary labour:[19]

Equation box 6.14

Employment_chance = Labour_demand/ Max(Temp_labour_supply,
Labour_demand)

The initial stock of temporary workers is increased by the process of temporary job search:

Equation box 6.15

> Temp_labour_supply(t) = Temp_labour_supply(t - dt) +
> (Temp_job_search) * dt

The total temporary job seekers' flow depends on size of the space seekers pool, as well as on the labour supplied by each household. At any time, labour supply decisions are taken on the basis of the previous period's value of the employment chance (which is expected to prevail in the current working season):

Equation box 6.16

> Labour_supply_per_Hhold[Hhold_type] = Delay(Employment_chance, 1)

Total supply of temporary labour is given by the dot product of per household labour supply times the total number of households of various types in the different ZAUs:

Equation box 6.17

> Temp_job_search = ARRAYSUM(Space_Seekers[*,New]) *
> Labour_supply_per_Hhold[New] +
> ARRAYSUM(Space_Seekers[*,Existing_NoTitle]) *
> Labour_supply_per_Hhold[Existing_NoTitle] +
> ARRAYSUM(Space_Seekers[*,Existing_Title]) *
> Labour_supply_per_Hhold[Existing_Title]

Migration and regular employment.
In this model, migration simply responds to excess demand for regular labour. Given a "labour gap" between the demand for permanent labour and the stock of regularly employed workers:

Equation box 6.18

> Perm_labour_gap = Perm_labour_demand - Regularly_employed

total migration will cover the employment gap; the distribution of migration across the different ZAUs will be proportional to each ZAU's share in the total space seekers pool:

Equation box 6.19

Migration[Zone,Hhold_type] = INT(Perm_labour_gap *
Space_Seekers[Zone,Hhold_type] / Max(1, Total_space_seekers))

Demand for livestock products

As discussed in the literature (Toledo, 1992; Barbier & Burgess, 1996), the expansion of cattle ranching activities depends on a variety of factors, including local, national and international demand for meat and dairy products, relative prices, public policies, and availability of suitable pasture land.

In the study area livestock development, widely encouraged by proactive public policies, has been one of the main driving forces of social change and natural habitat modification in the region. Most of the public programs supporting cattle ranching have been discontinued in the late 1990s; the future of ranching in the region is therefore likely to depend mainly on relative output and input prices, and patterns of demand.

On the unit margin front, prospects may improve because of the devaluation-induced increased competitiveness of the region's low-input ranching system. More uncertainty is associated with the evolution of demand in presence of stagnating or falling production (and hence income) in Mexico's economy, and in particular in Veracruz oil district. The present analysis therefore focuses on the impact of income (via demand for livestock products) on cattle ranching activities.

It is assumed that cattle herds adjust to variation in demand for livestock products.[20] In the absence of detailed information on the demand for individual products (milk, meat from various beef types, etc.), we have to use the number of heads of cattle as the actual dependent variable in the demand function. This may not be an implausible first order approximation: if the demand for meat or milk increases, there will need to be more animals to be milked or slaughtered.

Given the nature of the data collected during the field work of this research, it was not possible to estimate the demand for cattle numbers directly. Rather, it was assumed that, based on an underlying demand function in prices and income, cattle numbers adjust to changes in income via an elasticity coefficient. An initial value for this coefficient was borrowed from the Mexico study of Barbier and Burgess (Barbier & Burgess, 1996). Based on cross-country regressions estimated on state-level data, these authors find that a 1% increase in income generates a 0.09% increase in cattle numbers.[21] At the beginning of the simulation, there is a stock of cattle in the study area, which reflects previous patterns of demand for livestock products. Increase in demand for cattle in excess of the existing stock is given by the livestock demand's income elasticity, times the increase in income:

Equation box 6.20

Increase_Cattle_Demand = INT(Elasticity_cattle_demand*
DERIVN(Income_billion_N\$, 1) * Demand_for_Cattle/
Income_billion_N\$)

When the demand for cattle numbers increases, herd sizes in the different ZAUs are adjusted in proportion to their relative share in the regions' total herd size.

Equation box 6.21

Cattle_Expansion[Zone] = IF(Increase_Cattle_Demand >0) THEN
INT((Demand_for_Cattle-Total_Cattle) * Cattle[Zone]/Total_Cattle) ELSE
0

A6.1.4   The land use sector

This sector of the model studies the variation over time of a selected number of stocks of land uses: primary forest or *monte*, secondary forest or *acahual*, farm land or *milpa*, and pasture. In addition, it also examines the impact of human activities on the stock of a resource extracted from forested areas, Chamedor Palm.

Land conversion to agriculture
Based on the number of encroachers determined in the land tenure sector of the model, in any given zone conversion of *acahual* to *milpa* is given by:

Equation box 6.22

Conversion_Acahual_to_Milpa[Zone] =
IF(Encroachable_Acahual[Zone]>0) THEN
(Encroachers_Acahual[Zone,New] * Milpa_size[New] +
Encroachers_Acahual[Zone,Existing_NoTitle] *
Milpa_size[Existing_NoTitle] +
Encroachers_Acahual[Zone,Existing_Title] * Milpa_size[Existing_Title])
ELSE 0

That is, subject to space availability, conversion is equal to the dot product of the number of encroachers times the size of *milpa* area (as determined in the linear programming model referred to earlier) across the different household types. The same dot product applies to the conversion of primary forest to farm areas, which, as indicated in the tenure sector of the model, does not start before all encroachable areas under secondary vegetation have been cleared:

Equation box 6.23

Conversion_Monte_to_Milpa[Zone] = Encroachers_Monte[Zone,New] *
Milpa_size[New] + Encroachers_Monte[Zone,Existing_NoTitle] *
Milpa_size[Existing_NoTitle] + Encroachers_Monte[Zone,Existing_Title]
* Milpa_size[Existing_Title]

In addition to conversion carried out by community residents, primary forest areas may also be cleared by space seekers coming from other communities:

Equation box 6.24

Off_site_monte_conversion[Zone] = IF(Encroachable_Monte[Zone] -
Conversion_Monte_to_Milpa[Zone] >
ARRAYSUM(Milpa_needed_off_site[*]) * Perc_tot_encr_monte[Zone])

THEN ARRAYSUM(Milpa_needed_off_site[*]) *
Perc_tot_encr_monte[Zone] ELSE 0

Equation box 6.24 indicates that in any community, provided that even after local encroachment, there are still areas of primary forest available for outsiders, total demand for off-site *milpa* will translate into conversion in proportion to the community's share of total remaining forest. Demand for off-site *milpa*, in turn, will again be given by the dot product of off site encroachers times the size of *milpa* area across the different household types:

Equation box 6.25

Milpa_needed_off_site[Zone] = Off_site_encroachers[Zone,New] *
Milpa_size[New] + Off_site_encroachers[Zone,Existing_NoTitle] *
Milpa_size[Existing_NoTitle] + Off_site_encroachers[Zone,Existing_Title]
* Milpa_size[Existing_Title]

Pasture

Pasture is the largest use of land in the study area. Historical and current processes of land conversion to pasture are the result of a complex interplay of policy, tenure, social and technology factors, some of which have been studied in detail elsewhere in the literature on the region (Buckles, 1987; Chevallier and Buckles, 1995; Lazos, 1995). The analysis of the process provided by the rest of this subsection (and complemented by Annex 6.4) is a simplified one.

On the basis of the linear programming model of Chapter 5, households without tenure are unlikely to convert communal forested land for pasture; therefore, the present model focuses on ranches already established in private land. Inflows to the pasture stock come from (young and mature) a*cahual* lands, and both on-site and off-site conversion of m*onte*; outflows are related to the process of pasture abandonment.

Equation box 6.26

Pasture[Zone,Land_Type](t) = Pasture[Zone,Land_Type](t - dt)+
(Conversion_acahual_to_pasture[Zone,Land_Type] +
Conversion_Monte_to_Pasture[Zone,Land_Type] +
Conversion_off_site_monte_pasture[Zone,Land_Type] +
Conversion_Young_Acahual_pasture[Zone,Land_Type] -
Pasture_abandoning[Zone,Land_Type])*dt

Conversion of land from other uses to pasture may take place either to support a fixed herd when overgrazing leads to declining productivity in existing grazing lands, or to enable herd expansion. This model addresses both sources of demand for additional pasture land. At any point in time, conversion to pasture is given by the sum of pasture to be replenished following abandonment of overgrazed land, and of new pasture required to meet increase in the demand for cattle numbers (determined, as explained in section A6.1.3, in the off-site economy sector):

Equation box 6.27

Demand_for_pasture[Zone,Land_Type] =
Dummy_Private_space[Land_Type] * ((1 -
Percent_Undergrazed[Zone,Land_Type]) * Cattle_Expansion[Zone] /
SR_Max[Zone,Land_Type] + Pasture_abandoning[Zone,Land_Type])

Equation box 6.27 says that not all of the increased demand for cattle is met by pasture increase. In under-grazed lands, herds increase by simply increasing the stocking rate (heads of cattle per hectare).[22] Conversely, in overgrazed areas, conversion to pasture will be given by the ZAU's share in herd expansion divided by the going stocking rate.[23] Pasture expansion will typically take place in the first instance in areas already cleared for use. Depending on how far in the past conversion took place, those areas will be at different stages in the process of vegetation re-growth. For simplicity, the two stages of "young" and "mature" *acahual* will be considered here (see Annex 6.4 for details). The first option for meeting the demand for pasture is conversion of young *acahual*. In particular, there will be a fraction of young *acahual* that is converted to pasture:

Equation box 6.28

Conversion_Young_Acahual_pasture[Zone,Land_Type] = LEAKAGE
OUTFLOW; LEAKAGE FRACTION = Min(1,
(Demand_for_pasture[Zone,Land_Type]/ Max(1,
Young_Acahual[Zone,Land_Type])))

The fraction is given by the ratio between the demand for pasture and the stock of young *acahual*, if this is less than one; if the fraction is larger than one, then all the existing stock will be converted to pasture, and the difference will be made up for by the existing mature *acahual*:

Equation box 6.29

Conversion_acahual_to_pasture[Zone,Land_Type] =
IF(Acahual[Zone,Private]>0) then
(Demand_for_pasture[Zone,Land_Type] -
Conversion_Young_Acahual_pasture[Zone,Land_Type]) else 0

If the demand for replenishment or new pasture can not be met by conversion of *acahual* areas, conversion of primary forest takes place:

Equation box 6.30

Conversion_Monte_to_Pasture[Zone,Land_Type] =
Demand_for_pasture[Zone,Land_Type] -
(Conversion_acahual_to_pasture[Zone,Land_Type] +
Conversion_Young_Acahual_pasture[Zone,Land_Type])

If there is still an excess demand because all accessible land has been cleared in communities with herds in excess of going stocking rates, the deficit may be met by converting forested land in neighbouring communities, and renting the resulting pasture to the ranchers of the deforested communities. Conversion in communities with remaining forest will take place by distributing the pasture deficit in proportion to the community's share in total *monte*:

Equation box 6.31

Conversion_off_site_monte_pasture[Zone,Land_Type] =
*Dummy_Private_space[Land_Type] ***
ARRAYSUM(Pasture_deficit[,Private]) ***
Monte[Zone,Private]/(Max(1,Total_private_Monte))

Forest extraction
Settlers in the various zoning units extract a variety of products from forested areas; however, only Chamedor Palm's extraction will be modelled here.

On the basis of the recorded altitudinal distribution of extracted species, Palm populations are likely to be found in parts of the total area under primary forest in the core and buffer zones (approximately 50% of it).

Accretions to the stock of Palm are given by the process of generation. For simplicity, a simple logistic growth process is assumed here, whereby the stock grows at a given rate per annum, up to the attainment of the habitat's carrying capacity.

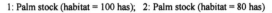

1: Palm stock (habitat = 100 has); 2: Palm stock (habitat = 80 has)

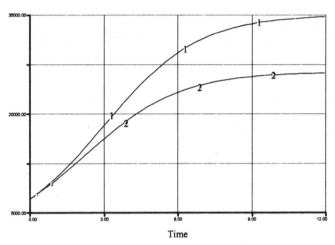

Time

Figure 6.11   Logistic growth of palm stock when the habitat shrinks

Once this level is reached, and in the absence of other perturbations, the population stabilizes. Carrying capacity is pragmatically determined by multiplying the observed density of plants per hectare, times the area of the habitat suitable for the species. As the latter decreases over time because of land conversion, the shape of the logistic growth function shifts downwards over time as well, as illustrated in Figure 6.11. The diagram assumes a density of 350 *gruesas* per ha, and a habitat of 100 has in the case of the upper curve, and of 80 has in the case of the lower curve. The equation for the process of Palm generation is thus:

Equation box 6.32

> *Palm_generation[Zone]* = *Palm_presence_per_zone[Zone]* *
> *Palm_stock[Zone]* * *Rate_of_Palm_generation[Zone]* * *(1 -*
> *(Palm_stock[Zone] / (1-Palm_presence_per_zone[Zone]* +
> *Habitat_carrying_cap[Zone])))*[24]

In each zone, a given percentage[25] of the various household types will be carrying out extraction activities. Extraction intensity figures (i.e. *gruesas* per household per annum) are based on the estimates of the linear programming model of Chapter 5. These, in turn, are sensitive to employment opportunities off site: the better the chance of temporary employment in the oil district, the lower the extraction of Palm from the wild.

Extraction takes place mostly under condition of open access; to capture this feature, it is assumed that extraction activities will be distributed across the different ZAUs in proportion to the relative availability of Palm (proxied by the ZAU's relative share of total Palm's habitat):

Equation box 6.33

> *Palm_extraction[Zone]* = *ARRAYSUM(Extraction_per_zone[*])* *
> *Relative_Palm_Habitat[Zone]*

Extraction per zone, in turn, is given by the usual dot product of extraction across household types:

Equation box 6.34

> *Extraction_per_zone[Zone]* = *Extractors[Zone,New]* *
> *Palm_per_Hhold[New]* + *Extractors[Zone,Existing_NoTitle]* *
> *Palm_per_Hhold[Existing_NoTitle]* + *Extractors[Zone,Existing_Title]* *
> *Palm_per_Hhold[Existing_Title]*

Extractors come from the settlers and landless farmers stocks:

Equation box 6.35

> *Extractors[Zone,Hhold_type]* = *INT((Landless_Hholds[Zone,Hhold_type]*
> + *Settlers[Zone,Hhold_type]) * Percent_gatherers[Hhold_type])*

ANNEX 6.2   ESTIMATING THE DEMAND FOR TEMPORARY WORK

The approach summarised by equations (6.3) and (6.4) (on page 215) can be applied in a straightforward way to labour regularly employed, by simply using census data on the number of regular workers as the denominator of y^L. The problem with non-regular labour is that the number of workers is not a good indicator of actual input to production, as the actual time of work of a temporary employee varies widely across individuals, time of the year, and production sector.

A better indicator is the *number of days* of temporary work employed in production.[26] No data of this nature was available in the 1994 Economic Census; therefore, a broad order of magnitude for total days of non-regular work employed in production was estimated on the basis of information from the 1990 General Census of Population and Housing (INEGI, 1991; INEGI, 1997).

The 1990 Census provides a breakdown, in classes of hours worked per week, of total employment in the municipalities under investigation. Assuming that services provided under temporary work arrangements do not exceed one third of a standard working week of 48 hours, only the classes 0 to 8, and 9 to 16 hours per week were considered. The mid point of these classes times total working weeks per year (43) divided by working hours per day (8) gives, for each class, average days worked per year.

The weighted average of days worked per year, with weights given by the share of workers in the total of the two classes of temporary employment, gives a figure of 43 days of work per year per temporary or non-regular worker. Multiplying this number by the 1994 Economic Census figure on total non-regular workers, we obtain an estimate of total number of days of temporary work in the trade, manufacture, mining and services industries sectors of the four municipalities considered as sources of temporary non-farm employment.

ANNEX 6.3   THE INCOME ELASTICITY OF CATTLE NUMBER DEMAND

It is assumed that livestock products and hence cattle numbers are superior goods, and hence their elasticity grows with income. However, it is not plausible that consumption of livestock products increases without limits as income grows. One way to avoid this result is to assume that the share of livestock products in the food budget (or in the overall budget) grows initially, but then levels off to a plateau, representing a "wealthy-status" level of meat and dairy products consumption. Using a simple logistic growth function, the income elasticity η of cattle numbers must obey the following differential equation:

$$\frac{d\eta}{dY} = r\eta(Y)\left(1 - \frac{\eta(Y)}{K}\right); \quad \eta(Y_0) = \eta_0 \tag{6.5}$$

where r is the elasticity growth rate, K is the ceiling, or maximum level of elasticity, and Y is income, measured by the value of total output of the trade, manufacture, mining and services industries in the four major municipalities of the region. The initial condition imposes that at the beginning-of-simulation level of income, elasticity is equal to its postulated initial value, η_0, borrowed from Barbier and Burgess (1996). The solution to (6.5), which is the expression for the elasticity used in the model, is:

$$\eta_t = \frac{e^{rY_t} K\eta_0}{e^{rY_0} K + e^{rY_t}\eta_0 - e^{rY_0}\eta_0} \tag{6.6}$$

The model uses a value of the maximum elasticity equal to three times the initial value; the rate of growth varies parametrically for use in scenario analysis, as discussed in section 6.2.

ANNEX 6.4   PASTURE ROTATION

As graphically illustrated in Chapter 2, pasture-driven frontier expansion and resulting deforestation are often explained in terms of nutrient mining: as nutrients decrease due to overgrazing, it is cheaper to convert new land to pasture than to invest in maintaining the productivity of existing pasture (for the case of Brazil, see Schneider, 1995). However, as better quality land becomes scarcer, and/or property rights on land become better defined, ranchers may also consider pasture rotation schemes as a management option complementary to land clearance.

Figure 6.12 depicts the basic approach used in this model to address this possibility. If there is insufficient investment in management, a certain proportion of pasture is overgrazed and then abandoned. As time goes by, second growth vegetation will start to form on idle pasture, and nutrients will start to be stored.

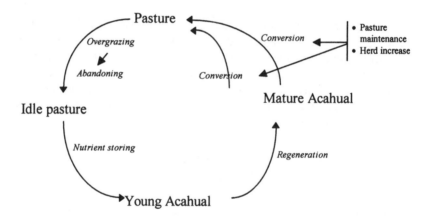

Figure 6.12   Pasture cycle

After some time (2 to 4 years), idle pasture will turn into young *acahual*; as the process of vegetation succession continues, woody species will tend to predominate over grassy ones, and young *acahual* will turn into mature *acahual* (after a period of say 5 to 10 years from the original pasture abandonment).

Both young and mature *acahual* may be reconverted to pasture.[27] Conversion is motivated both by the need for replacing abandoned pasture, so that existing herds can be supported, and by the need for increasing herd size, when demand for livestock products increases.

If the demand for livestock products is constant or grows slowly, if overgrazing time is long, and if nutrient storing and vegetation regeneration time is short, the system could be in dynamic equilibrium: pasture and *acahual* land fluctuate around steady state values. However, in the presence of growing demand for livestock, short overgrazing time, and long regeneration time, *acahual* tends to be depleted, and the pasture deficit will be met by conversion of primary forest.

In this model, the dynamics of pasture conversion and abandonment decisions revolves around variation in stocking rates (heads of cattle per hectare). For given cattle rearing and pasture management technology, there will be an optimal level of the stocking rate, s^*, which will vary across lands of different quality, slope, precipitation, and so forth. Ranches with rates below s^* are under-grazed, while ranches with rates in excess of s^* are overgrazed.[28]

The former have the potential of increasing herds without decreasing productivity, whereas in the latter nutrient exhaustion is bound to occur. The larger the stock of overgrazed pasture relative to under-grazed, the larger the need for converting land under vegetation cover, both for meeting increases in the demand for cattle numbers, and for replacing pasture eventually abandoned when nutrients are exhausted.

It then becomes important to estimate the percentage of overgrazed stock, and to determine its variation over time. For reasons of computation simplicity, it is assumed that stocking rates are distributed uniformly between a minimum and a maximum value: see Figure 6.13 for a graphical illustration.

The minimum value is constant, and equal to the minimum value obtained in the survey sample (0.15). The maximum varies over time, and is calculated using the expression of the average stocking rate $\bar{s}$, under the assumption of uniform distribution: $s_{max} = 2\,\bar{s} - s_{min}$

As shown in Figure 6.13, the percentage of under-grazed pasture is the area, under the distribution of stocking rate, to the left of the carrying capacity s^*, and is given by:

$$P_{under} = \frac{s^* - s_{min}}{s_{max} - s_{min}} \tag{6.7}$$

so that the percentage of overgrazed pasture is 1 - p_{under}. If more cattle are purchased than pasture can support, nutrient exhaustion does not occur immediately, but after a given period of time, T_e (or *Nutr_exhuast_time* in the model's terminology).

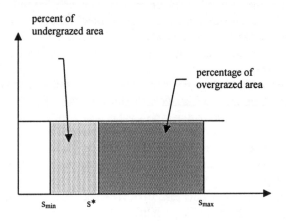

Figure 6.13   Distribution of stocking rates

Assuming that overgrazed pasture lands are distributed uniformly also across the range of times preceding exhaustion (0 - T_e), for every level of overgrazing maturity, overgrazed land will be:

Equation box 6.36

> *Overgrazing[Zone,Land_Type] = (1 -*
> *Percent_Undergrazed[Zone,Private]) * (Pasture[Zone,Private] -*
> *Idle_Pasture[Zone,Private]) / Nutr_exhaust_time*

The overgrazing flow adds to the stock of overgrazed land:

Equation box 6.37

> *Overgrazed_Pasture[Zone,Private](t) =*
> *Overgrazed_Pasture[Zone,Private](t - dt) + (Overgrazing[Zone,Private] -*
> *Pasture_depletion[Zone,Private]) * dt*

After T_e years, overgrazed land is depleted of nutrients and abandoned. Abandoned land flows in the Idle Pasture reservoir:

Equation box 6.38

> Idle_Pasture[Zone,Land_Type](t) = Idle_Pasture[Zone,Land_Type](t - dt)
> + (Abandoning[Zone,Land_Type] - Initial_succession[Zone,Land_Type])
> * dt

The earlier stage of the succession process (*Initial_succession*) lasts a certain number of years (*Nutrient_storing_time*), after which idle land turns into young *acahual*:

Equation box 6.39

> Young_Acahual[Zone,Land_Type](t) =
> Young_Acahual[Zone,Land_Type](t - dt) +
> (Initial_succession[Zone,Land_Type] -
> Acahual_regeneration[Zone,Land_Type] -
> Conversion_Young_Acahual_pasture[Zone,Land_Type]) * dt

Land flows out of this stock either through formation of mature *acahual* (after a regeneration time T_r, *Acahual_regeneration_time* in the model's terminology), or via conversion to pasture. In particular, there will be a fraction of young *acahual* that is converted to pasture:

Equation box 6.40

> Conversion_Young_Acahual_pasture[Zone,Land_Type] = LEAKAGE
> OUTFLOW; LEAKAGE FRACTION = Min(1,
> (Demand_for_pasture[Zone,Land_Type]/ Max(1,
> Young_Acahual[Zone,Land_Type])))

The fraction is given by the ratio between the demand for pasture and the stock of young *acahual*, if this is less than one; if it is larger than one, all the existing stock will be converted to pasture, and the difference will be made up for by the existing mature *acahual*:

Equation box 6.41

Conversion_acahual_to_pasture[Zone,Land_Type] =
IF(Acahual[Zone,Private]>0) then
(Demand_for_pasture[Zone,Land_Type] -
Conversion_Young_Acahual_pasture[Zone,Land_Type]) else 0

NOTES

1. Equations are reported directly in the format generated by the *Stella* software: variable names are the same, descriptive ones, used in the diagramming layer of the software (the source of Figure 6.2). Because of their array nature, several variables are in the form *Variable[Zone, Hhold_type]*; quantity appearing in square brackets are not arguments, but rather equivalents to subscripts denoting variation across dimensions. In more standard notation, the same expression would be *Variable$_{ij}$* , meaning value of the *variable* for zone i and household type j.
2. The simulation is carried out over a 20 year period, even though in some of the graphs included in the chapter, it ends after 18 or 15 years, as the relevant variables stabilise to their terminal values before the final simulation time. Initial values are set 1996 levels, i.e. right after data collection was completed in the study area.
3. See the discussion on "*avecindados*" in Chapter 4.
4. It is assumed that the adjustments in cattle numbers and thus pasture follow a short-term increase in price of livestock products caused, for given herd sizes, by higher demand.
5. Three separate agroforestry models are analysed, which can be applied to the different agro-ecological conditions of the buffer and influence zones of the study area. The models compare a "without", and "with" project situation, where the "without" is an average cropping pattern of a prototypical farm, and the "with" situation entails changes in the production technology and in the cropping pattern that entail lower conversion of forested land and lower extraction of forest products.
6. This was defined in section A6.1.2 as the threshold value for the continuation of the *minifundio* process; once the average farm size falls below the threshold level, households on existing farm land can no longer share it with landless farmers.
7. The very large values obtained in the last three scenarios are due to the fact that utility in the no-policy case (the denominator of the ratio) is close to zero for those scenarios.
8. Despite the practical difficulties in defining concepts such as "pristine" or "undisturbed" since human presence is almost ubiquitous across the world, it seems uncontroversial that the vast majority of land in the planet is subject to

some form of human intervention: for example, according to McNeely, Gadgil et al. (1995), only some 27% of the total land area is "undisturbed" (excluding rocks, ice and barren areas).

9. An important type of financing mechanism is represented by conservation trust funds. These consist of a capital endowment financing conservation activities either for a limited period of time (through the gradual "sinking" of the capital), or in perpetuity, by using the interests generated by the capital. Conservation funds are being increasingly established in various countries of the world (often with seed funds provided by the Global Environment Facility); in the Latin America region there are funds, among others, in Brazil, Bolivia, Peru, Mexico. For a discussion on financing instruments for biodiversity in general see Bayon, Lovink and Veening (2000); on conservation trust funds see GEF (1999). A very recent (end of 2000) experiment in developing countries to use trust funds as a source for compensating land owners for the foregone benefits of resource use is the Monarch Butterfly fund in Mexico. Using the annual returns to the fund's \$5 million donations capital, it purports to compensate holders of timber extraction permits for non-use.

10. In several of the equations specified in the model, "dummy" variables are used. These have in general the purpose of limiting the impact of given processes of change to selected components of arrayed variables. For example, the quantity *Dummy_New_Hholds[Hhold_type]* in Equation box 6.4, has the purpose of activating the household formation process only in the "New" component of the Household Type array.

11. In their study of deforestation in Mexico, Barbier and Burgess (1996) observe that a critical determinant of deforestation is the choice of whether to increase production in land already converted (previously cultivated and currently idle), or in "frontier" land. They argue that much of the forest loss is due to the fact that policies have been inducing farmers to prefer the second to the first option. In the present model, the choice of "frontier land" is not directly affected by policies, but is a result of the "space seekers" not having access to credit, and hence to land, markets.

12. Note that this is not necessarily a "space-efficient" allocation rule. A more efficient rule may be to allocate land across different user groups in a way that minimises the total space requirement of those who have to be excluded from the allocation.

13. Encroachment is likely to take place in land which has not yet been parcelled, as well as in private or parcelled land where topographical conditions make monitoring difficult. The percentages of encroachable land for the various zoning and administrative units of the region used in the present analysis are based on survey evidence of the communal land parcelling process.

14. In each ZAU, total space needed for *milpa* use is given by the dot product of space-seekers times *milpa* size across the different household types.

15. See Buckles and Erenstein (1996) for a discussion of causes of, and remedies for, the declining productivity of maize-based systems in the region.
16. For heuristic purposes, the numerical value of this minimum average *milpa* size threshold has been set at 2 has.
17. Initial values for this stock are taken from table 4.7, column "totally landless".
18. Constant farm-gate prices for Chamedor Palm will be assumed, on the grounds that (a) most of the sales are for exports outside the region, and in part outside the country, so that regional policy makers are unlikely to be able to exercise control on Palm's price; (b) the Sierra is a small producer, and hence unable to affect Palm prices.
19. In order for this ratio not to exceed one, the actual expression used in the model is: probability of employment = l_d / Max (l_d, l_s), where the subscripts refer to labour demand and supply, respectively.
20. See endnote 4. on the adjustment in cattle numbers and pasture.
21. However, it is plausible that, as income grows, the weight of meat consumption in the average diet increases. If this is the case, the income elasticity of cattle numbers will not be constant, but rather positively correlated with income. As explained in Annex 6.3, the model assumes a logistic growth of the elasticity of cattle numbers, from an initial to a ceiling level.
22. The division of pasture in over- and under-grazed land, and the process of regeneration of young and mature *acahual* are both explained in Annex 6.4.
23. The stocking rate used for determining conversion is the maximum, over a range of possible values prevailing in each ZAU: newly converted land is likely to be initially rich in nutrients, and thus able to a support relatively large number of animals. Additional details on the estimation of stocking rate ranges are provided in Annex 6.4.
24. In a standard logistic growth function, the term in the last denominator would normally be: *Habitat_carrying_cap*[*Zone*]; the term actually used (1- *Palm_presence_per_zone*[*Zone*] + *Habitat_carrying_cap*[*Zone*]) has the purpose of avoiding division by zero in the ZAUs with no recorded presence of Palm populations.
25. Based on field evidence, it is estimated that this percentage is 6.5% and 2% for the buffer and influence zone, respectively.
26. Days of work is also the unit of measurement of labour allocation decisions in the linear programming model of Chapter 5.
27. It is plausible that land with better conditions of accessibility will be reconverted first, so that mature *acahual* will be found in worst location areas.
28. Based on field evidence and existing literature (including the FAO report on livestock carried out in the context of the development of the GEF-PSSM study (Cervigni and Ramirez, 1997), an educated guess for "carrying capacity" stocking rate is of 0.75 and 1 heads/ha for the buffer and influence zone, respectively.

References

Aboumrad, G. (1993) *Oil Prices and the Real Business Cycle: The Case of Mexico*, Ph.D. dissertation, Duke University, Unknown.

Abramovitz, J. N. (1991), *Investing in biological diversity: U.S. research and conservation efforts in developing countries*, Washington, D.C: World Resources Institute.

Acosta-Perez, R., and Vazquez Torres, M. (1990) 'Análisis estructural del componente arbóreo de una hectárea de Selva alta perennifolía en la Sierra de Santa Martha' *Resumenes Soc. Bot. de México: XI Congreso Mexicano de Botánica.*

Adger, W. N., Brown, K., Cervigni, R. and Moran, D. (1995), 'Total economic value of forests in Mexico', *Ambio,* **24** (5), 286-296.

Aguilar-Ortiz, F. (1982). 'Estudio ecologico de las aves del cafetal', in E. Jimenez Avila, and A. Gomez Pompa (editors), *Estudios ecologicos en el agroecosistema* (INIREB)' Mexico DF: Compañia editorial continental.

Albers, H. J. (1992) *Economics of tropical forest management: uncertainty, irreversibility, and spatial relationships,* Ph.D. thesis, University of California, Berkeley

Albers, H. J. (1996), 'Modeling Ecological Constraints on Tropical Forest Management: Spatial Interdependence, Irreversibility, and Uncertainty', *Journal of Environmental Economics and Management,* **30** (1), 73-94.

Albers, H. J., Fisher, A. C. and Hanemann, W. M. (1996), 'Valuation and management of tropical forests: implications of uncertainty and irreversibility', *Environmental and Resource Economics,* **8,** 39-61.

Alcorn, J. B., and Toledo, V. M. (1995) The role of tenurial shells in ecological sustainability: property rights and natural resource management in Mexico prepared for the Property Rights and Performance of Natural Resource Systems program of the Beijer International Institute of Ecological Economics.

Allegretti, M. H., Hansen, S., Soberon, J., Salleh, M., Schei, P., and Seyani, J. (1996) Implementation of the Biodiversity Convention: the Ecosystem Approach As a Strategy to Achieve Sustainability in the Use of Biodiversity. Draft: STAP.

Aluja, A. G., and McDowell, R. E. (1984), *Decision making by livestock/ crop small holders in the state of Veracruz, Mexico,* Ithaca, N.Y.: Dept. of Animal Science, New York State College of Agriculture and Life Sciences.

Alvarez Del Castillo, G. C. (1976), *Estudio Ecológico y Florístico del cráter del Volcán San Martin Tuxtla, Veracruz, México,* Tesis Biólogo, Facultad de Ciencias, UNAM, Mexico.

Anderson, D. (1987), *The economics of afforestation : a case study in Africa,* Baltimore: published for the World Bank by Johns Hopkins University Press.

Andrle, R. F. (1964), *A biogeographical investigation of the Sierra de Tuxtla in Veracruz, Mexico,* Ph.D. dissertation, Lousiana State University.

Andrle, R. F. (1966), 'North American migrants in the Sierra de Tuxtla of southern Veracruz, Mexico', *The Condor,* **68,** 177-184.

Andrle, R. F. (1967), 'Birds of the Sierra de Tuxtla in Veracruz, Mexico', *The Wilson Bull* **79** (2), 163-187.

Antonovic, J. (1990), 'Genetically based measures of uniqueness', in G. H. Orians, G. M. Brown, W. E. Kunin, and J. E. Swierzinbinski (editors), *The Preservation and Valuation of Genetic Resources* (pp. 94-118), Seattle: University of Washington Press.

Arellano, J. (1985), *Una investigación sobre el conocimiento etnoecológico entre comunidades indigenas del sur de México,* Tesis Biólogo, Fac de Ciencias, UNAM, Mexico.

Arrow, K. (1968), 'Optimal capital policy with irreversible investment', in J. N. Wolfe (editor), *Value, capital and growth* (pp. 1-20), Chicago.

Arrow, K., Bolin, B., Costanza, R., Dasgupta, P., Folke, C., Holling, C. S., Jansson, S., Levin, S., Mäler, K. G., Perrings, C. and Pimentel, D. (1995), 'Economic growth, carrying capacity and the environment', *Ecological Economics,* **15** (2), 91-95.

Arrow, K. and Fisher, A. C. (1974), 'Environmental Preservation, Uncertainty and Irreversibility', *Quarterly Journal of Economics,* **88,** 312-319.

Bailey, R. G. and Hogg, H. C. (1986), 'A world ecoregions map for resource partitioning', *Environmental Conservation,* **13,** 195-202.

Banerjee, A. (1995), *Rehabilitation of degraded forests in Asia,* World Bank technical paper 270, Washington DC: World Bank.

Barbault, R., and Sastrapradja, S. D. (1995), 'Generation, maintenance and loss of biodiversity', in V. H. Heywood (editor), *Global biodiversity assessment,* Cambridge: Cambridge University Press.

Barbier, E. (1994), 'Tropical wetlands values and environmental functions', in C. Perrings, K. G. Mäler, C. Folke, C. S. Holling, and B. O. Jansson (editors),

Biodiversity Conservation: Policy Issues and Options, Amsterdam: Kluwer Academic Press.

Barbier, E. and Burgess, J. C. (1996), 'Economic Analysis of Deforestation in Mexico', *Environment and Development Economics,* **1** (2), 203-39.

Barbier, E., Burgess, J. C., and Folke, C. (1994), *Paradise lost? The ecological economics of biodiversity,* London: Earthscan.

Barnett, D., Blake, B. and McCarl, B. A. (1982), 'Goal Programming via Multidimensional Scaling Applied to Senegalese Subsistence Farming', *American Journal of Agricultural Economics,* **64** (4), 720-727.

Barnum, H., and Squire, L. (1979), *A model of an agricultural household: theory and evidence,* Baltimore: Johns Hopkins University Press.

Barrett, S. (1990), 'The Problem of Global Environmental Protection', *Oxford Review of Economic Policy,* **6** (1), 68-79.

Barrett, S. (1991), 'Economic Analysis of International Environmental Agreements. Lessons for a Global Warming Treaty', in OECD (edited by), *Responding to Climate Change: Selected Economic Issues,* Paris: OECD.

Barrett, S. (1994), 'The Biodiversity Supergame', *Environmental and Resource Economics,* **4** (1), 111.

Barrios, M. S. (1982), *Aspectos biológicos de Pripomorpha oleaginea Lichtenstein (AVES: Tyrannidae) en el área de Santa Marta, Los Tuxtlas, Veracruz, México,* Tesis Biólogo, Facultad de Ciencias UNAM, Mexico.

Bayon, R. Lovink, J. S, and Veening, W.J. (2000), 'Financing Biodiversity Conservation' Washington D.C.: Inter-American Development Bank.

Becker, H. (1990), 'Labor input decisions of subsistence farm households in southern Malawi', *Journal of Agricultural Economics,* **41,** 162-171.

Behrens, C. (1994), 'Recent Advances in the Regional Analysis of Indigenous Land Use and Tropical Deforestation: Introduction', *Human Ecology,* **22** (3), 243.

Berry, R. A., and Soligo, R. (1992), 'Rural-Urban Migration, Agricultural Output, and the Supply Price of Labour in a Labour-Surplus Economy', in D. Lal (editor), *Development economics* (Vol. 1). Aldershot, Hants, England: Elgar.

Bierregaard, R. O. Jr., Lovejoy, T. E., Kapos, V., Dos Santos, A. A. and Hutchings, R. W. (1992), 'The Biological Dynamics of Tropical Rainforest Fragments', *BioScience,* **42** (11).

Bisby, F. A., Coddington, J., Thorpe, J. P., Smartt, J., Hengeveld, R., Edwards, P. J., and Duffield, S. J. (1995), 'Characterization of biodiversity', in V. H. Heywood, and R. L. Watson (editors), *Global biodiversity assessment,* Cambridge; New York: Cambridge University Press.

Bishop, R. (1978), 'Endangered species and uncertainty: the economics of a safe minimum standard', *American Journal of Agricultural Economics,* **60,** 10-13.

Blakie, P. and Jeanrenaud, S. (1996), *Biodiversity and human welfare*, Discussion paper 72, Geneva, Switzerland: United Nations Research Institute for Social Development.

Bluffstone, R. A. (1995), 'The Effect of Labor Market Performance on Deforestation in Developing Countries under Open Access: An Example from Rural Nepal', *Journal of Environmental Economics and Management*, **29** (1), 42-63.

Bongers, F., Popma, J., Meave del Castillo, J. and Carabias, J. (1988), 'Structure and floristic composition of the lowland rain forest of Los Tuxtlas, Mexico', *Vegetatio*, (74), 55-80.

Boussard, J.-M. and Petit, M. (1967), 'Representation of farmer behavior under uncertainty with a focus loss constraint', *Journal of Farm Economics*, **49**, 869-80.

Bouzaher, A. and Mendoza, G. A. (1987), 'Goal Programming: Potential and Limitations for Agricultural Economics', *Canadian Journal of Agricultural Economics*, **35** (1), 89-107.

Brindis, Y., Buckles, D., Cervigni, R., Erenstein, O., Gutiérrez, R., Ledesma, M., Lozada, M.P., Paré, L., Ramírez, F., Ramos, M., and Velázquez H., E. (1997), *Sustainable development and biodiversity conservation: a case study in the Sierra de Santa Marta, Veracruz, Mexico* PRINCE-GEF, Washington DC.

Browder, J. O. (1989), 'Development alternatives for tropical rainforests', in H. J. Leonard (editor), *Environment and the poor: development strategies for a common agenda* New Brunswick, NJ: Transaction Books.

Brown, K. S., and Brown, G. G. (1992), 'Habitat alteration and species loss in Brazilian Forest', in T. C. Whitmore, and J. A. Sayer (editors), *Tropical deforestation and species extinction*. London; New York, NY: Chapman and Hall.

Brown, K., and Pearce, D. W. (editors) (1994), *The causes of tropical deforestation: the economic and statistical analysis of factors giving rise to the loss of the tropical forests*, London: UCL Press.

Brown, K., Pearce, D. W., Perrings, C., and Swanson, T. M. (1993), *Economics and the Conservation of Global Biological Diversity*, Washington DC: Global Environment Facility.

Brown, S. and Lugo, A. E. (1990), 'Tropical secondary forests', *Journal of Tropical Ecology*, **6**, 1-32.

Brown, S. and Lugo, A. E. (1994), 'Rehabilitation of tropical lands: a key to sustaining development', *Restoration Ecology*, **2** (2), 97-111.

Bruijnzeel, L. A. (1990), *Hydrology of moist tropical forests and effects of conversion: a state of knowledge review*, Amsterdam: UNESCO.

Buckles, D. (1987), *Cattle, corn and conflict in the Mexican tropics*, Ph.D. dissertation, Carleton University, Ottawa, Unknown.

Buckles, D., and Arteaga, L. (1993), 'Extension campesino a campesino de los abonos verdes en la Sierra de Santa Marta, Veracruz, Mexico. ', in D. Buckles (editor), *Gorras y Sombreros: Caminos hacia la Colaboracion entre Tecnicos y Campesinos*, Mexico, D.F.: CIMMYT.

Buckles, D., and Erenstein, O. (1996), *Intensifying Maize-Based Farming System in the Sierra De Santa Marta, Veracruz*, Mexico: CIMMYT. Study co-funded by CIMMYT and the PRINCE program of the Global Environment Facility

Bueno, S. J. (1980). Tricopteros de la zona de Los Tuxtlas, Veracruz (Insecta: Trichoptera) *Primer Simposio de Estaciones de Campo*, Mexico: Inst. de Biología, UNAM.

Buist, H., Fischer, C., Michos, J. and Abebayehu, T. (1995), 'Purchase of Development Rights and the Economics of Easements', *USDA Economic Research Service*, **718** .

Burgess, R. L. and Sharpe, D. M. (editors). (1981), *Forest island dynamics in man-dominated landscapes*, New York: Springer Verlag.

Burgess, R. L., and Sharpe, D. M. (1981), 'Summary and conclusions', in R. L. Burgess, and D. M. Sharpe (editors), *Forest Island Dynamics in man-dominated landscapes*, New York: Springer-Verlag.

Calatayud, G. A. (1990), *Estudio etnobotánico de plantas medicinales en una comunidad nahua de la Sierra de Santa Martha*, Veracruz, Tesis Bióloga, Universidad Veracruzana, Xalapa.

Candler, W. and Boehlje, M. (1971), 'Use of linear programming in capital budgeting with multiple goals', *Americam Journal of Agricultural Economics*, **53**, 325-30.

Carabias, J. (1979), *Analisis de la vegetacion de la selva alta perennifolia y comunidades derivadas de esta en una zona calido-humeda de Mexico, Los Tuxtlas, Veracruz*, Tesis Biólogo, Universidad Nacional Autonoma de Mexico, Mexico, DF.

Carlson, G. A., Zilberman, D., and Miranowski, J. A. (editors)(1993), *Agricultural and environmental resource economics*, New York: Oxford University Press.

Cavendish, W. (1997), The complexity of the commons: environmental resource demands in rural Zimbabwe, Mimeo, *Centre for the study of African Econommies, Oxford*.

Cervigni, R. (1993), *Mexico Forestry and Conservation Sector Review: Substudy of Economic Valuation of Forests. Annex 1: Tourism and Recreation*, Washington DC: The World Bank.

Cervigni, R. (1993), *Biodiversity, Incentives to Deforest and Tradeable Development Right*,. Global Environmental Change Working Paper GEC 93-07, University College London and University of East Anglia : Centre for Economic and Social Research on the Global Environment.

Cervigni, R. (1994), 'Aspectos Economicos de los Bosques Tropicales como Reservas de la Biodiversidad: la Comercialización de los Derechos de Explotación como Incentivo para su Conservación', *Agricultura y Sociedad*, **73**, 11-40.

Cervigni, R. (1995), *Incremental cost in the convention on biological diversity: a simple model*, Global Environmental Change Working Paper GEC 95-32, University College London and University of East Anglia: Centre for Economic and Social Research on the Global Environment.

Cervigni, R. (1997), *Biodiversity conservation, sectoral development and incremental cost: a case study in Mexico*, unpublished manuscript, Washington DC : Global Environment Facility.

Cervigni, R. (1997), Land use, resource extraction and subsistence farming in Mexico: a linear programming approach, paper submitted to the *First World Congress of Environmental and Resource Economists*, Venice, Italy.

Cervigni, R. (1997), Subsistence needs, non-farm employment and tenure conflicts: predicting land use change using dynamic stock-flow modelling techniques. Paper submitted to the *World Congress of Environmental and Resource Economists*, Venice, Italy.

Cervigni, R. (1998), 'Incremental cost in the convention on biological diversity', *Environmental and Resource Economics*, **11**, 217-241.

Cervigni, R. (1998), *Land use, national development and global welfare: the economics of biodiversitys conservation and sustainable use*, Ph.D. Dissertation, University College London.

Cervigni, R., and Ramírez, F. (1996), *Desarrollo Sustentable y Conservación De La Biodiversidad: Un Estudio En La Sierra De Santa Marta, Veracruz, México,.* Mexico City and Washington DC: Preliminary Report in Spanish, Global Environment Facility, Proyecto Sierra de Santa Marta AC, Centro Internacional para el Mejoramiento del Maíz y Trigo.

Cervigni, R. and Ramírez, F. (editors) (1997), *Desarrollo sustentable y conservacion de la biodiversidad: un estudio de caso en la Sierra de Santa Marta, Veracruz, Mexico.* Global Environment Facility, Proyecto Sierra de Santa Marta, Centro Internacional para el Mejoramiento del Maíz y Trigo ed., México DF: Instituto de Investigaciones Sociales, Universidad Nacional Autónoma de México (forthcoming).

Chaudhuri, A., and Vos, J. W. E. (1988), *Unified theory and strategies of survey sampling*, Amsterdam, New York: North-Holland.

Chevallier, J., and Buckles, D. (1995), *A land without Gods: Process theory, maldevelopment and the Mexican Nahuas*, London: Zed Books.

Chichilnisky, G. (1996), 'An Axiomatic Approach to Sustainable Development', *Social Choice and Welfare*, **13** (2), 231-57.

Chomitz, K. M. and Gray, D. A. (1996), 'Roads, land use and deforestation: a spatial model applied to Belize', *The World Bank Economic Review*, **10** (3), 487-512.

Ciriacy-Wantrup, S. V. (1952), *Resource conservation: economics and policies*, Berkeley: University of California Press.

Claridge, M. F. (1995), 'Introducing Systematics Agenda 2000', *Biodiversity and Conservation*, **4** (5), 950-961.

Clark, C. (1973a), 'The Economics of Overexploitation', *Science*, **181**, 630-4.

Clark, C. (1973b), 'Profit Maximisation and the Extinction of Animal Species', *Journal of Political Economy*, **81** (4), 950-61.

Clark, C., and Haswell, M. R. (1970), *The economics of subsistence agriculture*, London: Macmillan.

Clarke, H. R. and Reed, W. J. (1990), 'Land Development and Wilderness Conservation Policies under Uncertainty: A Synthesis', *Natural Resource Modeling*, **4** (1), 11-37.

Cleaver, K. (1992), 'Deforestation in the Western and Central African Forest: The Agricultural and Demographic Causes, and Some Solutions', in K. Cleaver (editor), *Conservation of West and Central African rainforests*. Washington, D.C.: World Bank.

Clüsener Godt, M., and Hadley, M. (1993), 'Ecosystem rehabilitation and forest regeneration in the humid tropics: case studies and management insights', in H. Lieth, and M. Lohmann (editors), *Restoration of tropical forest ecosystem*, Dordrecht: Kluwer.

Coates - Estrada, R., and Estrada. A. (1985), *Lista De Las Aves De La Estación De Biología "Los Tuxtlas"*. Mexico: Instituto de Biología, Univ. Nal. Autón. de México.

Coll de Hurtado, A. (1970), 'Carta geomorfológica de la región de Los Tuxtlas, Ver., *Bol. Inst. Geografía Univ. Nal. Autón. México*, **3**, 23-28.

Cortes, R. G. R. (1982). *Revisión taxonómica de los Bambusoides leñosos (Graminae: Bambusoideae) del Estado de Veracruz*, Tesis Biólogo, Universidad Veracruzana, Xalapa.

Costanza, R. (editor)(1991), *Ecological Economics: the Science and Management of Sustainability*, New York: Columbia Univ. Press.

Costanza, R. (1994), 'Three General Policies to Achieve Sustainability', in A. Jansson, M. Hammer, C. Folke, and R. Costanza (editors), *Investing in Natural Capital*, Washington, DC: Island Press.

Costanza, R. (1995), 'Economic growth, carrying capacity and the environment: forum', *Ecological Economics*, **15** (2), 89-90.

Costanza, R., d' Arge, R., de Groot, R., Farber, S., Grasso, M., Hannon, B., Limburg, K., Naeem, S., O'Neill, R. V., Paruelo, J., Raskin, R. G., Sutton, P. and van der

Belt, M. (1997), 'The Value of the World's Ecosystem Services and Natural Capital', *Nature*, **387** (15-May), 253-61.

Covarrubias, M. (1980), *El sur de México*, Mexico: INI.

Csuti, B., Polasky, S., Williams, P. H., Pressey, R. L., Camm, J. D., Kershaw, M., Kiester, A. R., Downs, B., Hamilton, R., Huso, M. and Sahr, K. (1997), 'A comparison of reserve selection algorithms using data on terrestrial vertebrates in Oregon', *Biological Conservation*, **80**, 83-97.

Dasgupta, P. (1993), *An inquiry into well being and destitution*, Oxford: Clarendon Press.

de Almeida, O. T. and Uhl, C. (1995), 'Developing a quantitative framework for sustainable resource-use planning in the Brazilian Amazon', *World Development*, **23** (10), 1745-1764.

De Groote, H. (1996), 'Optimal survey design for rural data collection in developing countries', *Quarterly Journal of International Agriculture*, **35**, 163-175.

De la Maza Elvira, R. G. and De la Maza R. (1979), 'Notas sobre los Papilionidae de Mexico. V: Zona de Los Tuxtlas, Veracruz. ', *Bol. Inf. Soc. Mex. Lepidopteridología*, **5** (3), 2-18.

de Miranda, E. E., and Mattos, C. (1992), 'Brazilian rain forest colonization and biodiversity', in M. G. Paoletti, and D. Pimentel (editors), *Biotic diversity in agroecosystems*, Amsterdam: Elsevier.

Deacon, R. T. (1995), 'Assessing the Relationship between Government Policy and Deforestation', *Journal of Environmental Economics and Management*, **28** (1), 1-18.

Deininger, K., and Heinegg, A. (1995), *Rural Poverty in Mexico*, mimeo, The World Bank

Deininger, K., and Minten, B. (1996), Poverty, policies and deforestation: the case of Mexico. Mimeo, The World Bank.

del Amo, S. (1991), 'Management of secondary vegetation for artificial creation of useful rainforest in Uxpanapa, veracruz, Mexico: an intermediate alternative between transformation and modification', in A. Gomez Pompa, T. C. Whitmore, and M. Hadley (editors), *Rain forest regeneration and management* (Man and the biosphere series ed.,) Paris: UNESCO.

Diewert, W. E. (1981), 'The economic theory of index numbers', in A. Deaton (editor), *Essays in the theory and measurement of consumer behaviour: in honour of Sir Richard Stone*, Cambridge ; New York: Cambridge University Press.

Dinerstein, E. (1995), *A Conservation assessment of the terrestrial ecoregions of Latin America and the Caribbean*, Washington, D.C.: The World Bank.

Dirzo, R. and Garcia, M. C. (1992), 'Rates of deforestation in Los Tuxtlas, a Neotropical area in Southeast Mexico', *Conservation Biology*, **6** (1), 84-90.

Dorfman, R., Samuelson, P. A., and Solow, R. M. (1958), *Linear programming and economic analysis*, New York: McGraw-Hill.

Downing, T. E. (editor) (1992), *Development or destruction: the conversion of tropical forest to pasture in Latin America*, Boulder, Colorado: Westview Press.

Dufournaud, C. M., Quinn, J. T., Harrington, J. J., Abeygumawardena, P. and Franzosa, R. (1995), 'A model of sustainable extraction of nontimber forest products in susbsistence societies', *Environment and Planning A*, 27, 1667-1676.

EarthWatch (1996), *Mexico Vanishing Rainforest*, Internet Web site: http://www.earthwatch.org./g/Gestrada.html.

Edwards, E. P. and Tashian, R. E. (1959), 'Avifauna of the Catemaco basin of sourthen Veracruz, Mexico', *The Condor*, 61, 325-337.

Edwards, S. R. (1995), 'Conserving biodiversity: resources for our future', in R. Bailey (editor), *The True State of the Planet* (pp. 212-65) New York, NY: The Free Press.

Ehrlich, P. R. (1988), The Loss of Diversity: Causes and Consequences. in E. O. Wilson (editor), *Biodiversity*, Washington, D.C.: National Academy Press.

Ehui, S. K., Erthel, T. W. and Preckel, P. V. (1990), 'Forest resource depletion, soil dynamics and agricultural productivity in the tropics', *Journal of Environmental Economics and Management*, 18, 136-154.

El-Serafi, S. (1994), *Incremental Cost: A Comment*, mimeo,The World Bank.

Ellis, F. (1988), *Peasant Economics*, Cambridge: Cambridge University Press.

Estrada. A. and Coates-Estrada, R. (1994), 'Las selvas de Los Tuxtlas, Veracruz: ¿islas de supervivencia de la fauna silvestre?', *Ciencia y Desarrollo*, 20 (116), 50-61.

Estrada. A. and Coates-Estrada, R. (1996), 'Tropical Rain Forest Fragmentation and Wild Populations of Primates at Los Tuxtlas, Mexico', *International Journal of Primatology*, 17 (5).

Estrada. A. and Coates-Estrada, R. (1997), 'Anthropogenic landscape changes and avian diversity at Los Tuxtlas, Mexico', *Biodiversity and Conservation*, 6 (1).

Estrada. A. Coates-Estrada, R., Meritt, D., Montiel, S. and Curiel, D. (1993), 'Patterns of frugivore species richness and abundance in forest islands and in agricultural habitats at Los Tuxtlas, Mexico', *Advances in Vegetation Science*, 15, 245-259.

Faith, D. P. (1994), 'Phylogenetic diversity: a general framework for the prediction of feature diversity', in P. L. Forey, C. J. Humphries, and R. I. Vane-Wright (editors), *Systematics and conservation evaluation*, Oxford: Clarendon Press.

Fearnside, P. M. (1993), 'Deforestation in Brazilian Amazonia: The Effect of Population and Land Tenure', *Ambio*, 22 (8), 537-545.

Feder, G., and Feeny, D. (1993), 'The theory of land tenure and property rights', in K. R. Hoff, A. Braverman, and J. E. Stiglitz (editors), *The Economics of rural organization : theory, practice, and policy* (World Bank ed.,), New York, N.Y.: Oxford University Press.

Feltenstein, A. (1992), 'Oil Prices and Rural Migration: The Dutch Disease Goes South', *Journal of International Money and Finance*, **11** (3), 273-91.

Fields, G. S. (1975), 'Rural-urban migration, urban employment and underemployement, and job-search activity in LDC', *Journal of Development Economics*, **2**, 165-187.

Firschein, I. L. and Smith, H. M. (1956), 'A new fringelimbed *Hyla* (Amphibia: Anura) from a new Faunal District of Mexico', *Herpetologiaca*, **12**, 17-21.

Fisher, A. C. (1988), 'Key aspects of species extinction: Habitat loss and over exploitation', in V. K. Smith (editor), *Environmental Resources and Applied Welfare Economics. Essays in Honor of J.V. Krutilla*. Washington, DC: Resources for the Future.

Fisher, A. C. and Hanemann, W. M. (1986), 'Option Value and the Extinction of Species', *Advances in Applied Micro-Economics*, **4**, 169-190.

Fisher, A. C. and Hanemann, W. M. (1990), 'Option Value: Theory and Measurement ', *European Review of Agricultural Economics*, **17** (2), 167-180.

Fisher, A. C., and Krutilla, J. V. (1985), 'Economics of Nature Preservation', in A. V. Kneese, and J. L. Sweeney (editors), *Handbook of Natural Resource and Energy Economics* (Vol. I), Amsterdam: North-Holland.

Fisher, A. C., Krutilla, J. V. and Cicchetti, C. J. (1972), 'The Economics of Environmental Preservation: a Theoretical and Empirical Analysis', *American Economic Review*, **62**, 605-619.

Flores Villela, O. (1988), *Conservación en México: Síntesis sobre vertebrados terrestres, vegetación y uso del suelo*, Mexico: INIREB Conservación Internacional.

Flores Villela, O., and Gerez, F. (1989), *Patrimonio Vivo de México*, New York: Conservation International.

Forester, D. and Machlis, G. E. (1996), 'Modelling human factors that affect the loss of biodiversity', *Conservation Biology*, **10** (4), 1253-1263.

Forey, P. Ł., Humphries, C. J. and Vane-Wright, R. I. (editors) (1994), Systematics and conservation evaluation, Oxford: Clarendon Press.

Fox, J. and Atok, K. (1997), 'Forest-dweller demographics in West Kalimantan, Indonesia.', *Environmental Conservation*, **24** (1).

Freeman, A. M. I. (1984). 'Methods for assessing the benefits of environmental programs', in A. V. Kneese, and J. L. Sweeney (editors), *Handbook of natural resources and energy economics* (Vol. I). Amsterdam: North-Holland.

Frontsys (1997), *A tutorial on spreadsheet optimization*, WEB site document (http://www.frontsys.com/tutorial.htm#problems).

Fujisaka, S., Bell, W., Thomas, N., Hurtado, L. and Crawford, E. (1996), 'Slash and-burn agriculture, conversion to pasture, and deforestation in two Brazilian Amazon colonies', *Agriculture, Ecosystems and Environment*, **59** (1-2), 115.

Gajaseni, J., Matta-Machado, R., and Jordan, C. F. (1996), 'Diversified agroforestry systems: buffers for biodiversity reserves and landbridges for fragmented habitats in the tropics', in R. C. Szaro, and D. W. Johnston (editors), *Biodiversity in managed landscapes: theory and practice*, New York, Oxford: Oxford University Press.

GEF (1999), *Experience with Conservation Trust Funds*, Washington D.C.: The Global Environment Facility.

Gentry, A. H. (1982), 'Bigoniaceae', in *Flora de Veracruz* (fasciculo 24 ed.,), Xalapa, Veracruz: Inst. Nal. de Investigaciones sobre Recursos Bióticos.

Gentry, A. H. (1996), 'Species expirations and current extinction rates: a review of the evidence', in R. C. Szaro, and D. W. Johnston (editors), *Biodiversity in managed landscapes: theory and practice*, New York, Oxford: Oxford University Press.

Georgiadis, N. and Balmford, A. (1992), 'The calculus of conserving biological diversity', *Tree*, **7** (10), 321-322.

Giesen, W. and King, K. (editors) (1997), *Incremental cost of conserving wetland biodiversity*, Kuala Lumpur: Wetland Internationals and Global Environment Facility.

Global Environment Facility, (1994), Instrument for the Establishment of the Restructured GEF, Washington DC: GEF.

Global Environment Facility, (1994), *Report by the Chairman to the Participants' Meeting,* Washington DC: Global Environment Facility.

Global Environment Facility, (1995), Joint Summary of the Chairs, document GEF/C.4, *Proceedings of the GEF Council Meeting.* Washington DC.

Global Environment Facility, (1996), *Incremental Costs (document GEF/C.7/Inf.5)* Web page URL http://www.gefweb.org/meetings/council7/c7inf5.htm.

Global Environment Facility, (1996), *Operational Strategy,* Washington DC: GEF.

Global Environment Facility, (1996b), Financing of GEF Projects (document GEF/C.7/Inf.4). *Proceedings of the GEF Council Meeting.* Washington DC.

Global Environment Facility. (1997), *Quarterly Operational Report,* Washington DC: GEF.

Global Environment Facility. (1997), *Streamlined Procedures for Incremental Cost Assessment,* Web page URL http://www.gefweb.org/prince/strmline1.htm.

Global Environment Facility. (2000), *Operational Report on GEF Projects,* Web page URL http://www.gefweb.org/html/map.html.

Glomsrød, S., Monge, M. D., and Vennemo, H. (1997), Structural adjustment and deforestation in Nicaragua, mimeo, submitted to Environment and Development.

Glowka, Burhenne-Guilmin, F., Synge, H., McNeely, J. A., and Guendling, L. (1994), *A Guide to the Convention on Biological Diversity,* Gland: IUCN.

Gobierno del Estado de Veracruz, (1995), *Plan Sectorial Forestal del Estado de Veracruz (1996 - 2034),* Xalapa, Veracruz: Gobierno del Estado de Veracruz; Secretaria de Medio Ambiente, Recursos Naturales y Pesca.

Gomez Pompa, A., and Burley, F. W. (1991), 'The management of natural tropical forests', in A. Gomez Pompa, T. C. Whitmore, and M. Hadley (editors), *Rain forest regeneration and management* (Man and the biosphere series ed.,), Paris: UNESCO.

Gomez Pompa, A., and del Amo, S. (editors) (1985), *Investigaciones sobre las selvas altas en Veracruz, Mexico* (INREB ed.), Xalapa: Editorial Alhambra.

Gomez Pompa, A., Kaus, A., Jimenez-Osornio, J., Bainbridge, D., and Rorive, V. M. (1993), 'Country Profile: Mexico', in National Research Council (US) *Sustainable agriculture and the environment in the humid tropics,* Washington DC: National Academy Press.

Gomez Pompa, A., and Vazquez Yanez, C. (1985), 'Estudios sobre la regeneracion de selvas en regiones calido-humedas de Mexico', in A. Gomez Pompa, and S. del Amo (editors), *Investigaciones sobre las selvas altas en Veracruz, Mexico*(INIREB ed., Vol. II), Xalapa: Editorial Alhambra.

Gomez Pompa, A., Vazquez Yanez, C. and Guevara, S. (1972), 'The Tropical rain forest: a non renewable resource', *Science,* 117, 762-765.

Gomez Pompa, A., Whitmore, T. C., and Hadley, M. (editors)(1991), *Rain forest regeneration and management* (Man and the biosphere series ed.), Paris: UNESCO.

Gonzalez Christensen, A. R. L. E. (1986), Los mamiferos tropicales de la Sierra de Santa Martha, Veracruz, *Memorias UNAM y Asoc. de Zoologicos y Acuarios de la Rep. Mexicana IV Simposio sobre Fauna Silvestre,* Mexico: UNAM.

Gonzalez, R. M. C. (1989), *Estudio etnobotánico de plantas comestibles de cuatro ejidos zoque - popolucas de la Sierra de Santa Marta, Veracruz,* Tesis Bióloga, Universidad Veracruzana, Xalapa.

Gonzalez, S. E., and Villeda C., M. P. (1980), Odonata de la Región de Los Tuxtlas, Veracruz, México. *Resumenes Primer simposio de Estaciones de Campo,* Mexico: Inst. de Biología, UNAM.

Gordon, H. S. (1954), "The Economic Theory of a Common Property Resource: the Fishery', *Journal of Political Economy,* 62, 124-142.

Graham, A. (1977), 'The tropical rain forest near its northern limits in Veracruz, Mexico: Recent or ephemeral?', *Bol. Soc. Bot. Mexico,* 36, 13-21.

Graham-Tomasi, T. (1994), 'Quasi-Option Value', in D. Bromley (editor), *Handbook of Environmental Economics,* Oxford: Basil Blackwell.

Grainger, A. (1993), 'Population as Concept and Parameter in the Modeling of Deforestation', in G. D. Ness, W. D. Drake, and S. R. Brechin (editors), *Population-environment dynamics: Ideas and observations*. Ann Arbor: University of Michigan Press.

Grime, J. P. (1997), 'Biodiversity and Ecosystem Function: the Debate Deepens', *Science*, **277** (August 29, 1997), 1260-1261.

Groombridge, B. (editor) (1992), *Global biodiversity : status of the earth's living resources*, A report compiled by the World Conservation Monitoring Centre; in collaboration with the Natural History Museum, London; and in association with IUCN, the World Conservation Union; UNEP, United Nations Environment Programme; WWF, World Wide Fund for Nature; and the World Resources Institute.

Guevara, S. (1995), 'Connectivity: key in maintaining tropical rain forest landscape diversity. A case study in Los Tuxtlas, México', in P. Halladay, and D. A. Gilmour (editors), *Conserving biodiversity outside protected areas: the role of traditional agro-ecosystems* (IUCN Forest Conservation Programme ed.,), Gland, Switzerland; Cambridge: IUCN.

Gutierrez-Carbajal, L. (1983), *Los factores del medio ambiente físico y al vegetación de los alrededores de la Laguna de Ostión (Municipio de Pajapan, Veracruz)*, Tesis Bióloga, Universidad Veracruzana, Xalapa.

Gutiérrez, R. (1994), *Geología de la Sierra de Santa Marta*, mimeo, Xalapa: Internal Report, Proyecto Sierra de Santa Marta, IDRC.

Gutiérrez, R. (1994)), *Morfoedafología de la Sierra de Santa Marta*, mimeo Xalapa: Internal Report, Proyecto Sierra de Santa Marta, IDRC.

Hadley, G. (1962), *Linear programming*, Reading, Mass.: Addison-Wesley Pub.

Hall, E. R. and Dalquest, W. W. (1963), 'The mammals of Veracruz', *Univ. Kansas Publ. Mus. Nat. Hist.,* **14** (4), 165-362.

Hamilton, L. S. (1983), *Tropical forested watersheds: hydrologic and soils response to major uses or conversions, Boulder*, Colo : Westview Press.

Hammer, J. S. (1986), 'Subsistence first: farm allocation decisions in Senegal', *Journal of Development Economics*, **23**, 355-369.

Hanemann, W. M. (1989), 'Information and the Concept of Option Value', *Journal of Environmental Economics and Management*, **16**, 23-37.

Hansen, M. H., Hurwitz, W. N., and Madow, W. G. (1953), *Sample survey methods and theory*, New York: Wiley.

Hargreaves Heap, S., Hollis, M., Lyons, B., Sugden, R., and Weale, A. (1992), *The Theory of choice: a critical guide*, Oxford: Blackwell.

Harper, J. L. and Hawksworth, D. L. (1994), 'Biodiversity: measurement and estimation. Preface', *Philosophical Transactions of the Royal Society of London Series B*, (345), 5-12.

Harrys, L., and Silva-Lopez, G. (1992), 'Forest fragmentation and the conservation of biological diversity', in P. L. Fiedler, and S. K. Jain (editors), *Conservation Biology: the theory and practice of nature conservation, preservation and management*, New York and London: Chapman and Hall.

Hartwick, J. (1977), 'Intergenerational equity and the investing of rents from exhaustible resources', *American Economic Review*, **66**, 972-974.

Hartwick, J., and Olewiler, N. D. (1986), *The Economics of Natural Resource Use*, New York: Harper and Row.

Hatch, U., Atwood, J. and Segar, J. (1989), 'An Application of Safety-First Probability Limits in a Discrete Stochastic Farm Management Programming Model', *Southern Journal of Agricultural Economics*, **21** (1), 65-72.

Hawksworth, D. L., and Kalin-Arroyo, M. T. (1995), 'Magnitude and distribution of biodiversity', in V. H. Heywood, and R. L. Watson (editors), *Global biodiversity assessment*. Cambridge; New York: Cambridge University Press.

Hazell, P. B. R. and Norton, R. D. (1986), *Mathematical programming for economic analysis in agriculture*, New York, London: MacMillan.

Heath, J. R. (1992), 'Evaluating the impact of Mexicos land reform on agricultural productivity', *World Development*, **20** (5), 685-711.

Henry, C. (1974), 'Investment Decisions under Uncertainty: the Irreversibility Effect', *American Economic Review*, **66** (6), 1006-1012.

Heywood, V. H. (1992), 'The measurement of biodiversity and the politics of implementation', in P. L. Forey, C. J. Humphries, and R. I. Vane-Wright (editors), *Systematics and conservation evaluation*. Oxford: Clarendon Press.

Heywood, V. H. (executive editor) (1995), R. H. Watson (chair), *Global biodiversity assessment*, Cambridge ; New York: Cambridge University Press.

Heywood, V. H., and Baste, I. (1995), 'Introduction', in V. H. Heywood (editor), *Global biodiversity assessment*, Cambridge: Cambrideg University Press.

Heywood, V. H., and Stuart, N. H. (1992), 'Species extinction in tropical forests', in T. C. Whitmore, and J. A. Sayer (editors), *Tropical deforestation and species extinction*, London; New York, NY: Chapman and Hall.

Hicks, J. R. (1946), *Value and capital*, Oxford: Oxford University Press.

Holdridge, L. (1967), *Life zone ecology*, San Jose, Costa Rica: Tropical Science Center.

Horn, H. S. (1974), 'The ecology of secondary succession', *Annals of the Review of Ecological Syst.*, **5**, 25-37.

Horn, H. S. (1975). 'Markovian properties of forest succession', in M. L. Cody and J. M. Diamond (editors), *Ecology and evolution of communities*, Cambridge, Mass.: Harvard University Press.

Howard, R. A. (1968), 'The ecology of an elfin forest in Puerto Rico. 1: Introduction and composition studies. ', *J. Arnold Arboretum*, **49**, 381-418.

HPS (1997),Stella 5.0 Research for Windows, Hanover, NH: High Performance System.

Hudson, W. E. (editor). (1991), *Landscape linkages and biodiversity*, Washington, D.C.: Island Press.

Humphries, C. J., Williams, P. H. and Vane-Wright, R. I. (1995), 'Measuring biodiversity value for conservation', *Annual Review of Ecology and Systematics*, **26**, 93-111.

Huston, M. A. (1994), *Biological diversity: the coexistence of species on changing landscapes*, Cambridge, New York: Cambridge University Press.

Hyde, W. F., Amacher, G. S. and Magrath, W. (1996), 'Deforestation and Forest Land Use: Theory, Evidence, and Policy Implications', *The World Bank Research Observer*, **11** (2), 223.

Ibarra - Manriquez, G., and Sinaca Colin, S. (1995), *Lista florística comentada de la Estación de Biología Tropical 'Los Tuxtlas', Veracruz, México*, Instituto de Biología de la Univ. Nal. Autón. de México, Unpublished manuscript.

INEGI (1991), *XI Censo General de Poblacion y vivienda, 1990*, Mexico, DF: Instituto Nacional de Estadistica, Geografia e Informatica (INEGI).

INEGI (1994), *Censos Economicos 1994, resultados definitivos*, Mexico, DF: Instituto Nacional de Estadistica, Geografia e Informatica (INEGI).

INEGI (1997), Sistema Municipal de Bases de Datos (SIMBAD), Mexico, DF: Instituto Nacional de Estadistica, Geografia e Informatica (INEGI).

Instituto Nacional de Ecología, *Los Tuxtlas, Reserva de la Biosfera*, (2000), Web page URL: http://www.ine.gob.mx/ucanp/data/consultaFicha.php3?anp=92

Jeffers, J. N. R. (1988), *Practitioner's Handbook on the modelling of dynamic change in ecosystem*, New York: John Wiley and Sons.

Jimenez Avila, E. and Gomez Pompa, A. (editors) (1982), *Estudios ecologicos en el agroecosistema cafetalero*, Instituto Nacional de investigaciones sobre recursos bioticos (INIREB) ed., Mexico DF: Compañia editorial continental.

Johansson, P. O. (1987), *The Economic Theory and Measurement of Environmental Benefits*, Cambridge: Cambridge University Press.

Johns, A. D. (1983), 'Wildlife can live with logging', *New Scientist*, (99), 206-11.

Johns, A. D. (1985), 'Selective logging and wildlife conservation in tropical rain forest: problems and recommendations', *Biological Conservation*, (31), 355-75.

Johns, A. D. (1992). 'Species conservation in managed tropical forests', in T. C. Whitmore, and J. A. Sayer (editors), *Tropical deforestation and species extinction*. London; New York, NY: Chapman and Hall.

Johns, R. J. (1992), 'The influence of deforestation and selective logging operations on plant diversity in Papua New Guinea', in T. C. Whitmore, and J. A. Sayer (editors), *Tropical deforestation and species extinction*, London; New York, NY: Chapman and Hall.

Kaimowitz, D, and Angelsen, A. (1998), *Economic Models of Tropical Deforestation: A Review*, Bogor, Indonesia: Center for International Forestry Research (CIFOR).

Kalton, G. (1983), *Introduction to survey sampling*. Beverly Hills, California: Sage Publications.

Karr, J. A. (1982), 'Population variability and extinction in the avifauna of a tropical bridge island', *Ecology*, (63), 1975-8.

Kask, S., Shogren, J., and Morton, P. (1994), 'Valuing Ecosystem Changes', in J. Van den Bergh, and J. Van Straaten (editors), *Economy and Ecosystems in Change: Analytical and Historical Perspectives* Island Press.

Katzman, M. T. and Kale, W. G. J. (1990),'Tropical Forest Preservation Using Economic Incentives', *Bioscience*, **40** (11), 827-832.

Kemp, R. H. (1992), 'The conservation of genetic resources in managed tropical forests', *Unasylva*, **169** (43), 244-49.

Kerr, J. and Currie, D. (1994), 'Effects of Human Activity on Global Extinction Risk', *Conservation Biology*, **9** (6), 1528-1538.

King, K. (1993), *Incremental Cost as an Input to Operational Decision Making*, *Working Paper*, **4**, Washington, DC: *Global Environment Facility*.

King, K. (1993), 'Issues to be addressed by the Program for measuring Incremental Costs for the Environment' (PRINCE), Working Paper 8, Washington DC : Global Environment Facility.

Kish, L. (1989), *Sampling methods for agricultural surveys*, Rome: Food and Agriculture Organization of the United Nations.

Krebs, C. J. (1994), *Ecology*, Harper Collins.

Krutilla, J. V. (1967), 'Conservation reconsidered', *American Economic Review*, **57**,777-786.

Kumari, K. (1995), 'An environmental and economic assessment of forest management options: a case study in Malaysia ', *World Bank Environment Department Papers*, **026** .

Kumari, K. (1995), 'Mainstreaming biodiversity conservation: a peninsular Malaysian case', *International Journal of Sustainable Development and World Ecology* (2), 182-198.

Kumari, Kanta and King, Kenneth (1997), *Paradigm Cases to Illustrate the Application of the Incremental Cost Assessment to Biodiversity,* Web page URL http://www/gefweb.org/prince.

Kydland, F. E. and Prescott, E. C. (1996), 'The computational experiment: an econometric tool', *Journal of Economic Perspectives,* **10** (1), 69-85.

Lazos, E. (1995), La ganaderización de dos comunidades veracruzanas: condiciones de la difusión de un modelo agrario, Mexico.

Lipton, M. (1968), 'The theory of the optimizing peasant', *Journal of Development Studies,* 327-51.

Lira, S. R. and Riba, R. (1984), 'Aspéctos fitogeográficos y ecológicos de la flora pteridológica de la Sierra de Santa Marta, Veracruz, México. ', *Biotica,* **9** (4), 451-467.

Lorence, H. D. and Castillo-Campos, G. (1988), '*Rondeletia tuxtlensis,* una nueva especie para el Estado de Veracruz, México', *Bol. Soc. Bot. Mexico,* **46**, 128-128.

Lorence, H. D. and Castillo-Campos, G. (1988), 'Tres nuevas especies y una combinación en el género Rondeletia (Rubiaceae: Rondeletieae) de Veracruz y Oaxaca, México', *Biotica,* **13** (1-2), 147-157.

Lorence, H. D. and Dwyer, J. D. (1987), 'New taxa and new name in Mexican and Central American Randia (Rubiaceae, Gardenieae)', *Bol. Soc. Bot. Mexico,* **47**, 37-48.

Lorence, H. D. and Nee, M. (1987), 'Randia retoflexa (Rubiaceae), new species from southern Mexico', *Brittonia,* **39** (3), 371-375.

Loucks, D. P. (1975), 'Planning for multiple goals', in C. R. Blitzer, P. B. Clark, and L. Taylor (editors), *Economy-wide models and development planning* (The World Bank ed.,) London: Oxford University Press.

Lovejoy, T. E. and Oren, D. C. (1981), 'The minimum critical size of ecosystems', in R. L. Burgess, and D. M. Sharpe (editors), *Forest Island Dynamics in man-dominated landscapes,* New York: Springer-Verlag.

Lovelock, J. (1987), *The ages of Gaia,* Oxford: Oxford University Press.

Low, A. R. C. (1974), 'Decision taking under uncertainty: a linear programming model of peasant farm behavior ', *Journal of Agricultural Economics,* **62**, 311-320.

Low, A. R. C. (1982), 'A comparative advantage theory of the subsistence farm-household: application to Swazi farming', *South African Journal of Economics,* **50** (2), 136-157.

Ludeke, A. K., Maggio, R. C. and Reid, L. M. (1990), 'An Analysis of Anthropogenic Deforestation Using Logistic Regression and GIS', *Journal of Environmental Management,* **31** (3), 247.

Lugo, A. E. (1988), 'Estimating Reduction in the Diversity of Tropical Forest Species', in E. O. Wilson (editor), *Biodiversity*, Washington, D.C.: National Academy Press.

Lugo, A. E., and Brown, S. (1996),'Management of land and species richness in the tropics', in R. C. Szaro, and D. W. Johnston (editors), *Biodiversity in managed landscapes: theory and practice*, New York ; Oxford: Oxford University Press.

Lugo, A. E., Parrotta, J. and Brown, S. (1993), 'Loss in species caused by tropical deforestation and their recovery through management', *Ambio* (22), 106-109.

Lutz, E. and Young, Michael (1992), 'Integration of environmental concerns into agricultural policies of industrial and developing countries', *World Development*, **20** (2), 241-253.

Lutz, W. (editor) (1994), *Population-Development-Environment: Understanding their interactions in Mauritius*, New York; Heidelberg and London: Springer.

MacArthur, R. H., and Wilson, E. O. (1967), *The theory of island biogeography*, Princeton: Princeton University Press.

Machlis, G. E., and Forester, D. (1996), 'The relationship between socio-economic factors and the loss of biodiversity: first effort at theoretical and quantitative models', in R. C. Szaro and D. W. Johnston (editors), *Biodiversity in managed landscapes: theory and practice*, New York; Oxford: Oxford University Press.

Magurran, A. E. (1988), *Ecological diversity and its measurement*, Princeton: Princeton University Press.

Mahar, D. (1989), *Government Policies and Deforestation in the Brazil's Amazon Region*, Washington DC: The World Bank.

Mäler, K. G. (1990), 'International Environmental Problems', *Oxford Review of Economic Policy*, **6** (1), 80-108.

Mann, C. (1991), 'Extinction: are ecologists crying wolf?', *Science*, **253**, 736-738.

Markanyda, A. (1998), 'Poverty, Income Distribution and Policy Making', *Environmental and Resource Economics*, **11** (3-4), 459-472.

Martinez De Pison, E. (1983), *El relieve de la Tierra*, Madrid: Salvat.

Martinez Ramos, M. (1994), 'Regeneración natural y diversidad de especies arbóreas en selvas húmedas', *Bol. Soc. Bot. Mexico*, **54**, 179-224.

Mata, P. S. (1985), *Estudio etnobotánico de las plantas medicinales entre los zoque popolucas de Piedra Labrada, Veracruz*, Tesis bióloga, Escuela Nacional de Estudios Profesionales de Iztacala, UNAM, Mexico.

McCarl, B. A. and Blake, B. (1983), 'Goal Programming via Multidimensional Scaling Applied to Senegalese Subsistence Farming: reply', *American Journal of Agricultural Economics*, 832-833.

McInerney, J. P. (1969), 'Linear programming and game thory: some extensions', *Journal of Agricultural Economics*, **20**, 269-278.

McNeely, J. A., Gadgil, M., Leveque, C., Padoch, C., and Redford, K. (1995). 'Human influences on biodiversity', in V. H. Heywood, and R. L. Watson (editors), *Global biodiversity assessment*, Cambridge; New York: Cambridge University Press.

McNeely, J. A., Miller, K., Reid, W., Mittermeier, R. A., and Werner, T. (1990), *Conserving the worlds biological diversity*, Washington DC: International Union for Conservation of Nature and Natural Resources, World Resources Institute, Conservation International, World Wildlife Fund (U.S.), World Bank.

Mendelsohn, R. (1994), 'Property Rights and Tropical Deforestation', *Oxford Economic Papers*, **46**, 750.

Menendez, F. L. (1976), *Los manglares de la Laguna de Sontecomapan, Los Tuxtlas, Veracruz*, Tesis Biólogo, Fac. de Ciencias, UNAM, Mexico.

Meyer, W. B. and Turner, B. L. (1992), 'Human population growth and global land use/ cover change', *Annual Review of Ecology and Systematics*, (23), 39-61.

Michael, R. T. and Becker, G. (1973), 'The new theory of consumer behavior', *Swedish Journal of Economics*, **75** (4).

Miller, K. (1996), *Balancing the scales: guidelines for increasing biodiversity's chances through bioregional management*, Wasington DC: World Rsources Institute.

Miller, K., Allegretti, M. H., Johnson, N., and Jonsson, B. (1995), 'Measures for conservation of biodiversity and sustainable use of its components', in V. H. Heywood, and R. L. Watson (editors), *Global biodiversity assessment*, Cambridge; New York : Cambridge University Press.

Mitchell, R. C., and Carson, R. (1989), *Using Surveys to Value Public Goods: The Contingent Valuation Method*, Washington D.C.: Resource for the Future.

Mittermeier, R. A. and Werner, T. B. (1990), 'Wealth of Plants and Animals Unites 'Megadiversity Countries', *Tropicus*, **4** (1), 4-5.

Montgomery, C. A. and Pollack, R. A. (1996), 'Economics and Biodiversity: Weighing the Benefits and Costs of Conservation', *Journal of Forestry*, **94** (2).

Mooney, H. A., Lubchenco, J. L., Dirzo, R., and Sala, O. E. (1995), 'Biodiversity and Ecosystem Functioning: Basic Principles', in V. H. Heywood, and R. L. Watson (editors), *Global biodiversity assessment*, Cambridge; New York: Cambridge University Press.

Moran, D. (1996), Investing in biological diversity: economic valuation and priorities for development, Ph dissertation, University College London, London.

Moran, D., and Pearce, D. W. (1996), 'The economics of biodiversity', in T. Tietenberg, and H. Folmer (editors), *International Yearbook of Environmental and Resource Economics: a Survey of current issues* Edward Elgar, forthcoming.

Moran, D., Pearce, D. W. and Wendelaar, A. (1996), 'Global biodiversity priorities. A cost-effectiveness index for investments', *Global Environmental Change*, **6** (2).

Munasinghe, M., and Shearer, W. (editors) (1995), *Defining and measuring sustainability: the biogeophysical foundations*, Washington DC: The United Nations University (UNU) and the World Bank.

Murgueitio, E. (1990), 'Intensive Sustainable Livestock Production: An Alternative to Tropical Deforestation', *Ambio*, **19** (8), 397.

Myers, N. (1983), *A wealth of wild species: storehouse for human welfare*, Boulder, Colorado: Westview Press.

Myers, N. (1994), 'Tropical deforestation: rates and patterns', in K. Brown, and D. W. Pearce (editors), *The causes of tropical deforestation: the economic and statistical analysis of factors giving rise to the loss of the tropical forests*, London: UCL Press.

Myers, N., Mittermeier, R. A., Mittermeier, C. G., da Fonseca, G. A. B. and Kents, J. (2000), 'Biodiversity hotspots for conservation priorities', *Nature*, **403**, 853-858.

Myles, G. D. (1995), *Public economics*, Cambridge; New York: Cambridge University Press.

Nair, P. K. R. (1991), 'State-of-the-art of agroforestry systems', *Forest Ecology and Management*, (45), 5-29.

Nakajima, C. (1969), 'Subsistence and commercial family farms: some theoretical models of subjective equilibrium', in C. R. Wharton (editor), *Subsistence agriculture and economic development*, Chicago: Aldine Pub.

National Research Council (US) (1993), *Sustainable agriculture and the environment in the humid tropics*, Washington DC: National Academy Press.

Navarro, D. (1981), *Mamíferos de la Estación de Biología Tropical Los Tuxtlas, Veracruz*, Tesis Biólogo, Fac. de Ciencias, UNAM, Mexico.

Nepstad, D. C., Uhl, C. and Serrao, E. A. S. (1991), 'Recuperation of a degraded Amazonian landscape: forest recovery and agricultural restoration', *Ambio*, **20** (6), 248-255.

Nerlove, M. (1991), 'Population and the Environment: A Parable of Firewood and Other Tales', *American Journal of Agricultural Economics*, **73** (5), 1334-47.

Ness, G. D., Drake, W. D., and Brechin, S. R. (editors) (1993), *Population-environment dynamics: Ideas and observations*, Ann Arbor: University of Michigan Press.

Nestel, D. (1995), 'Coffe in Mexico: international market, agricultural landscape and ecology', *Ecological Economics*, **15** (2), 165-178.

Newcombe, K. (1987), 'Economic justification for rural afforestation: the case of Ethiopia', *Annals of Regional Science*, **21**, 80-99.

Nicholson, C. F., Blake, R. W. and Lee, D. R. (1995), 'Livestock, Deforestation, and Policy Making: Intensification of Cattle Production Systems in Central America Revisited', *Journal of Dairy Science*, **78** (3).

Nir, M. A. (1988), 'The survivors: orchids on a Puerto Rican coffefinca', *American Orchid Society Bulletin* (57), 989-995.

Norton, B. G. (1994). 'On what we should save: the role of culture in determining conservation targets', in P. L. Forey, C. J. Humphries, and R. I. Vane-Wright (editors), *Systematics and conservation evaluation*, Oxford: Clarendon Press.

Norton, B. G. and Ulanowocz, R. E. (1992), 'Scale and Biodiversity Policy: A Hierarchical Approach', *Ambio*, **21** (3), 244-249.

Noss, R. F. (1990), 'Can we maintain biological and ecological integrity?', *Conservation Biology*, (4), 241-244.

O'Riordan, T. (1993), 'The politics of sustainability', in R. K. Turner (editor), *Sustainable environmental econommics and management: principles and practice*, London: Belhaven Press.

Oldfield, M. L. (1984), *The value of conserving genetic resources*, Washington DC: U.S. Dept. of the Interior, National Park Service.

Ortega - Ortiz, J. F. (1996), Aristolochiaceae de Veracruz. *Fasciculo de la Flora de Veracruz*, Forthcoming, Inst. de Ecología and California University.

Ostrom, E. (1995), 'A framework relating human "driving forces" and their impact on biodiversity', paper presented at International Symposium on Measuring and monitoring forest biological diversity: the international network of biodiversity plots, Washington DC.

Page, T. (1988), 'Intergenerational equity and the social rate of discount', in V. K. Smith (editor), *Environmental Resources and Applied Welfare Economics. Essays in Honor of J.V. Krutilla*, Washington, DC: Resources for the Future.

Palacios-Rios, M. (1990), 'New Pteridophyte records for the State of Veracruz, Mexico ', *American Fern Journal*, **80** (1), 29-32.

Panayoutou, T. (1994),'Conservation of Biodiversity and Economic Development: The Concept of Transferable Development Right', in C. Perrings, K. G. Mäler, C. Folke, C. S. Holling, and B. O. Jansson (editors), *Biodiversity Conservation: Policy Issues and Options*, Amsterdam: Kluwer Academic Press.

Paoletti, M. G., and Pimentel, D. (1992), *Biotic diversity in agroecosystems*, Amsterdam: Elsevier.

Paoletti, M. G., Pimentel, D., Stinner, B. R., and Stinner, D. (1992), 'Agroecosystem biodiversity: matching production and conservation biology', in M. G. Paoletti, and D. Pimentel (editors), *Biotic diversity in agroecosystems*, Amsterdam: Elsevier.

Paré, L. (editor), J. L. Blanco, D. Buckles, J. Chevallier, R. Gutiérrez, H. Perales, F. Ramírez, and E. Velázquez H. (co-authors). (1993), *La Sierra de Santa Marta: hacia un desarrollo sustentable* (translat. *The Sierra De Santa Marta: Towards Sustainable Development)*, Xalapa, Veracruz, Mexico: Proyecto Sierra de Santa Marta.

Paré, L. (1997). *Las plantaciones forestales de eucalipto en el sureste de mexico ¿ una prioridad nacional?* mimeo, IIS - Universidad Nacional Autonoma de Mexico.

Parrotta, J. (1993), 'Secondary forest regeneration on degraded tropical lands: the role of plantations as foster ecosystem', in H. Lieth, and M. Lohmann (editors), *Restoration of tropical forest ecosystem*, Dordrecht: Kluwer.

Parrotta, J., and Jones, N. (1996), *Report on Bank-Sponsored Symposium on Tropical Forest Rehabilitation and Restoration*, World Bank office memorandum, Washington DC: The World Bank.

Pearce, D. W. (1993), *Economic Values and the Natural World*, London: Earthscan.

Pearce, D. W. (1994), *Economic values and the natural world*, London: Earthscan.

Pearce, D. W. and Atkinson, G. (1993), 'Capital theory and the measurement of weak sustainability', *Ecological Economics*, **8**, 103-108.

Pearce, D. W., and Atkinson, G. (1994). 'Measuring sustainable development', in D. Bromley (editor), *Handbook of Environmental Economics*, Oxford: Basil Blackwell.

Pearce, D. W., and Barrett, S. (1993), *Incremental Cost and Biodiversity Conservation*, London: Centre for Social and Economic Research on the Global Environment, University College London.

Pearce, D.W. and Cervigni, R. (1994), *North-South Transfers, Incremental Cost and the Rio Environment Conventions*, Global Environmental Change Working Paper GEC 95-33, University College London and University of East Anglia : Centre for Economic and Social Research on the Global Environment.

Pearce, D. W., and Moran, D. (1994), *The economic value of biodiversity*, London: Earthscan.

Pearce, D. W., and Warford, J. (1993), *World without end*, New York: Oxford University Press.

Pemberton, M. (1996), *The measurement of biodiversity*, mimeo, Department of economics, University College London.

Pérez-Higareda, G. and Navarro, D. (1980), 'The faunistic districts of the low plains of Veracruz, Mexico, based on reptilian and mammalian data', *Bulletin Maryland Herpetological Society*, **16** (2), 54-69.

Pérez-Higareda, G., Vogt, R. C., and Flores V O.A.. (1987), *Lista anotada de los anfibios y reptiles de la Región de Los Tuxtlas, Veracruz,* Estación de Biología Tropical "Los Tuxtlas". Inst. de Biología, UNAM.

Perrings, C. (1991), 'Reserved rationality and the precautionary principle: technological change, time and uncertainty in environmental decision making', in R. Costanza (editor), *Ecological Economics: the Science and Management of Sustainability,* New York: Columbia Univ. Press.

Perrings, C. (1998), 'Resilience in the Dynamics of Economy-Environment Systems', *Environmental and Resource Economics,* **11** (3-4), 503-520.

Perrings, C., Barbier, E., Brown, G. M., Dalmazzone, S., Folke, C., Gadgil, M., Hanley, N., Holling, C. S., Lesser, W. H., Mäler, K. G., Mason, P., Panayoutou, T., Turner, R. K., and Wells. M. (1995), 'The Economic Value of Biodiversity', in V. H. Heywood (editor), *Global biodiversity assessment,* Cambridge: Cambridge University Press.

Perrings, C., Mäler, K. G., Folke, C., Holling, C. S. and Jansson, B. O. (editors). (1994), *Biodiversity Conservation: Policy Issues and Options,* Amsterdam: Kluwer Academic Press.

Perrings, C., Mäler, K. G., Folke, C., Holling, C. S., and Jansson, B. O. (editors) (1994), *Biodiversity Conservation: Problems and Policies,* Amsterdam: Kluwer Academic Press.

Perrings, C. and Opschoor, H. (1994), 'The Loss of Biological Diversity: Some Policy Implications', *Environmental and Resource Economics,* **4** (1), 1.

Perrings, C. and Pearce, D. W. (1994), 'Threshold Effects and Incentives for the Conservation of Biodiversity', *Environmental and Resource Economics,* **4** (1), 13.

Persson, A. and Munasinghe, M. (1995), 'Natural resource management and economywide policies in Costa Rica: a computable general equilibrium (CGE) modelling approach', *The World Bank Economic Review,* **9** (2), 259-285.

Pezzey, J. (1989), *Economic analysis of sustainable growth and sustainable development,* Environment department working paper 15, Washington DC: The World Bank.

Pimentel, D., Stachow, U., Tackacs, D. A., Brubaker, H. W., Dumas, A. R., Meraney, J. J., O'Neil, J. A. S. and Onsi, D. E. (1992), 'Conserving biological diversity in agricultural/ forestry systems', *Bioscience,* (42), 354-362.

Pimm, S. L., Russell, G. J., Gittleman, J. L. and Brooks, T. M. (1995), 'The Future of Biodiversity', *Science,* **269** (5222), 347-350.

Polasky, S., Jaspin, M., Szentandarasi, S., Bergeron, N., and Berrens, R. (1996), *Bibliograpy on the Conservation of Biological Diversity: Biological/ Ecological, Economic and Policy Issues,* draft prepared in part for and with support from the Agricultural Experiment Station, Oregon State University, Project 143 and the

Environment, Infrastructure and Agriculture Division, Policy Research Department, World Bank, RPO #679-40.

Polasky, S., Solow, A. and Broadus, J. (1993), 'Searching for uncertain benefits and the conservation of biological diversity', *Environmental and Resource Economics*, 3, 171-181.

Porter, R. C. (1982), 'The new Approach to Wilderness Conservation Through Cost-Benefit Analysis', *Journal of Environmental Economics and Management*, 9, 59-80.

Prescott-Allen, R. and Prescott-Allen, C. (1983), *Genes from the wild : using wild genetic resources for food and raw materials*, London : International Institute for Environment and Development.

PSSM (1995), *Sistema de Información Geográfica de la Sierra de Santa Marta* (Geographical Information System of the Sierra de Santa Marta), [IDRISI/ ARC-INFO] Xalapa, Veracruz, Mexico: Proyecto Sierra de Santa Marta.

PSSM – GEF (1995), *Sustainable development and biodiversity conservation in the Sierra de Santa Marta, Veracruz, Mexico* [Computer database of households and key informants surveys], Xalapa, Mexico and Washington DC: Proyecto Sierra de Santa Marta and Global Environment Facility.

Pulliam, H. R. (1995), 'Managing landscapes for sustainable biodiversity', in M. Munasinghe, and W. Shearer (editors), *Defining and measuring sustainability: the biogeophysical foundations*, Washington DC: The United Nations University (UNU) and the World Bank.

Ragsdale, C. T. (1995), *Spreadsheet Modeling and Decision Analysis: A Practical Introduction to Management Science*, South-Western College Publishing.

Ramamoorthy, P. T. (1984), 'A new species of Salvia (Lamiaceae) from the Sierra de Los Tuxtlas, México', *Pl. Syst. Evol.* 146, 141-143.

Ramirez, B. A., Pérez-Higareda, G., and Casas A., G. (1980), Lista de anfibios y reptiles de la región de Los Tuxtlas, Veracruz, México. *Resumenes Primer Simposio de estaciones de Campo*, Mexico: Inst. de biología. UNAM.

Ramírez, F. (1984), Plan conceptual para el manejo y desarrollo de una Reserva de la Biósfera en la Sierra de Santa Marta, Veracruz, *Inst. Nac. de Invest. sobre Recursos Bióticos*, unpublished note.

Ramírez, F. (1993), Biodiversidad y estado de conservación de la Reserva Especial de la Biósfera 'Sierra de Santa Marta'. *Memoria de resúmenes del Primer Congreso sobre Parques Nacionales y Areas Naturales Protegidas de México: pasado, presente y futuro*, (pp. 305-307), Universidad Autónoma de Tlaxcala.

Ramos, M. (1982), *Conservation of tropical rain forest birds in the lowlands of Mexico and Central America*. Washington DC: World Wildlife Fund.

Ramos, M., and Warner, D. W. (1980), 'Analysis of North American subspecies of migrant birds wintring in Los Tuxtlas, southern Veracruz, México', in A. Keast, and Morton (editors), *Migrant birds in the Neotropics*. Washington DC: Smithsonian Institution Press.

Randall, A., and Castle, E. (1985), 'Land Resources and Land Market', in A. V. Kneese, and J. L. Sweeney (editors), *Handbook of Natural Resource and Energy Economics*. Amsterdam: NorthHolland.

Reardon, T. and Vosti, S. (1995), 'Links between Rural Poverty and the Environment in Developing Countries: Asset Categories and Investment Poverty', *World Development*, **23** (9), 1495-1506.

Reed, W. J. (1989), 'Optimal Investment in the Protection of a Vulnerable Biological Resource', *Natural Resource Modeling*, **3** (4), 463-480.

Reed, W. J. (1992), 'Uncertainty and the conservation or destruction of natural forests and wilderness', *Invited paper at First SPRUCE Conference*, Lisbon.

Reed, W. J. and Ye, J. J. (1994), 'Cost-Benefit Analysis Applied to Wilderness Preservation: Option Value Uncertainty and Ditonicity', *Natural Resource Modeling*, **8** (4), 335-372.

Rees, R. (1985), 'The Theory of Principal and Agent: Part I', *Bulletin of Economic Research*, **37** (1), 3-25.

Reid, W. (1992), 'How many species will be there?', in T. C. Whitmore, and J. A. Sayer (editors), *Tropical deforestation and species extinction*, London; New York, NY: Chapman and Hall.

Reid, W. (editor) (1993), *Biodiversity prospecting: using genetic resources for sustainable development*, Washington, D.C.: World Resources Institute (WRI).

Reid, W. (1994), 'Setting objectives for conservation evaluation', in P. L. Forey, C. J. Humphries, and R. I. Vane-Wright (editors), *Systematics and conservation evaluation*, Oxford: Clarendon Press.

Reid, W. McNeely, J. A., Tunstall, D., Bryant, D., and Winograd, M. (1993), *Biodiversity Indicators for PolicyMakers*, Washington D.C.: World Resources Institute.

Reid, W. and Miller, K. (1989), *Keeping options alive: the scientific basis for conserving biodiversity*, Washington, DC: World Resources Institute.

Repetto, R. and Gillis, M. (1988), *Public policies and the misuse of forest resources*, Cambridge: Cambridge University Press.

Resendez, M. A. (1982), 'Hidrología e Ictiofauna de la Laguna de Sontecomapan, Veracruz, México', *An. Inst. Biol. Univ. Nal. Autón. De Méx.*, **53** (1), 385-417.

Riba, R. (1989), 'A new species of *Thelypteris* subg. *Goniopteris* from the State of Veracruz, Mexico', *American Fern Journal*, **79** (3), 122-124.

Richards, M. (1997), 'The potential for economic valuation of watershed protection in mountainous areas: a case study from Bolivia', *Mountain Research and Development,* **17** (1).

Richards, P. W. (1952), *The tropical rain forest and ecological study,* Cambridge: Cambridge University Press.

Rios Macbeth, F. (1952), 'Estudio geológico de la región de los Tuxtlas', *Boletín De La Asociación Mexicana De Geólogos Petroleros,* **IV** (9-10), 325-373.

Rodriguez Luna, E., Cortés Ortiz, L., and Miller, P. (1995), *Population and Habitat Viability Assessment for the Mantled Howler Monkey (Alouatta Palliata Mexicana).* Puebla, Mexico: A collaborative workshop of Asociación de Zoologicos Criaderos y Acuarios de la Republica Mexicana (AZCARM), Asociación Mexicana de Primatologia, Universidad Veracruzana, Primate Specialist Group IUCN, Conservation Breeding Specialist Group IUCN.

Romero, C. and Rehman, T. (1983), 'Goal Programming via Multidimensional Scaling Applied to Senegalese Subsistence Farming: comment', *American Journal of Agricultural Economics,* 829-831.

Romero, C. and Rehman, T. (1984), 'Goal programming and multiple criteria decision making in farm planning', *Journal of Agricultural Economics,* **35,** 177-190.

Ross, G. N. (1967), *A distributional study of the Butterflies of the Sierra de Tuxtla in Veracruz, Mexico,* Ph. dissertation, Lousiana State University and Agricultural and Mechanical Collage.

Roughgarden, J., May, R. M. and Levin, S. A. (editors) (1989), *Perspectives in ecological theory,* Princeton, N.J. Princeton University Press.

Roumasset, J. A., Boussard, J.-M., and Singh, I. (editors) (1979), *Risk, uncertainty and agricultural development,* New York: Southeast Asian Regional Center for Graduate and Agricultural Development Council.

Roy, A. D. (1952), 'Safety-first and the holding of assets', *Econometrica,* **20,** 431-439.

Rudd, E. V. (1981), 'Ormosia (Leguminosae) in Mexico, including a new species from Oaxaca', *Bol. Soc. Bot. Mexico,* **41,** 153-159.

Rudel, T. K. and Horowitz, B. (1993), *Tropical deforestation: small farmers and land clearing in the Ecuadorian Amazon,* New York: Columbia University Press.

Ruitenbeek, H. J. (1992), 'Economic Analysis of Tropical Forest Conservation Initiatives: Examples from West Africa', in K. M. Cleaver (editor), *Conservation of West and Central African rainforests,* Washington DC: The World Bank.

Ruitenbeek, H. J. (1996), 'Distribution of Ecological Entitlements: Implications for Economic Security and Population Movement', *Ecological Economics,* **17** (1), 49-64.

Ruiz, A. E. d. B., and Pérez P. A. (1993), *Catalogo preliminar de especies vegetales en peligro de extinción en la zona tropical del Veracruz*, Inst. Nal. de Invest. Forestales y Agropecuarias. Centro Regional del Golfo Centro.

Rzedowski, J. (1978), *La Vegetación de México*, Mexico: Ed. Limusa.

Sagoff, M. (1997), 'Do we consume too much?', *Athlantic Monthly*, 80-96.

Samuelson, P. A. (1954), 'The Pure Theory of Public Expenditure', *Review of Economics and Statistics*, **36**, 387-389.

Sanchez - Vindas, P. (1986), 'Mirtaceas Mexicanas', *Phytologia*, **61** (3), 136-145.

Santos R. M.A. (1988), *Etnobotánica (plantas medicinales) de los zoquepopolucas de los ejidos de San Fernando, Santa Martha, Ocotal Chico y Ocotal Grande, Municipio de Soteapan, Veracruz*, Tesis Bióloga, Universidad Veracruzana, Xalapa.

Sarmiento, F. O. (1997), 'Arrested succession in pastures hinders regeneration of Tropandean forests and shreds mountain landscapes', *Environmental Conservation*, **24** (1).

Sarukhan, J. (1968), *Estudio sinecológico de las selvas de Terminalia amazonia en la planicie costera del Golfo de México*. Tesis M. en C., Colegio de Postgraduados de Chapingo.

Scheaffer, R. L., Mendenhall, W., and Ott, L. (1986), *Elementary survey sampling*, Boston: Duxbury.

Scherr, S. J. (1989), 'Agriculture in an Export Boom Economy: A Comparative Analysis of Policy and Performance in Indonesia, Mexico and Nigeria', *World Development*, **17** (4), 543-60.

Schneider, R. (1992), *An Analysis of Environmental Problems in the Amazon*, Washington DC: The World Bank.

Schneider, R. (1995), *Government and the Economy on the Amazon Frontier*, World Bank Environment Paper, Washington DC: 11. The World Bank.

Sen, A. (1992), *Inequality reexamined*, New York: Russell Sage Foundation.

Shafer, C. L. (1990), *Nature reserves: island theory and conservation practice*, Washington DC: Smithsonian Institution Press.

Shah, A. (1995), *The Economics of Third World National Parks: Issues of Tourism and Environmental Management*, Aldershot: Edward Elgar.

Sharif, M. (1986), 'The concept and measurement of subsistence: a survey of the literature', *World Development*, **14** (5), 555-577.

Silva-Lopez, G. (1987), *La situación actual de las poblaciones de monos araña (Ateles geoffroyi) y aullador (Alouatta palliata) en la Sierra de Santa Martha, (Veracruz, México,.* Tesis Biólogo, Universidad Veracruzana, Xalapa.

Simberloff, D. S. (1986), 'Are we on the verge of a mass extinction in tropical rain forests?', in D. K. Elliot (editor), *Dynamics of extinction*, New York : J. Wiley.

Simberloff, D. S. (1992), 'Do species-area curves predict extinction in fragmented forests?', in T. C. Whitmore, and J. A. Sayer (editors), *Tropical deforestation and species extinction*. London; New York, NY: Chapman and Hall.

Simpson, R. D. (2000). 'The Economic Value of Ecosystem Services: a Review of Literature and Issues'. Resources for the Future, Washington D.C. Mimeo.

Simpson, R. D., Sedjo, R. and Reid, W. (1996), 'Valuing Biodiversity for use in New Product Research', *Journal of Political Economy*, **104**, 163-185.

Singh, I., Squire, L., and Strauss, J. (1986), *Agricultural household models : extensions, applications, and policy*, Baltimore: The Johns Hopkins University Press.

Singh, I., Squire, L., and Strauss, J. (1992), 'A Survey of Agricultural Household Models: Recent Findings ', in D. Lal (editor), *Development economics* (Vol. 2). Aldershot, Hants, England: Elgar.

Sisk, T. D., Launer, A. E., Switky, K. R. and Ehrlich, P. R. (1994), 'Identifying Extinction Threats', *BioScience*, **44** (9), 592-604.

Skole, D. and Tucker, C. (1993), 'Tropical deforestation and habitat fragmentation in the Amazon: satellite data from 1978-1988', *Science*, (260), 1905-1909.

Smith, F. D. M., May, R. M., Pellew, R., Johnson, T. H. and Walter, K. S. (1993), 'Estimating extinction rates', *Nature*, **364** (6437), 494-96.

Smith, N. J. H. (1996). 'Effects of Land use systems on the use and conservation of biodiversity', in J. P. Srivastava, N. J. H. Smith, and D. A. Forno (editors), *Biodiversity and agriculture intensification*, Washington DC: The World Bank.

Solow, A. and Polasky, S. (1994), 'Measuring biological diversity', *Environmental and Ecological Statistics*, **1** (2).

Solow, A., Polasky, S. and Broadus, J. (1993), 'On the Measurement of Biological Diversity', *Journal of Environmental Economics and Management*, **24**, 60-68.

Solow, R. M. (1986), 'On the intergenerational allocation of natural resources', *Scandinavian Journal of Economics*, **88**, 141-149.

Soulé, M. E. (editor) (1987), *Viable populations for conservation*, Cambridge: Cambridge University Press.

Soulé, M. E. (1991), 'Theory and strategy', in W. E. Hudson (editor), *Landscape linkages and biodiversity*, Washington, D.C.: Island Press.

Sousa, M. (1968), 'Ecología de las leguminosas de Los Tuxtlas, Veracruz', *An. Inst. Biol. Univ. Nal. Auton. México Ser. Bot.* **39**, 121-161.

Sousa, M. (1993), 'El Genéro Inga (Leguminosae: Mimosidae) del sur de México y Centroamérica, estudio previo para la Flora Mesoaméricana', *Ann. Missouri Bot. Gard.* **80**, 223-269.

Sousa, M. and Rudd, V. E. (1993), 'Revisión del genéro Styphnolobium (Leguminosae: Papilionidae: Sophorae)', *Ann. Missouri Bot. Gard.* **80**, 270-283.

Southgate, D. (1990), 'The Causes of Land Degradation along "Spontaneously" Expanding Agricultural Frontiers in the Third World ', *Land Economics*, **66** (1), 93-101.

Southgate, D. (1991), *Tropical deforestation and agricultural development in Latin America*. London Evironmental Economics Centre. LEEC Discussion Paper 91-01, London .

Southgate, D. (1995). 'Economic progress and habitat conservation in Latin America', in T. M. Swanson (editor), *The econommic and ecology of biodiversity decline: the forces driving global change*(pp. 91-98). Cambridge: Cambridge University Press.

Southgate, D. (1996), *Can Habitats Be Protected and Local Living Standards Improved by Promoting Ecotourism, Non-Timber Extraction, Sustainable Timber Harvesting and Genetic Prospecting?* Washington D.C.: Report to the Inter-American Development Bank.

Srivastava, J. P., Smith, N. J. H., and Forno, D. A. (1996), *Biodiversity and agriculture intensification,*. Washington DC: The World Bank.

Stedman-Edwards, P. (1997), *Socio-economic root causes of biodiversity loss: an approach paper,* mimeo, WWF - MPO, Washington D.C.

Stern, P., Young, O. and Druckman, D. (editors). (1992). Global Environmental Change: Understanding the Human Dimension, Washington D.C.: National Academy Press.

Stiglitz, J. E. (1988), 'Sharecropping', John M. Olin Program for the Study of Economic Organization and Public Policy Discussion Paper, **11**, 1-23.

Stone, S. (1996), *Economic Trends in the Timber Industry of the Brazilian Amazon: Evidence From Paragominas,*. Collaborative Research in the Economics of the Environment and Development (CREED) Working Paper Series, 6, International Institute for Environment and Development.

Swanson, T. M. (1990), *The International Regulation of Extinction*, London: Macmillan.

Swanson, T. M. (1992), *The International Franchise Agreement Option, mimeo, Centre for Social and Economic Research on the Global Environment*, University of East Anglia, University College London .

Swanson, T. M. (1994), 'The Economics of Extinction Revisited and Revised: A Generalised Framework for the Analysis of the Problems of Endangered Species and Biodiversity Losses', *Oxford Economic Papers*, **46** (Supplementary Issue), 800-821.

Swanson, T. M. (1995). 'Uniformity in development and the decline of biological diversity', in T. M. Swanson (editor), *The economic, and ecology of biodiversity decline: the forces driving global change*(pp. 41-54) Cambridge: Cambridge University Press.

Swanson, T. M., and Cervigni, R. (1996). 'Policy Failures and Resource Degradation', in T. M. Swanson (editor), *The economics of environmental degradation,* Edward Elgar.

Swanson, T. M., International Union for Conservation of Nature and Natural Resources, and World Wide Fund for Nature (1997), *Global action for biodiversity: an international framework for implementing the convention on biological diversity.* London: Earthscan.

Swanson, T. M., Pearce, D. W., and Cervigni, R. (1994). *The Appropriation of the Benefits of Plant Genetic Resources for Agriculture: an Economic Analysis of the Alternative Mechanisms for Biodiversity Conservation,* Background Study Paper 1, Rome: Food and Agriculture Organization, Commission on Plant Genetic Resources.

Szaro, R. C. (1996), 'Biodiversity in managed landscapes: principles, practice and policy', in R. C. Szaro, and D. W. Johnston (editors), *Biodiversity in managed landscapes: theory and practice,* New York ; Oxford: Oxford University Press.

Taylor, J. E. and Adelman, I. (1996), *Village economies: The design, estimation, and use of villagewide economic models,* New York and Melbourne: Cambridge University Press.

Taylor, J. E. and Wyatt, T. J. (1996), 'The Shadow Value of Migrant Remittances, Income and Inequality in a Household-Farm Economy', *Journal of Development Studies,* **32** (6), 899-912.

Thiesenhusen, W. C. (1991), 'Implications of the Rural Land Tenure System for the Environmental Debate: Three Scenarios', *Journal of Developing Areas,* **26** (1), 1-23.

Toledo, V. M. (1969), *Diversidad de especies en las selvas altas de la plasnicie costera del Golfo de México,* Tesis Biólogo, Fac. de Ciencias UNAM, Mexico.

Toledo, V. M. (1982), 'Pleistocene changes of vegetation in tropical Mexico', in T. G. Prance (editor), *Biological diversification in the tropics,* New York: Columbia University Press.

Toledo, V. M. (1992), 'Bio-economic costs', in T. E. Downing (editor), *Development or destruction : the conversion of tropical forest to pasture in Latin America.* Boulder, Colorado: Westview Press.

Toledo, V. M., Ortiz, B. and Medellin, S. (1994), 'Biodiversity islands in a sea of pasturelands: indigenous resource management in the humid tropics of Mexico', *Etnoecologica,* **2** (3), 37-49.

Tricart, J., and Kilian, J. (1982), *La ecogeografía y la ordenación del medio natural,* Barcelona: Anagrama.

Udvardy, M. D. F. (1975), 'A classification of the biogeographical provinces of the world', *IUCN Occasional Papers*, **18**.

Uhl, C., Nepstad, R., Buschbacher, K. C., Jaufman, B., and Subler, S. (1990). 'Studies of ecosystem response to natural and anthropogenic disturbances provide guidelines for designing sustainable land-use systems in Amazonia', in A. B. Anderson (editor), *Alternatives to deforestation: steps toward sustainable use of the Amazon rain forest*, New York: Columbia University Press.

UNCED (1993), *Agenda 21: programme of action for sustainable development*, Rio de Janeiro, Brazil: United Nations Conference on Environment and Development.

UNEP (1992), *Convention on biological diversity*, Nairobi: United Nations Environment Programme, Environmental Law and Institutions Programme Activity Centre.

Valerio, E. C. (1991), *La biodiversidad de Costa Rica*, San José, Costa Rica: Editorial Heliconia, Fundación Neotrópica .

Van Kooten, G. C., and Bulte, E. H. (2000), *The Economics of Nature*, Oxford: Blackwell.

Vandeveer, L.R. and Drummond, H.E. (1978), *The use of Markov process in estimating land use change*, Agricultural experimental station, *Technical Bulletin* **148**, Oklahoma.

Vane-Wright, R. I., Humphries, C. J. and Williams, P. H. (1991), 'What to protect? - Systematics and the Agony of choice', *Biological Conservation*, **55**, 235-254.

Varian, H. (editor) (1996), *Computational Economics and Finance: Modeling and Analysis with Mathematica*, TELOS/Springer-Verlag.

Vega - Rivera, J. H. (1982), *Aspectos biológicos de Myiobius sulphureipygius (AVES:Tyrannidae) en el área de Santa Marta, Región de Los Tuxtlas, Ver., México*, Tesis Biólogo, ENEP iztacala, UNAM, Mexico.

Velázquez H., E. (1992), 'Política, ganadería y recursos naturales en el trópico húmedo veracruzano: el caso del municipio de Mecayapan', *Relaciones, El Colegio De Michoacán*, **50**, 23-64.

Velázquez H., E. (1995), *La tierra: eje de la historia social en la sierra de Santa Marta*.

Velázquez H., E., and Ramírez, F. (1995), 'Usos económicos de la selva de montaña en una reserva de la biósfera', in E. Boege, H. García, and P. Gerez (eds.), *Alternativas al manejo de laderas en Veracruz*, (pp. 203-222) Mexico: SEMARNAP/Fundación Friedrich Ebert.

Vosti, S., and Witcover, J. (1996), 'Arresting Deforestation and Resource Degradation in the Forest Margins of the Humid Tropics: Policy, Technology and Institutional Options', *Multi-country research program: Review of methodology*, Washington DC: International Food Policy Research Institute.

Weisbrod, B. A. (1964), 'Collective-consumption services of individual consumption goods', *Quarterly Journal of Economics*, **78**, 471-477.

Weitzman, M. (1992), 'On diversity', *Quarterly Journal of Economics*, May, 363-405.

Weitzman, M. (1993), 'What to preserve? An application of Diversity Theory to Crane Conservation', *Quarterly Journal of Economics*, **CVIII** (Feb), 157-183.

Wendt, T. (1993), 'Composition, floristic affinities, and origins of the canopy tree flora of the Mexican Atlantic slope rain forest', in P. T. Ramamoorthy, R. Bye, and A. Lot (editors), *Biological diversity of Mexico: origins and distribution*, New York: Oxford University Press.

Werber, E. J. (1957), 'A new lizard of the genus *Lepidophyma*, from Volcan San Martin Pajapan, Veracruz', *Herpetologica*, **13** (3), 223-226.

Western, D. and Pearl, M. C. (1989), *Conservation for the twenty-first century*, New York: Oxford University Press.

Wetmore, A. (1943), 'The birds of southern Veracruz, Mexico', *Proc. U.S. Natl. Mus.* **93**, 215-340.

Wharton, C. R. (editor) (1969), *Subsistence agriculture and economic development*, Chicago: Aldine Pub.

Wharton, C. R. (1969), 'Subsistence agriculture: concepts and scope', in C. R. Wharton (editor), *Subsistence agriculture and economic development*, Chicago: Aldine Pub.

Whitmore, T. C., and Sayer, J. A. (1992), 'Deforestation and species extinction in tropical moist forests', in T. C. Whitmore, and J. A. Sayer (editors), *Tropical deforestation and species extinction* London; New York, NY: Chapman and Hall.

Wilen, J. E. (1985), 'Bioeconomics of renewable resource use', in A. V. Kneese, and J. L. Sweeney (editors), *Handbook of natural resources and energy economics* (Vol. I) Amsterdam; New York: North-Holland.

Wille, C. (1994), 'The birds and the beans', *Audubon* (November - December), 58-64.

Williams Linera, Halffter, G., and Ezcurra, E. (1992), 'Conservación en México: Síntesis sobre vertebrados terrestres, vegetación y uso del suelo', *Acta Zoológica Mexicana, Volume especial sobre la Diversidad Biológica de Iberoamérica*, 285-312.

Williams, P. H. (1996), *WORLDMAP iv WINDOWS: Software and user document 4.1*, London: Privately distributed.

Williams, P. H., and Humphries, C. J. (1994), 'Biodiversity, taxonomic relatedness, and endemism in conservation', in P. L. Forey, C. J. Humphries, and R. I. Vane-Wright (editors), *Systematics and conservation evaluation*, Oxford: Clarendon Press.

Williams, W. T., Lance, G. N., Tracey, J. G. and Connell, J. H. (1969), 'Studies in the numerical analysis of complex rain-forest communities. IV. A method for the elucidation of small scale forest pattern', *Journal of Ecology*, **57**, 635-654.

Wilson, E. O. (editor). (1988). *Biodiversity,*. Washington, D.C.: National Academy Press.

Winker, K., Oehlenschlager, R. J., Ramos, M., Zink, R. M., Rappole J.H. and Warner, D. W. (1992), 'Avian distribution and abundance records for the Sierra de Los Tuxtlas, Veracruz, Mexico', *Wilson Bull,* **104** (4), 699-718.

Wolfram, S. (1996), *The Mathematica Book,* Wolfram Media, Inc. and Cambridge University Press.

World Bank (1994), *Mexico: resource conservation and forest sector review,* Washington DC: Agriculture and natural resources operations division, Country department II, Latin America and the Caribbean Regional Office.

World Bank (1995), *Mexico: Issues in agriculture, natural resources and rural poverty,* Washington DC: Agriculture and natural resources operations division, Country department II, Latin America and the Caribbean Regional Office.

World Bank (1995a), *Mainstreaming biodiversity in development: a World Bank assistance strategy for implementing the Convention on Biological Diversity,* Washington, D.C. : The World Bank, Environment Department.

World Bank (1995b), *Mexico: rural financial markets,* Washington DC: Natural resources and rural poverty division, Country department II, Latin America and the Caribbean Regional Office.

World Bank (1996), *Mainstreaming Biodiversity in Agricultural Development*: Toward Good Practice, draft, Washington DC

World Bank (1996a), *Mexico: rural poverty,* Washington DC: Agriculture and Environment Sector Leadership Group, Latin America and the Caribbean Regional Office.

World Bank (1997), *Monitoring environmental progress: expanding the measure of wealth,* Washington DC: Indicators and environmental valuation unit, environment department, the World Bank.

World Resources Institute (1992), *Global biodiversity strategy: guidelines for action to save, study, and use earth's biotic wealth sustainably and equitably,* Washington DC: World Resources Institute (WRI), the World Conservation Union (ICUN), United Nations Environment Programme (UNEP) in consultation with Food and Agriculture Organization (FAO), United Nations Education, Scientific and Cultural Organization (UNESCO).

World Resources Institute (1992), *World Resources 1992-93: A Guide to the Global Environment,* New York: Oxford University Press.

World Resources Institute (1994), World Resources. *A guide to the Global Environment*. People and the Environment, New York: Oxford University Press.

Wunderlee, J. M. and Waide, R. B. (1993), 'Distribution of overwintering nearctic migrants in the Bahamas and Greater Antilles', *The Condor* (95), 904-933.

Index

acahual (second growth forest in Mexico), 156, 159, 173, 174, 184, 197, 210, 220, 221, 222, 223, 231, 232

agricultural household models, 160

Amazon, 42, 43, 51, 59, 176

Arrow, K., 22

Barbier, E., 15, 16, 19, 23, 177, 187, 205, 219, 227, 233

Barrett, S., 61, 90

bid-rent function, 41, 43

Biodiversity
causes of loss, 23
community level, 10
economic definitions of, 11
ecosystem functions, xiii, 18
genetic level, 9
objective functions for conservation, xiii, 28, 140
species level, 9
sustainable use, xv, 202
valuation, 15

Buckles, D., xviii, 129, 130, 131, 137, 198, 221, 234

Burgess, J., 23, 176, 177, 187, 205, 219, 227, 233

Centre for Social and Economic Analysis on the Global Environment (CSERGE), 3, xvii, xviii

Centro Internacional para el Mejoramiento del Maíz y Trigo (CIMMYT), xvii, 127, 135, 175

Cervigni, R., 3, 69, 89, 90, 91, 122, 127, 144, 146, 177, 198, 234

Chevallier, J., 129, 131, 137, 221

Clark, C.W., 24

Climate change, 61, 89

Convention on Biological Diversity, xiv, xix, 3, 5, 7, 30, 61, 64, 65, 68, 72, 80, 83, 84, 90, 95, 206

Convention on International Trade in Endangered Species (CITES), 105

Costanza, R., 19, 205

Deininger, K., 177

Dinerstein, E., 103

ejido (Mexican communal land tenure unit), 108, 126

El-Serafy, S., 91

Erenstein, O., 198, 234

extinction, 12
theories of, 24

Folke, C., 23, 205

Food and Agriculture Organisation (FAO), 25

Food and Agriculture
Organization (FAO), 25, 171,
234
franchise agreements, 51, 159
Gadgil, M., 23, 35, 233
Gaia hypothesis, 6
Gentry, A., 30
Global Environment Facility
(GEF), xvii, xviii, xix, 61, 62,
83, 89, 90, 109, 112, 115, 116,
118, 119, 120, 122, 123, 127,
233
Glowka, L., 69, 91
Gomez Pompa, A., 60
Hanemann, M., 22, 30
Hartwick, J., 39
Henry, C., 22
Heywood, V.H., 3, 8, 30
incremental cost, xiv, 30, 55, 60,
61, 62, 63, 66, 69, 70, 71, 72,
73, 74, 76, 78, 80, 81, 82, 83,
84, 85, 90, 95
baseline, 69
price distortions, 77
Instituto Nacional de Estadistica y
Geografía (INEGI), 112, 215
Island bio-geography theory, 25,
39
Kaimowitz, D., 26, 27, 177
King, K., xvii, xviii, 90, 91
land tenure, 107, 134
in Mexico, 125
linear programming models, xv,
142, 145, 146, 147, 160, 162,
164, 168, 188, 209, 211, 216,
220, 221, 225, 234
safety-first constraints, 142,
143, 164, 180

Los Tuxtlas, 96, 102, 103, 104,
105, 127, 137, 175, 176
Lovejoy, T., 13
Lugo, A., 35, 37, 60, 180
McNeely, J., 23, 30, 35, 233
Miller, K., 30
milpa (maize-based farming
system), 148, 149, 150, 151,
152, 154, 156, 157, 158, 159,
173, 174, 175, 210, 211, 212,
220, 221
monte (primary forest in Mexico),
156, 172, 173, 174, 184, 192,
197, 211, 220, 221, 223
Moran, D., xvii, 15, 23, 89, 90, 91
Myers, N., 13, 59
non-timber forest products, 42,
47, 64, 77, 118
North American Free Trade
Agreement (NAFTA), 125,
133, 134, 156
open access, 24, 45, 54, 225
Ostrom, E., 23
Panayotou, T., 51
Paré, L., xviii, 128, 129, 210
Pearce, D.W., xvii, 15, 23, 26, 69,
83, 89, 90, 91, 128, 205
Perrings, C., xiv, 15, 16, 19, 30,
205
Polasky, S., 3
Programa de Apoyo al Campo
(PROCAMPO), 134, 135, 136
Programa de Certificación de
Derechos Ejidales y Titulación
de Solares Urbanos
(PROCEDE), 125, 126, 134,
139, 140, 152, 182, 198, 208

Programa Nacional de Solidaridad (PRONASOL), 175

Proyecto Sierra de Santa Marta (PSSM), xvii, xviii, 96, 98, 99, 108, 109, 112, 113, 115, 116, 118, 119, 120, 122, 123, 127, 128, 135, 175

Quasi-option value, 22

Ramirez, F., xviii, 90, 105, 122, 127, 144, 177, 198, 234

Ramos, M., xviii, 105

Randall, A., 39

Repetto, R., 83

road building, 40, 43, 45, 131

Safe Minimum Standards (SMS), 22, 29

Schneider, R., 42, 59, 176, 228

Sedjo, R., 18

shifting agriculture, 44

Sierra de Santa Marta, xv, xvii, xviii, 95, 96, 97, 102, 104, 107, 121, 127, 128, 133, 134, 135, 139, 175, 198, 202, 204
  biodiversity, 102
    fauna, 104
    flora, 104
  cattle ranching, 137
  forest products, 117
  hunting, 119
  indigenous groups, 107
  land tenure, 107
  land use, 112

  process of change, 129
  social and economic aspects, 106, 120
  trapping of live animals, 117
  zoning, 97

Simpson, D., 18, 19

Singh, I., 179

Southgate, D., 59

Species-area relationship, 13, 25, 30, 35, 36, 37, 38

Stedman-Edwards, P., 23

Stella modeling software, 181, 232

Swanson, T., 24, 51

Toledo, V., 103, 175

tradable development rights, 51, 52

United Nations, 83

Van Kooten, G.C., 18, 19, 30

Velázquez, E., 130

Veracruz (Mexican State), xviii, 95, 96, 103, 104, 120, 121, 124, 131, 135, 176, 218

Warford, J., 83, 128

Weitzman, M., 30

Wilson, E.O., xviii, 30, 35

World Bank, 3, 4, 52, 84, 103, 124, 128, 144, 169, 177, 178, 205

World Resources Institute (WRI), 23, 30, 36, 38